Cambridge Studies in American Literature and Culture

William Faulkner:
The Art of Stylization

D1605407

Cambridge Studies in American Literature and Culture

Editor

Albert Gelpi, Stanford University

Advisory Board

Nina Baym, University of Illinois, Champaign-Urbana
Sacvan Bercovitch, Harvard University
Richard Bridgman, University of California, Berkeley
David Levin, University of Virginia
Joel Porte, Harvard University
Mike Weaver, Oxford University

Other books in the series

Robert Zaller: *The Cliffs of Solitude*
Peter Conn: *The Divided Mind*
Patricia Caldwell: *The Puritan Conversion Narrative*
Stephen Fredman: *Poet's Prose*
Charles Altieri: *Self and Sensibility in Contemporary American Poetry*
John McWilliams: *Hawthorne, Melville, and the American Character*
Barton St Armand: *Emily Dickinson and Her Culture*
Mitchell Robert Breitwieser: *Cotton Mather and Benjamin Franklin*
Albert von Frank: *The Sacred Game*
Beth McKinsey: *Niagara Falls*
Marjorie Perloff: *The Dance of the Intellect*
Albert Gelpi: *Wallace Stevens*
Karen Rowe: *Saint and Singer*
Paul Giles: *Hart Crane*
Richard Gray: *Writing the South*
David Wyatt: *The Fall into Eden*
George Dekker: *The American Historical Romance*
Lawrence Buell: *New England Literary Culture*
Ann Kibbey: *The Interpretation of Material Shapes in Puritanism*
Sacvan Bercovitch and Myra Jehlen: *Ideology and Classic American Literature*
Jerome Loving: *Emily Dickinson*
Steven Axelrod and Helen Deese: *Robert Lowell*
Brook Thomas: *Cross-Examinations of Law and Literature*
Brenda Murphy: *American Realism and American Drama*
Warren Motley: *The American Abraham*
Lynn Keller: *Remaking it New*
Margaret Holley: *The Poetry of Marianne Moore*

William Faulkner:
The Art of Stylization in his Early Graphic and Literary Work

LOTHAR HÖNNIGHAUSEN

University of Bonn

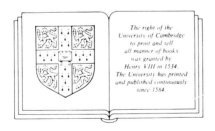

CAMBRIDGE UNIVERSITY PRESS

CAMBRIDGE
NEW YORK   NEW ROCHELLE
MELBOURNE   SYDNEY

Published by the Press Syndicate of the University of Cambridge
The Pitt Building, Trumpington Street, Cambridge CB2 1RP
32 East 57th Street, New York, NY 10022, USA
10 Stamford Road, Oakleigh, Melbourne 3166, Australia

First published 1987

Printed in Great Britain at
The University Press, Cambridge

British Library cataloguing in publication data
Hönnighausen, Lothar
William Faulkner: the art of stylization
in his early graphic and literary work. –
(Cambridge studies in American literature
and culture).
1. Faulkner, William – Criticism and
interpretation
I. Title
813′.52   PS3511.A86Z

Library of Congress cataloguing in publication data
Hönnighausen, Lothar.
William Faulkner: the art of stylization in his
early graphic and literary work
(Cambridge studies in American literature and culture)
Bibliography.
Includes index.
1. Faulkner, William, 1897–1962 – Style.   2. Faulkner,
William, 1897–1962 – Knowledge – Art.   3. Art and
literature – United States.   I. Title.   II. Series.
PS3511.A86Z83   1987   813′.52   87–6401

ISBN 0 521 33280 X

WV

For my American Friends

Contents

viii   Contents

Appendix 2

Plates

For purposes of identification I have given my own titles to the plates from *Mayday* and *The Marionettes*.

SOURCES

I am indebted to Mrs Jill Faulkner Summers and to the following institutions for permission to use copyright material and for providing photographic prints:

Mississippi Collection, University of Mississippi: 22, 33, 34, 35, 36, 37, 38, 39, 40, 41, 42, 43, 44, 45, 46, 47, 48, 49, 50, 51, 52, 53, 54, 55, 56, 57, 58; William Faulkner Collections, University of Virginia Library: 1, 2, 3, 9, 10, 11, 12, 13, 14, 15, 16, 17, 18, 19, 20, 21, 97; Wisdom Collection, Tulane, New Orleans: 23, 24, 25, 26, 27, 28, 29, 30; Academic Center Library, University of Texas at Austin: 31; Louis Daniel Brodsky Collection: 4, 5, 6, 7, 8, 32, 104, 105, 106; Whitney Museum of American Art Collection, New York: 90, 93, 103; Fogg Art Museum, Harvard: 87; Louise and Walter Arensberg Collection, Philadelphia Museum of Art: 95; Musée National du Louvre, Paris: 102; The Library of Congress, Washington: 61; Archives photographiques, Paris: 96; Dover Publications: 62, 63, 64, 65, 66, 67, 68, 69, 70, 71, 72, 73, 74, 75, 76, 80, 83; Mathews and Lane: 77, 78, 79, 81, 82; Keysersche Verlagsbuchhandlung: 88, 91, 92, 99, 100; Princeton University Press: 89, 94, 101; Holle Verlag: 86, 98; The Arden Library: 84; Gerd Hatje Verlag: 85.

Preface

THIS BOOK takes Faulkner's artwork as a starting-point to approach his early poetry and prose, and derives its focal point from Faulkner's fascination with "the art of stylization." His Arts and Crafts affinities, his drawings in the Beardsley style, and his cartoons for the student yearbook *Ole Miss* have a certain interest in themselves; but the reason why they are studied here in detail (for the first time) is that they help us to achieve a more balanced appraisal of how his imitative early poetry and prose prepares the ground for the style of his great novels. When we relate the binding and lettering of the *Lilacs* volume in the Brodsky Collection to the text of the poems, or examine how in *The Marionettes* the meaning of the words and the form of their presentation work together to achieve the total aesthetic effect, we may come to see the poetic arrangement of the narrative in *Absalom, Absalom!* or the "wordy mannerism" of the Ike Snopes episode in *The Hamlet* in a different light. It is not then from the traditional perspective of source and influence studies that I shall look closely at Faulkner's "debts" to Swinburne and Wilde, to Verlaine, Aiken and Eliot. Rather, I propose to study Faulkner's assimilation of the highly stylized poetry and prose that went before him to observe how his own stylizing power formed itself. The assessment of this process of formation may lead us to a more intimate acquaintance with that element of Faulkner's imagination which added a Symbolist dimension to the realism of his novels.

In writing the book, I became aware how strongly influenced I was by a European academic tradition. This seemed natural, however, and indeed more appropriate than imitating what the native American Faulkner scholar can do better. Throughout the work I have enjoyed the friendship and unstinted support of American friends to whom I dedicate the book. I am particularly grateful to Thomas L. McHaney whose expert help and kind interest were invaluable from the conception of the book to its final draft. James B. Meriwether gave encouragement and expert advice in extensive discussion in Bonn and Columbia SC. I am greatly indebted to Noel Polk not only for his introduction to and edition of *The Marionettes*, which opened up the field, but also for his valuable suggestions and kind interest in my book. Louis Daniel Brodsky generously shared information with me and provided photographic material from his collection. Joseph Blotner, André Bleikasten, Ursula Brumm, Hans Bungert, Harold Kolb, Ilse Lind,

Patrick Samway and Mike Weaver all in various ways but with equal kindness supported the project. I am grateful also to William B. Ferris and Ann Abadie of the Center for the Study of Southern Culture, to Evans Harrington of the English Department at the University of Mississippi, to Elinor Shaffer of the University of East Anglia, and to Waldemar Zacharasiewicz of the University of Vienna, for giving me the opportunity to try out parts of the book in lectures and discussions.

My sincere thanks go to Mrs Jill Faulkner Summers for graciously granting permission to use copyright material, and to Mr Edward Berkeley, Ms Joan St C. Crane, and the staff of the University of Virginia Library for giving expert assistance and for making my work there so pleasant. Mr Thomas M. Verich of the John Davis Williams Library, the University of Mississippi, was most helpful in allowing me to use material from *Ole Miss* and *The Scream*. I should like to express my thanks to Mr John Muirhead and the library of the John F. Kennedy Institute for American Studies (Free University, Berlin) for their efficient help. Thanks are due to Dr Judith L. Sensibar, who sent me a copy of her dissertation before the publication of her book, *The Origins of Faulkner's Art*, to which specific reference is made in the appropriate sections of this book. I am grateful to Robert W. Hamblin for providing photographic material from the Brodsky Collection, and I should like to thank the Deutsche Forschungsgemeinschaft and Dr Briegel for a travel grant enabling me to work in American Faulkner Collections.

Throughout the various stages of the manuscript, Chr. Brost, E. Denton, R. Glasgow, S. Gülicher, B. Honrath, Chr. Irmscher, T. Langston, S. Taubeneck, and Jo van Vliet acted as dedicated research assistants. C. Daufenbach did valuable work on the index. Great thanks are due to Albert Gelpi, the editor of the series, for his close and very helpful reading of the typescript. I should also like to express my deep gratitude to Andrew Brown and copy editor Penny Wheeler of Cambridge University Press who gave excellent editorial guidance. My most profound thanks go to my wife Gisela for her expert advice, her good humor, and her suggestion for the design of the dust jacket.

Abbreviations

References in the text to works by William Faulkner are to these editions, and are abbreviated as follows:

AA	*Absalom, Absalom!* New York: Random House, 1936.
CS	*Collected Stories.* New York: Random House, 1950.
ELM	*Elmer.* Edited by James B. Meriwether and Dianne L. Cox. *Mississippi Quarterly*, 36 (1983), 337–460.
EPP	*Early Prose and Poetry.* Edited with an introduction by Carvel Collins. London: Jonathan Cape, 1962.
FAB	*A Fable.* New York: Random House, 1950.
FD	*Flags in the Dust.* Edited with an introduction by Douglas Day. New York: Random House, 1973.
HAM	*The Hamlet.* New York: Random House, 1940.
HO	"Hong Li." Quoted in Noel Polk, "William Faulkner's 'Hong Li' on *Royal Street.*" *The Library Chronicle of the University of Texas at Austin*, 13 (1980), p. 29.
LA	*Light in August.* New York: Smith and Haas, 1932; reissued Vintage, 1972.
MF & GB	*The Marble Faun and A Green Bough.* New York: Random House, 1965.
MAR	*The Marionettes.* Edited with an introduction and textual apparatus by Noel Polk. Charlottesville: University Press of Virginia, 1977.
MAY	*Mayday.* Introduction by Carvel Collins. Notre Dame and London: University of Notre Dame Press, 1976.
MOS	*Mosquitoes.* London: Chatto and Windus, 1964.
NOS	*New Orleans Sketches.* Edited with an introduction by Carvel Collins. New York: Random House, 1968.
REQ	*Requiem for a Nun.* New York: Random House, 1951.
SANC	*Sanctuary. The Original Text.* Edited with an afterword and notes by Noel Polk. New York: Random House, 1981.
SAR	*Sartoris.* London: Chatto and Windus, 1954.
SF	*The Sound and the Fury.* New, corrected edition. Edited by Noel Polk. New York: Random House, 1984.

SL   *Selected Letters of William Faulkner*. Edited by Joseph Blotner.
            London: The Scolar Press, 1977.
SP   *Soldiers' Pay*. London: Chatto and Windus, 1954.
TWN   *The Town*. New York: Random House, 1957.
US   *Uncollected Stories of William Faulkner*. Edited by Joseph Blotner.
            New York: Random House, 1979.
VS   *Vision in Spring*. Edited with an introduction by Judith Sensibar.
            Austin: University of Texas Press, 1984.
WP   *The Wild Palms*. New York: Random House, 1939.

Introduction
Faulkner and the Art of Stylization

FROM HIS FIRST NOVEL *Soldiers' Pay*, in which the mythic pattern of satyr and nymph informs realistic characters, to that litany of mythical *femmes fatales* surrounding the country girl from Frenchman's Bend, Faulkner's work is characterized by stylizing features. His specific artistic genius lies in the productive tension between the concreteness of realistic description and various means of stylization: mythic method, momentary freeze, silhouette effect, intervention in the flow of time and plot, manneristic image and sound clusters, unnatural sentences, and esoteric vocabulary. Stylization is, of course, a characteristic feature of all art, but in certain epochs like the Middle Ages or in certain genres such as the Elizabethan sonnet it proves to be a more influential or intense force. It becomes a useful category in literary criticism only when its historical modes and specific forms are considered and its degrees differentiated. Faulkner's early literary and graphic works, for example, display more intense features of stylization than his novel trilogy *The Hamlet*, *The Town*, and *The Mansion*, and his parody of Malory's medieval style in *Mayday* produces a more homogeneous, if less subtle, system of stylization than that used in *Absalom, Absalom!* The awareness of the power of stylization of major twentieth-century authors like Joyce and Faulkner is related to their ambition of restoring to the epic genre the poetic dimension it had lost in the Naturalistic novel. The new insights of the times of Freud, Frazer, and Bergson demanded a more flexible lyrical imagination of the fiction writer and so it is probably no coincidence that the two greatest English language novelists of the early twentieth century began with experiments in lyric poetry. Joyce's *Chamber Music* and Faulkner's *The Marble Faun* or *Vision in Spring* do not constitute great poetry. Yet they are of significance because they reveal the later novelists' search for more intense forms of expression, a prerequisite for the genesis of the modern novel.

Faulkner's integration of modes of expression from the modern novel and the lyric tradition of late English Romanticism has been recognized by Edmund Wilson:

... he belongs . . . to the full-dress post-Flaubert group of Conrad, Joyce, and Proust. . . . To their kind of highly complex fiction he has brought the rich and lively resources, appearing with amazing freshness, of English lyric verse and romantic prose . . . [1]

The young Faulkner's affinities not only with Eliot but also with Swinburne's poetry and Beardsley's art become more apparent when we recall that he rejected Carl Sandburg's and Vachel Lindsay's poems as unpoetic and accepted only the more lyrical Conrad Aiken from among his countrymen. Faulkner's partiality for Aiken is consistent with his predilection for Swinburne, Verlaine, and the Keats imitators of the *fin de siècle*. Aiken's distortions of the modern world are so guarded that the stylized beauty of his Impressionistic imagery and his late Romantic sonority are never seriously threatened. Faulkner's admiration of Aiken's moderate Modernism raises the question of his escape from the American present of 1920 to the outmoded forms and tropes of the European late Romantic tradition.

Before attempting to explain what the young Faulkner believed he could find in English literature and what he thought lacking in his American surroundings, it should perhaps be mentioned that Swinburne and the English *fin de siècle* were not so out of the way for an American of that time as would seem today. Besides the general American interest in English literature of the nineteenth century, there was, understandably, in the South of the post-Reconstruction era a particular receptiveness for the retrospective, melancholic idealism of late English Romanticism.

In this respect William A. Percy's volume of poetry *In April Once*, reviewed by Faulkner in *The Mississippian* of November 10, 1920, proves to be a revealing document. It is interesting to note that what Faulkner considers problematic in Percy's work are the same tendencies visible in his own lyric production of the time:

Mr. Percy – like alas! how many of us – suffered the misfortune of having been born out of his time. He should have lived in Victorian England and gone to Italy with Swinburne, for like Swinburne, he is a mixture of passionate adoration of beauty and as passionate a despair and disgust with its manifestations and accessories in the human race . . . The influence of the frank pagan beauty worship of the past is upon him, he is like a little boy closing his eyes against the dark modernity which threatens the bright simplicity and the colorful romantic pageantry of the middle ages with which his eyes are full. (*EPP*, 71–2)

The need for a stylized world of sensual beauty characterizes both Faulkner's appraisal of Percy and the early phases of his own work of around 1920. In the gray reality of the economically and culturally undeveloped South, a utilitarian and rigidly religious world distrustful of the sensuous richness of art – Mencken's "Sahara of the Bozart" – Faulkner chooses to emphasize the "influence of the frank pagan beauty worship of the past" in Percy's poetry. He himself was obviously drawn toward the colorful world of William Morris's romanticized Middle Ages, and the sensuousness of the Pre-Raphaelite Keats, of Swinburne and Oscar Wilde, which in Percy's work are set against a present-day atmosphere perceived as threatening and antagonistic toward beauty: "the dark of modernity." The pain of existence felt by sensitive artistic temperaments in such an uncongenial atmosphere is further intensified by the feeling of "malaise" of the "lost generation." Faulkner notes that Percy had seen action in the First World

War – as Hemingway had and he alas had not – and, because of his longing for beauty, Percy thus is in conflict with the present ("born out of his time"). So it is not surprising to see Faulkner in early works like *Lilacs* and *Vision in Spring* experiment with late Romanticism and early Modernism side by side. If we take the historical context into account, the combination of heroic and sentimental poses, of the quietistic vocabulary of Pre-Raphaelitism and the distorted imagery of Modernism becomes believable and understandable.

Although the young Faulkner cannot escape the spirit of the post-war, Modernist twentieth century, or the fascination of correspondingly new modes of expression (Eliot, Aiken, and Joyce), both historical and personal reasons hold him under the spell of late Romanticism and the specific forms of its idealism for a relatively long time.[2] The lifelong predilection of the ostensibly Realistic Faulkner for heroes like Don Quixote and Cyrano de Bergerac simply reflects in another way the problem of ideality versus reality, one for which he ultimately finds a convincing solution in the ironic constellation Gavin Stevens-Ratliff.

In that early review of his fellow Mississippian Percy's work, Faulkner describes with remarkable clearsightedness major tensions in both his own works and in those of many of his contemporaries. It is the reaction to these tensions that produces the increased desire for stylization in the works and lives of many artists of the day. Not only in Europe, but also in the United States, the great cultural changes brought about by the First World War and its aftermath help to explain the peculiar brand of disappointed idealism and aestheticism characterizing so many sensitive young artists of the time: "a mixture of passionate adoration of beauty and as passionate a despair and disgust with its manifestations and accessories in the human race," as Faulkner puts it. Keeping these tendencies in mind we begin to understand why the American twenties should have turned to the European "l'art pour l'art" aesthetic and to the masks and motifs, forms and language of the *fin de siècle*.

Faulkner's own use of this tradition makes even more sense when we attempt to discover not just influences, but the underlying needs and forces that made him submit to them. What his early drawings and poems show above all is his fascination with "beautiful" and often esoteric modes of expression. Apparently it was only through this tradition of stylization that he became able to express himself artistically for the first time. His amazingly long, and as the manuscripts show, tireless work with late Romantic materials of secondary quality makes clear that he realized mere exposure to the reality of his native soil probably would have left him poetically inarticulate. Evidently, under the strains of his cultural and personal situation, art was only art when explicitly "beautiful," in delicate if somewhat pale colors and forms and in any case very remote from everyday reality. A *Gesamtkunstwerk* like *The Marionettes*, in which picture, text, and binding create a small cosmos, shows that art signifies not primarily a representation, but a *transformation* of reality for the young artist. From our perspective, the particular forms may seem unoriginal, the assimilation of turn-of-the-century attitudes juvenile, yet what matters is the undeniable seriousness of the young man's interest in form and style. In this the juvenilia reveal the developing professionalism of the great artist.

Faulkner's beginnings as a poet and graphic artist are of interest, because he became a great novelist afterward. This fact has had two decisive consequences for the scholarly debate on the early works.[3] Critics have approached Faulkner's initial phase almost exclusively from the perspective of the major works and from the perspective of influences, since in the early work, sources of inspiration and literary models for the later works are more abundant and easier to identify. This tradition includes not only the first stocktaking by Richard P. Adams, but also the respective chapters in Blotner's biography and in Cleanth Brooks's *William Faulkner: Toward Yoknapatawpha and Beyond*.[4] Paradoxically, since all influences are ostensibly known by now, critics bound to the concept of individual influences seem to be losing interest in them. Characteristically, in one of the most recent books, *William Faulkner: The Making of a Novelist*, Martin Kreiswirth, after first carefully registering the individual influences, ends by emphasizing Faulkner's rejection or outgrowing of them.[5] A more daring influence study is *The Origins of Faulkner's Art* by Judith Sensibar, who derives the structures of the later novels directly from the influence of Aiken's poetic polyphony on Faulkner's lyric cycle of 1921, *Vision in Spring*.[6] In addition to these more recent studies we are indebted to the posthumous editions and introductions of Faulkner's early work by Noel Polk (*The Marionettes*), Judith Sensibar (*Vision in Spring*), and particularly Carvel Collins (*Early Prose and Poetry, New Orleans Sketches*, and *Mayday*) for a knowledge of Faulkner which now extends much further than *The Marble Faun* and *A Green Bough*.

This expanded awareness of the early works has led to a much more accurate overall conception of Faulkner. Those critics familiar with the influence of Swinburne, Wilde, and Verlaine, of Eliot, Aiken, and Joyce, no longer regard Faulkner as the natural genius from the American South. Our concern today is not whether Faulkner was a literarily conscious artist, but rather how and why he undertook those specific exercises in imitation and adaptation of which we are now acutely aware. As Thomas McHaney in his review of Cleanth Brooks's *William Faulkner: Toward Yoknapatawpha and Beyond* has put it:

I am not sure how Faulkner came to balance his sense of place with his artistic ambitions, his knowledge of north Mississippi with his sophisticated aesthetic, or his native and circumambient language with the late nineteenth- and early twentieth-century poetry and prose he had been reading. It was clearly more than stumbling into possession of his "postage stamp of native soil."[7]

This book attempts to provide an answer to McHaney's implied question: how Faulkner became a literary artist and not simply a vehicle for some rural muse. He did so by virtue of a relatively long apprenticeship to identifiable traditions and styles, notably the late Romantic movements referred to by such terms as *fin de siècle*, "Pre-Raphaelite," "Symbolism," "Arts and Crafts," *art nouveau*, and "Modernism." To be sure, when a young Mississippian uses Pre-Raphaelite motifs and stylistic devices during the years 1918–25, under the influence of an epigone of English Romanticism like the now little known Robert Nichols, the Pre-Raphaelitism must be differently motivated and of a different type than the mode followed by the Pre-Raphaelite Brotherhood (1848). On the other hand, certain features of Faulkner's early works must be labeled "Pre-Raphaelite," as they would otherwise remain unidentified.[8] The term *art nouveau* for Faulkner's drawings may seem unjustified for those who know their countryman Faulkner, and it would, of course, be mistaken to use the term with Faulkner in the same sense as it applies to artists in Vienna or Brussels, or to the American illustrator William Bradley. But if the provincial modifications which the international *art nouveau* movement receives in the student yearbook *Ole Miss* are seen, the applicability of the term *art nouveau* to Faulkner becomes quite apparent.[9]

Judging from these examples, it is clear that such terms ought not to be understood as mutually exclusive concepts, but as mutually defining components of a semantic field. The designations *fin de siècle* and "late Romantic," which are made concrete by their contexts, express different relations to "Modernism," and in turn describe the network of historical tensions in which Faulkner worked.[10] The term "Symbolist," for example, is generally used in connection with the problem of correspondences,[11] whereas "Pre-Raphaelite" is employed to refer to the specific color effects or archaic rhyming patterns derived from the corresponding English tradition. To apply the term "Modernist" to certain aspects of Faulkner's early work seems justified not only because of the Aiken and Eliot influences, but even more so in view of the new overall picture of the Southern contribution to twentieth-century literature.[12]

Establishing a manner of writing and painting in imitation of an already existent mode of perception and style is of primary importance for most artists. From the reworking of the transmitted style, together with the new thematic content, a distinctly individual mode of expression arises during further stages of development. In Faulkner's case this development begins after the initial phase focused on here (1919–21), with the New Orleans sojourn of 1925, a rich subject for further study.

A writer like Faulkner, who as a youth was so devoted to the close observation of his native world, apparently needed experience in dealing with strong stylizing elements to offset his realism and to establish a controlling artistic consciousness that fitted the Modernistic paradigm. Without his experiments in describing and drawing stylized scenery and figures in such works as *The Marble Faun* and *The Marionettes*, the Mississippi landscapes later portrayed by Faulkner in *Sartoris*, *Sanctuary*, and *The Sound and the Fury* could have been neither structured nor symbolically charged. Similarly, without the experience with manneristic image and sound patterns in *The Marionettes*, until now rejected by critics as artificial and pointless, the subtle structuring of imagery so central to *Light in August*, *Absalom, Absalom!* and *A Fable* could not have been perfected. Faulkner's artistic learning processes encompass not only the imitation of motifs and paraphrase, but also the adoption of masks and role-playing.[13] In this respect it will be very illuminating when we discuss the various Pierrot personae as a mode of artistic vision in Faulkner's texts as well as in his drawings.

In the following study we will look at the works of the initial phase not primarily as preparation for Faulkner's major works but in themselves and as related to their literary and graphic traditions. Like other artists, Faulkner, in his early phase, shows more clearly recognizable affinities with contemporary fashions and trends than in his mature works. His interest in Swinburne and Verlaine, for example, appears in a different light when we bear in mind that Fitzgerald, Wallace Stevens, and Joyce all turned to the same sources for inspiration.

In each of the following four parts I will attempt to see Faulkner's individual place in the contemporary panorama, including the specifically American and local variants of the great international movements which inspired him and so many other artists of the time. In Part I, Faulkner's handmade and handwritten book manuscripts are discussed in connection with the Arts and Crafts movement and the drawings related to *art nouveau* and cartoon drawings of the American twenties. In Part II, a group of early poems, that, unlike those in *The Marble Faun* and *A Green Bough*, have so far received little attention, are discussed within the context of the late Romantic, Pre-Raphaelite tradition on the one hand, and Modernism on the other. In Part III, Faulkner's one-act play *The Marionettes*, closely related to his stylized artwork and poetry, is seen against the background of the Little Theater movement and its concern with the mask and a new poetic voice. Finally, in Part IV, Faulkner's poetic prose in *The Marionettes* and the prose poems will be discussed in connection with image patterns and scenes from *Soldiers' Pay*, *Flags in the Dust*, *The Sound and the Fury*, *Light in August*, *Absalom, Absalom!*, *The Hamlet*, and *A Fable* to demonstrate how an understanding of Faulkner's self-education in the art of stylization can inform current criticism and illuminate Faulkner's most challenging fictional works.

PART I

Faulkner's Artwork

1

Faulkner, *Fin de Siècle*, and Early Modernism

I went particularly to see Oscar Wilde's tomb, with a bas-relief by Jacob Epstein.
Faulkner, *Selected Letters*, 12

TODAY most critics realize that many of the supposedly new elements in Modernist works were latent in the *fin de siècle*, and that Modernist artists continued to use *fin de siècle* motifs and forms, but actual instances in the works of the great twentieth-century authors still tend to elicit surprise. This is certainly true in the case of Faulkner's *A Fable*. There is not only a "savage and slumbrous head" by Gaudier-Brzeska (*FAB*, 283), but also a young RAF pilot reading Walter Pater's *Gaston de la tour* (*FAB*, 101). In this late novel, where Faulkner attempts to structure the apocalyptic visions called up by totalitarianism and the horrors of the Second World War, a number of motifs such as the Harlequin and the Hermaphrodite, the dream of Cathay or showers of confetti still show how formative the transitional phase between *fin de siècle* and Modernism had been for him. The mature author, of course, puts these images, familiar from his early works, to a very different use. Hermaphroditism no longer illustrates that peculiar *fin de siècle* ideal of beauty, but the "phenomenon of war," whose "principles of victory and defeat inhabit the same body" (*FAB*, 344). In *A Fable*, Harlequin ("like Harlequin *solus* on a second- or third-act stage," *FAB*, 236) no longer serves as a mask for the late Romantic–early Modernist ego, as in the early Picasso or in the early Faulkner's own Pierrot figure, but helps to caricature the inauthentic existence of the old general's aide, and the RAF pilot reads Pater not because he is a Decadent, but because he cannot reconcile his idealistic patriotism with the strategic exigencies of modern mass warfare.

The attitudes of Modernists like Eliot, Schoenberg, and Matisse toward their predecessors were in many respects not as antagonistic as they liked to claim. Pound, for instance, refers on the one hand ironically to Swinburne in several poems and uses the review of Gosse's book on Swinburne as a platform to define his Modernist poetics.[1] On the other hand, major aspects of Pound's early poetry, including the *Cantos*, can only be fully understood in the light of the Pre-Raphaelite influence. Lincoln Kirstein, in a book on Pound and the visual arts, stresses Pound's roots in the *fin de siècle* and its influences – Ruskin, Quattrocento Tuscan art, Walter Pater, Salomon Reinach, Whistler, Charles Ricketts, and Charles Shannon – and maintains that "Pound's early preferences were a logical issue of the Nineties; Elkin Matthews of *The Yellow Book* was his first English publisher."[2] Wallace Stevens's *Harmonium* shows the influence of Pre-

Raphaelitism, Verlaine, and Imagism to be quite complementary. One critic has perceptively located Stevens's *fin de siècle* interests in the context of the Arensberg circle, which as part of its "taste for the exquisite" held Wilde and Beardsley in the same esteem as Baudelaire, Mallarmé, and Verlaine.[3] Like the young James Joyce, Stevens was fascinated with the older, complicated verse forms rediscovered by Théodore de Banville and by minor English poets such as Austin Dobson. These interests were widespread: there are, for example, traces of Swinburne influences in Joyce's *A Portrait of the Artist as a Young Man* and in John Dos Passos's war novel *Three Soldiers*. The avant-garde poet e. e. cummings speaks of his own attraction to the verbal intelligence and stylistic mannerism of Rossetti's sonnets.[4] The same tendency is manifested in Joyce's *Chamber Music*, Edna St Vincent Millay's experiments with Elizabethan verse, and the young Faulkner's search for a new stylized prose, in which he utilizes Swinburnian motifs and the rhetoric of Wilde's *Salome*. Seen against this historical background, Faulkner's seemingly eclectic *études* like "Sapphics" and "Une Ballade des femmes perdues" and his one-act play *The Marionettes* begin to take on their real significance for his artistic development.

The New Orleans avant-garde journal *The Double Dealer* exemplifies the juxtaposition of the old and the new with American contributors like Sherwood Anderson, Hemingway, and the young Faulkner appearing alongside the Decadent Arthur Symons, who had been instrumental in bringing the new French poetry to the attention of English writers in the nineties and in introducing Yeats to the works of the Symbolists.[5] A year after the First World War, when Hemingway was in his major gestation period, James Branch Cabell's *Jurgen* came out, with its bizarre content and parodistic wit.[6] Faulkner's enthusiasm for this novel, as reflected in *Mayday* and *Soldiers' Pay*, fits into the pattern of his interest in Beardsley's art and Wilde's *Salome*. The same tendency underlies Faulkner's explicitly acknowledged debt to Thomas Beer, whose witty opening to *The Mauve Decade* – "They laid Jesse James in his grave and Dante Gabriel Rossetti died immediately" – is characteristic of the inner affinity between the American twenties and Wilde's *fin de siècle*.[7]

Certain features of American university life at the time also reveal an interest in the *fin de siècle*. Malcolm Cowley, well-known to Faulknerians, reports in his memoir *Exile's Return*: "the Harvard Aesthetes of 1916 were trying to create in Cambridge, Massachusetts, an after-image of Oxford in the 1890s."[8] Judging from the *Nassau Literary Magazine*, to which F. Scott Fitzgerald contributed such an essentially *fin de siècle* poem as "The Cameo Frame," the atmosphere at Princeton was quite similar. And at Yale, where Faulkner visited his mentor Phil Stone in 1918, undergraduate interest in Oscar Wilde remained high until the American entry in the First World War, when the infatuation with the Aesthetic movement in the *Yale Literary Magazine* gave way to wartime propaganda. Yet even the World War did not become an absolute boundary between the *fin de siècle* and Modernist trends in America; in fact, it had no effect on the style of the drawings and sketches in the *Yale Record*, the undergraduate humor magazine, which shows a lively appreciation of Beardsley and *art nouveau* throughout the period. Even at more provincial schools like the University of Mississippi, the European *fin de siècle* had a considerable impact. *Ole Miss*, the student yearbook, contains, as we shall see, a remarkable number of drawings influenced by *fin de siècle* and *art nouveau*, many by Faulkner himself.

Little wonder that fashionable magazines like *Vanity Fair* and literary journals like *The Dial* flirted with *fin de siècle* attitudes. Characteristically, in 1918 *Vanity Fair* ran a full-page photograph of Madame Yorska as Salome in a production of the Washington Square Players as part of its regular feature on actresses (Pl. 1). This in turn provides the background for the influence of Wilde's one-act play on Faulkner's *The Marionettes* and also for the deadly wit of Millay's play *Aria Da Capo*, which combines the spirit of Pirandello's modern drama with the irony of Wilde's comedies and counts as another of the sources for Faulkner's play.

Faulkner's roots in this period of transition and the impact of its tendency towards highly stylized forms of expression become more clearly apparent if we approach his first literary endeavors through such artwork as *The Marionettes* booklet. This hand-crafted and illustrated one-act play is by no means an exception among Faulkner's early works, but belongs to an entire group of such booklets: *Dawn, an Orchid, a Song* (1918), *The Lilacs* (1919–20), *Vision in Spring* (1920), *Mayday* (1926), *Helen: A Courtship* (1926; Pls. 2, 3), *Royal Street: New Orleans* (1926; Pl. 4) and *The Wishing Tree* (1927; Pl. 5). Faulkner may well have bound the six extant copies of *The Marionettes* himself, since this was the only way to "publish" the work,[9] and the fact that he illustrated the text can obviously be explained away by the biographical coincidence of multiple talents. But it is rather striking that the young would-be playwright should strive for a calligraphic script, illustrate this work like a volume of esoteric poetry, and bind it himself. Both the form of the hand-crafted booklets and the persistence of these efforts over an extended period of time (1918–27) suggest that these works correspond to a more widespread concept, the holistic ideal of the Arts and Crafts artist, who, in the words of Rossetti's allegorical tale, works with "Hand and Soul." *The Marionettes* and the handbound and illustrated *Lilacs* manuscript in the Brodsky Collection together with the other booklets reveal how much the idea of a book as a multimedia creation, a *Gesamtkunstwerk*, informs Faulkner's early work.[10]

The larger context is evoked in Sherwood Anderson's *The Modern Writer* (1925), a lecture that Anderson delivered at about the time that he and Faulkner were friends in New Orleans. In this little volume, whose conception corresponds altogether to Arts and Crafts ideals (Pl. 6), Anderson characterizes the beginnings of the modern movement in literature and the visual arts. Like the disciples of William Morris, he sees the new movement essentially as a protest against the anti-artistic standardization of industrial production: "The Modern Movement . . . is in reality an attempt on the part of the workman to get back into his own hands some control over the tools and materials of his craft."[11] Similarly, this development combining Arts and Crafts, Aestheticism, and Modernism, which was so productive for the new poetological concept of the *poeta faber*, appears in

1. "Mme Yorska as Salome," from *Vanity Fair*, June 1918

an essay by Elinor Wylie in 1923 with the revealing title "Jewelled Bindings": "The design of the back cover is equally brilliant and contains . . . eight opals, eight moonstones . . . twelve blue chalcedonies . . ." Wylie's delight in precious metals and stones is just as evident as that in Amy Lowell's poetry, Wilde's *Salome*, and Faulkner's *The Marionettes*. Wylie does not, however, stop with appreciation, but goes on to draw a connection between precious bindings and certain features of contemporary poetry:

. . . I believe we are *good workmen*, *dexterous* and *clean* in our handling of *gold* and *silver* and *precious* – or even semi-precious – *stones* . . . As to the decoration, the *setting* of *words* transparent or opaque in a *pattern* upon our jewelled bindings; I am by no means ready to discard it. It is a *deliberate art*, perhaps, but as such it is a *discipline* and a struggle not to be too impetuously scorned.[12]

Wylie uses this analogy to the art of making jewelry in the same way as Oscar Wilde in his essay "The Critic as Artist": as a call for sensuousness and awareness of form in poetry.

Wylie's essay points especially to the appropriate context for understanding Faulkner's illustrated, calligraphic works. Although precious stones take only a literary form in *The Marionettes*, the book's imagery, decoration, and calligraphy place it well within the movement Wylie describes. Faulkner's hand-crafted *art nouveau* booklets relate to a new ideal of the artist, one which manifests itself in different variations in the development of Modernism: to Wilde's or Wylie's goldsmith and bookbinder, to Anderson's conception of the artist as a workman, which essentially derives from the Morris tradition, and finally, to the Modernistic ideal of the *poeta faber*, which figures prominently in Eliot's dedication of *The Waste Land* to Pound ("il miglior fabbro").

That Faulkner did indeed subscribe to this ideal of the artist as a craftsman is well illustrated by a striking item in the Brodsky collection, Faulkner's copy of

2–3. Faulkner, cover and title page of *Helen: A Courtship*, 1926

HONG LI

 It is written that a man's senses are as bees which, while hiving the indiscriminate honey of his days, cement unawares the imperishable edifice of his soul. What matter if at times the honey seem oversweet to him, or seem to his inferior clay, bitter even? The honey's sweetness is but comparable: soon sweet becomes pallid and without taste; oversweet, but sweet; and at last bitterness strikes no responding chord and man is as a gorged reptile supine before the croaching rumor of worms.

Misfortune is man's greatest gift: happiness is as the orchid that rots the trunk to which it clings and which, removed, dies, leaving the soul a battened pig grunting and jaded in its own filth. Sorrow purges it, and the soul is as the imperishable willow, grave without sadness nor desire. Bereavement? a thing for unlettered beasts to lift yowling inarticulate faces to the remote contemplation of Cosmos. Bereavement of woman, of a little parcel of scented flesh, an articulation of minute worms? Beasts yowling for beasts in the accumulate mud of Time. But for one of the fourth degree? Heh!

The husbandman winnows his grain ere he sow it; the wise husbandman destroys the seed of tares. So do I, in the nurtured garden of my soul, winnow carefully the grain given me; so do I root out and destroy the tares which her dead and delicate feet sowed across my heart, that my soul may be as a garden beyond the rumors of the world

4. Faulkner, "Hong Li," from *Royal Street: New Orleans*, 1926

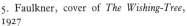

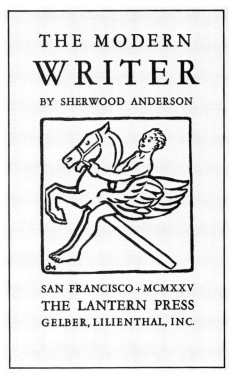

5. Faulkner, cover of *The Wishing-Tree*, 1927

6. Title page of Sherwood Anderson's *The Modern Writer*, 1925

the Imagist anthology of 1915 (Pls. 29–31) (see Robert W. Hamblin, Louis D. Brodsky, *Selections from the William Faulkner Collection of Louis Daniel Brodsky*, Charlottesville, 1979, 20). Apparently Faulkner himself re-bound and hand-lettered this characteristic document of Modernism in the *art nouveau* manner of his own hand-crafted booklets.

Simply to maintain that art movements like *art nouveau* made an impression on Faulkner's Oxford does not imply that its inhabitants and the students at the university were aware of the significance of these movements or gave much thought to them. It seems clear that Faulkner and the students who worked on the University of Mississippi yearbook *Ole Miss* must have come into contact with diverse and fashionable art forms more by chance and instinct than by theoretical considerations. Faulkner may have learned of new trends in art and literature from Phil Stone, whom he visited at Yale in 1918, or discovered them himself through his own reading in contemporary books and magazines. He probably would have had little to say about the relationship between abstract terms like *art nouveau*, *fin de siècle* Aestheticism, and Arts and Crafts movement. As a practicing artist, however, he made recognizable contributions to this tradition with works like his illustrated poem "Nocturne" and the *Dramatis Personae* of *The Marionettes*.

Yet it must be emphasized that Oxford, home of the University of Mississippi, was by no means as cut off from new modes in the artistic world as is generally assumed. The student publications of Faulkner's Alma Mater, including the newspaper *The Mississippian*, the annual *Ole Miss*, and the humor magazine *The Scream*, are of great interest because they reveal varying degrees of influence by *art nouveau* and *fin de siècle* elements. The student newspaper *The Mississippian*, for example, is much farther removed from the Aesthetic movement than *Ole Miss*. This can partly be explained by the fact that artwork, the medium in which such influences are most noticeable, appears only in the annual. Faulkner's poems and translations published in *The Mississippian* stand out rather conspicuously from other contributions and from the mostly humorous verse of his fellow students. His lyric paraphrase of Swinburne, "Sapphics," is placed incongruously among advertisements for clothing and hardware.[13] Faulkner's esoteric poetry and personal mannerisms were the subjects of parody and ridicule; in the same issue in which his "L'Après-midi d'un faune" appears, jokes are made about him in the *Hayseed Letters*: "Sounds like poetry of the Hon. Count Will Faulkner to me . . . "[14] On the other hand, reviews in the *Books and Things* column like those by Paul Rogers of Maeterlinck and by Ben Wasson of one-act plays and the Little Theater Movement indicate that Faulkner was not totally lacking kindred spirits in Oxford.[15] The overall impression left by *The Mississippian* remains, however, that Faulkner's studies in the *fin de siècle* style were exceptions to the rule.

Ole Miss presents an entirely different picture. In this yearbook Faulkner is only one among many students who contributed drawings influenced by Aestheticist tendencies. The use of motifs demonstrating some degree of familiarity on the part of Mississippi students with international trends in art and literature, such as peacocks and *femme fatale* figures, is immediately apparent. L. R. Somerville's contribution, *A New World Symphony – Dvorak*, appears in the same volume as Faulkner's sketch *Fish, Flesh, Fowl*.[16] In his poem "To an Ole Miss Co-ed," Ben Wasson relates the co-ed to a sphinx, a motif used by Victorian painters and by Wilde in poetry.[17] Wasson's final compliment, with its humorous contrast of "free verse" and "sonnet," also reveals his familiarity with contemporary trends in poetry. The combination of *fin de siècle* attitudes and Modernist traits, characteristic of both *Ole Miss* and the twenties in general, is again clearly evident in M. B. Howorth's drawing of a dandy, with a Japanese kimono thrown over his formal wear, sitting in an easy chair covered with an abstract print (Pl. 7).[18]

Howorth's dandy suggests the kind of connoisseurship which encouraged a number of *art nouveau* touches in *Ole Miss*. A 1916–17 cover vignette (Pl. 8) displays typical *art nouveau* motifs (a candle, arabesque flames, stylized flowers) and attempts to unify ornament and script. With its symmetrical, tree-like forms and its Gothic landscape with ruins, the 1920–1 *Ex Libris* (Pl. 9) closely follows *art nouveau*. Lettering and decoration are brought together, while balance is established between geometric and organic forms. The *art nouveau* nature of the graphic work in *Ole Miss* is carried over into its advertisements. An ad for

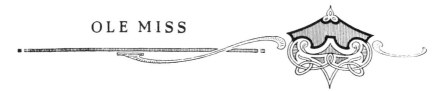

OLE MISS

7. M. B. Howorth, drawing of a dandy, *Ole Miss*, 26, 1921–2

Kennington's (Pl. 10) reveals that the Mississippi business world was familiar with that odd coupling of beauty in design and commercial intentions responsible for some of the finest achievements of European and American *art nouveau* (for example, Bradley's bicycle posters).[19] In the typical *art nouveau* manner, the ad weaves organic forms into arabesques without neglecting their symmetrical order. The script, beginning "The Best Styles . . ." and placed directly above the ornamentation, becomes an integral part of the decoration through positioning, as it seems to rest on the floral arrangement and lettering (especially the shapes of 'T,' 'Q,' 'y,' 's,' and 'B'). Another characteristic trait of *art nouveau* scripts is the combination of latinate-curved lettering with arabesque-like gemmations. This quite reserved ensemble of word and picture forms an aesthetic contrast to the large, simple, bold-face lettering which makes the store's name prominent, "Jackson's Best Store: Kennington's."

The Kennington advertisement illustrates one of the ways in which international art influences, with their origins in the commercial and cultural centers of Europe and America, made an impact on more provincial areas as well. The significance of such indirect channels should not be underestimated. Advertising is one medium in which *art nouveau* made an immediate and frequent impression on people's lives. An advertisement like that for Kennington's would have appeared somewhat earlier in Vienna and Berlin, New York or Chicago, but there would have been little difference in design.

Supplementary material such as the graphic work in *Ole Miss* is of importance

8. Cover vignette from *Ole Miss*, 21, 1916–17

9. *Ex Libris*, from *Ole Miss*, 25, 1920–1

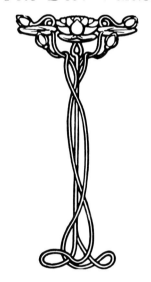

KENNINGTON'S

JACKSON'S BEST STORE

The Best Styles
The Best Quality
The Best Values

The Only Complete Department Store in Mississippi

10. Advertisement for Kennington's, *Ole Miss*, 24, 1919–20

because it provides new insights into *The Marionettes*. It helps us to visualize the artistic milieu of the young Faulkner and clearly demonstrates that even in the Mississippi of the 1920s a young artist trying out various means of expression would have had access to *art nouveau*. Few of his fellow students were prepared or capable of matching Faulkner's preoccupation with Wilde, Beardsley, and other aspects of *fin de siècle* and *art nouveau*, yet the same interests which inspired him were widespread enough to appear in various guises in the college yearbook. Naturally, the yearbook of a provincial university cannot be compared to avant-garde magazines like *Savoy*, *The Chap-Book*, *Jugend*, or *Pan*. In a publication like *Ole Miss*, a certain number of adolescent elements are unavoidable: an emphasis on undergraduate club life, manifestations of social status and snobbery, attempts to assert a sense of self-importance, and second-rate contributions. Precisely these elements, however, make the artwork in *Ole Miss* representative of contemporary taste. In the process of reconstructing an artistic environment like that of the young Faulkner, it is just as important to trace the indirect, diluted, often banalized effects of artistic modes and movements as to pinpoint the direct, consequential influences of such models as Beardsley's brilliant black-and-white art. Another look at *Ole Miss*, where most of Faulkner's known graphic work takes its place among similar drawings from his fellow students, brings us much closer to the world of *The Marionettes*.

It was characteristic of the cultural environment of Faulkner's college days to foster young artists like Howorth, who were able to accommodate *fin de siècle* types such as the *femme fatale* and the dandy to the spirit of the twenties (Pls. 7, 102).[20] In his illustration for the title page of the 1921–2 *Ole Miss* (Pl. 11), Howorth proves just as skillful in his treatment of the neo-rococo style. This scene, showing a cavalier courting a lady in an eighteenth-century park, is a prelude to the neo-rococo decoration giving an air of elegance and modish sophistication to the plainness of the seniors' photographs. The moon and the rising form of a pine tree, which finds an echo in the hanging Spanish moss, recall similar effects in illustrations by Beardsley and Faulkner. Two other *art nouveau* elements are clearly evident: the arabesque shape of the branches on the left side and the use of leaves as organic patterns. It is hardly conceivable that many Mississippi students would turn to rococo art for the inspiration Faulkner or Wallace Stevens found in Verlaine's *Fêtes galantes* or in Beardsley's illustrations for *The Rape of the Lock*. Nevertheless, some of these students shared, if not the artistic purpose, at least the same taste.

The table of contents for the 1921–2 *Ole Miss* (Pl. 12) shows the influence of the Japanese style which, like *fin de siècle* and *art nouveau* tendencies, reached Faulkner's Oxford with a certain provincial lateness. It is not the Japanese motifs, however, but the ensemble-like unity of illustration and script that connects this illuminated page to the *Dramatis Personae* of *The Marionettes* (Pl. 41). Like Faulkner, the anonymous young artist emulates the *art nouveau* style by treating the lettering as part of the decoration. Numerous details contribute to this final integration. The rising curtain, for instance, provides the sense of a beginning

1922 OLE MISS Vol. XXVI

Published Annually by
The Senior Class of all Departments
of the University of Mississippi

11. M. B. Howorth, title page of *Ole Miss*, 26, 1921–2

12. Table of contents, *Ole Miss*, 26, 1921–2

appropriate to the table of contents. The painted Japanese screens themselves foreshadow elements in the text, corresponding to the table of contents in function as well as in format and in the decoration of the cords by which they hang. The distinctly handwritten character of the script and the affinity between the floral ornamentation and the organic, uneven letters in the table of contents for the 1921–2 *Ole Miss* (Pl. 12) provide further parallels to *The Marionettes*. The general tendency followed in forming the letters and particular decorative details (for example, the low position of the middle bars in the 'E' and 'F,' the arabesque-like curves of the 'S') are reminiscent of Faulkner's ornate script. Unlike the exotic aspect of his literary tastes, this attraction to calligraphy was apparently shared by many of his fellow students. There are numerous examples of this common interest in *Ole Miss*. In a sketch by Durfey for the Clubs section (Pl. 15), the *art nouveau* script is carried up by pipe smoke, and together they make an effective contrast to the geometric shape and abstract patterns of the Modernist furniture.[21] In another sketch for this section (Pl. 13), the form of the script mirrors tree and shrubbery in a quite original manner.[22] A sketch accompanying the Juniors section (Pl. 14) is equally successful in capturing the spirit of the Fitzgerald generation; through the elongated tail of the initial 'J' and the curve of the final 'S,' the script closely connects the two figures of a Japanese girl and her beau.[23] On the basis of the graphic works and the illustrated, calligraphic pages in *Ole Miss*, it is clear that Faulkner's artwork is far from being a singular, inexplicable phenomenon, but has its roots in a cultural and artistic environment which was not as isolated from international art movements as the provincial setting of *Ole Miss* might suggest.

The beginnings of the Arts and Crafts tradition can be traced back to William Morris and his attempt to reconcile body and spirit by means of an integration of art and craftsmanship; his spiritual godfather was the Victorian prophet of art, John Ruskin. Ruskin's theories essentially formed the basis for a new philosophy of life, the aim of which was to resolve the social and individual dilemmas posed by industrial civilization. A desire for wholeness prompted artists of the Arts and Crafts movement to make multimedia artworks of books and houses; in doing so, they were reacting against the alienation and suppression of imagination which they experienced in modern society. By taking complete charge of their books and assuming the roles of writer, illustrator, calligrapher, and bookbinder, artists like Morris and Walter Crane believed they could overcome the division of labor which Carlyle, Arnold, and Ruskin, as well as Sherwood Anderson for that matter, had diagnosed as the main evil of industrial society.

As a result of such works as Roger Stein's study of the reception of Ruskin, it has become evident that in America similar attempts were being made to relate art and life in a new and meaningful way.[24] As early as 1902, Oscar Lovell Triggs's *Chapters in the History of the Arts and Crafts Movement* had provided the American public with a committed survey of the socio-political and aesthetic concepts of Carlyle, Ruskin, Morris, and Charles Ashbee.[25] Triggs placed certain trends in America within the same tradition. More far-reaching than his book was the

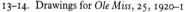

13–14. Drawings for *Ole Miss*, 25, 1920–1

15. Durfey, drawing for *Ole Miss*, 24, 1919–20

journal *The Craftsman*, which appeared from 1910 to 1916 and was edited by the designer Gustav Stickley. This magazine gave its American readers access to the entire spectrum of the Arts and Crafts movement, encompassing both the Anglo-American variety and the continental European variation of *art nouveau*. Despite the difficulties in distinguishing between them and bringing them into agreement, the terms "Arts and Crafts movement" and *art nouveau* refer to different aspects of a single, comprehensive phenomenon, which developed over an extended period and left its mark on everything from housing projects to esoteric book designs.

As early as the Chicago Exhibition in 1893, America had demonstrated to the world that there was not only interest in English Arts and Crafts (Oscar Wilde made his famous lecture tour of America in 1882; Walter Crane lectured there in 1890), but that Americans were also in a position to make their own contributions. It was no accident that Chicago, the center of the Prairie School of American architecture, was "among the earliest and most important centers of arts and crafts in America."[26] In fact, Frank Lloyd Wright (1867–1959), the great architect of modern America who began his work in Chicago, explicitly linked himself to William Morris.[27] Among the American contributions to the *art nouveau* movement, the work of Tiffany and Bradley is particularly worthy of mention. The glasswork and jewelry of Louis Comfort Tiffany (1848–1933) and the posters and illustrations of William H. Bradley (1868–1961) measure up to the best work of European *art nouveau* (Pl. 16). In examining the background of Faulkner's experiments with *art nouveau*, attention should above all be focused on such comparable American examples in printing, poster art, and calligraphy. Bradley is especially important; like Faulkner, he fell under the influence of Beardsley, and at one point was even called "the American Beardsley."[28]

William Morris's founding of the Kelmscott Press in 1890 began a change in America as well as in England, as American printers soon realized. "From 1890 to 1914 the spirit of adventure seized the printers . . . in no similar length of time was so much interesting and stimulating work issued from the American press."[29] Book designers and printers like Daniel Berkeley Updike, Bruce Rogers, Frederic Goudy, W. A. Dwiggins, Carl P. Rollins, and T. M. Cleland won international respect and acclaim for American printing.[30] The publishing of exquisitely beautiful books became fashionable and was cultivated by such publishers as Elbert Hubbard, Thomas B. Mosher, Stone and Kimball, Way and Williams, and Copeland and Day. Even the more conservative Harvard University Press, under William Dana Orcutt, published important Arts and Crafts books; "the Arts and Crafts book became a symbol for the values of production by hand-quality and individuality."[31] Artists and writers soon took to founding presses themselves. William Bradley founded the Wayside Press in Springfield, Massachusetts in 1895, and Philip Green Wright began the Asgard Press. Seen within this context it is no longer surprising that even a poet like Carl Sandburg, whom Faulkner naughtily associated with the Beef Butchers' Union (*EPP*, 85), identified with the "Arts and Crafts" goals of his friend Wright ("Arts-Crafts! . . . an almost holy word") and, as the cover design of his *The Plaint of a Rose* (Pl. 17) shows, actively contributed to the movement.[32] Sandburg's volume of poems as a graphic and literary ensemble points to the same tradition as Faulkner's handcrafted booklets like *The Marionettes* and *Mayday*.

Many artists of the *art nouveau* generation first became aware of the effectiveness of integrating illustration, ornament, and script through illuminated medieval manuscripts and Japanese and Chinese art.[33] Morris, for example, saw illustration and bookbinding as intrinsically connected following his conviction that craftsmanship and the spirit of the artist move together. Only through this holistic combination could the artist overcome the fragmentation resulting from a world of division of labor and rediscover a natural, harmonious life. The pleasure taken in handwritten and handmade books corresponds to the longing for organic works that led Ruskin to postulate an ideal of imperfection in opposition to the deadening perfection of machine-made objects.[34]

The delight in handmade books as multimedia works of art (*Gesamtkunstwerke*) in content and presentation, along with the appreciation of the organic forms of

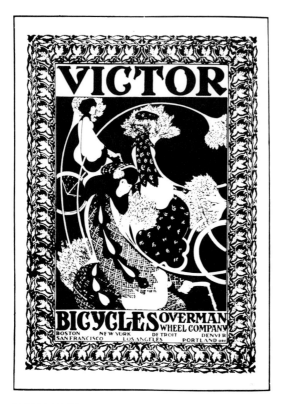

16. William H. Bradley, poster for Overman Wheel Company

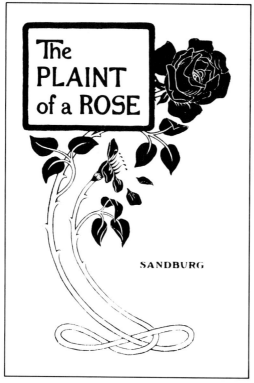

17. Carl Sandburg, cover of *The Plaint of a Rose*, 1908

handwritten texts, are also manifested in Faulkner's collection of poetry *The Lilacs* (Pls. 18–22). As with the one-act play *The Marionettes*, he illustrated the volume of poems himself. In addition to a pen and ink drawing of a nude woman, there is a watercolor of a female figure, whose coloring and flowing forms resemble the *Mayday* illustrations (Pls. 77, 78). The small drawing of a nude can be connected to the poem "A Dead Dancer" (Pl. 22) and understood as an ornamental apotheosis of the lover, along with a corresponding illustration from *The Marionettes* (Pl. 97). But the figure is far too abstract for the picture to be interpreted as the illustration of only a single poem. Instead, it is to be seen as an appropriate final vignette for the entire cycle, which, although named after the Modernistic initial poem "The Lilacs," is governed in general by Pre-Raphaelite motifs and forms and a late Romantic, elegiac tone:

> . . . she danced
> On slender gilded feet;
>
> . . .
> The notes weave back and forth across
>   the growing shadows
> Like gold threads in a dim old tapestry.[35]

The drawing shows an ornamental white nude on a diamond-shaped, black surface, which includes a white border. The figure, whose head remains in an unclear, mask-like shape, and whose arms form a symmetrical triangle, corresponds in length to the elongated diamond shape. With its strong emphasis on the axis, the drawing recalls the symmetry of inkblot art. As in Faulkner's advertisement for the drama club "The Marionettes" in *Ole Miss* (Pl. 55), the figure is obviously shaped to fit the format. Through its emphatic stylization, and the black, diamond-shaped background derived from the cross form, the vignette is reminiscent of cult images. The symmetry, together with the reduction of the physicality to ornament and the interaction of white and black forms on a single plane, correspond to the *art nouveau* ideals that Faulkner found in Beardsley's art.

Faulkner's sensitivity to the contemporary style of the Arts and Crafts movement becomes clear when we realize that the little nude in the final vignette appears as a decorative echo of the watercolor of a female figure at the beginning of the little book. Not only the illustrations, but the "red velvet" binding as well, contribute to the effect of an ensemble arrangement and reflect the preference of the time for beautifully bound works. Faulkner's dedication of the volume to his friend and mentor, Phil Stone, is equally characteristic. Such dedications correspond to tendencies in both *fin de siècle* and Modernism towards literary friendship and esoteric groups of literary friends. A further element becomes apparent in the inclusion of a French quotation in the dedication (". . . quand il fait sombre"; Pl. 19). The table of contents for *The Lilacs* manifests the same tendency, with the clearly recognizable preference for French or "exotic" titles: "L'Après-midi d'un faune," "Une Ballade des femmes perdues," "Cathay" (comparable to the title of Pound's versions of Chinese poems), "O Atthis," and "Sapphics."

18–21. Faulkner, fragments from *The Lilacs*, 1919–20: title page; dedication to Phil Stone; leaf; watercolor

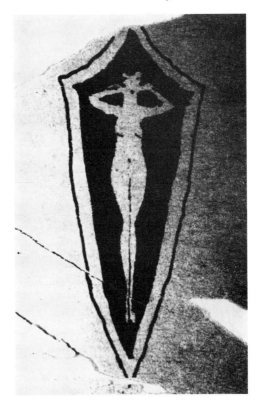

22. Faulkner, drawing from *The Lilacs*, 1919–20

The impression of pronounced esotericism is heightened by such titles, which would not have been accessible to every fellow student at "Ole Miss," as well as by the overall presentation of the work and, not least, through the handwriting. The script is essentially the same decorative type as in *The Marionettes* (Pl. 23). In both cases, the most remarkable features are the spiral 'S' forms. As we shall see in *The Marionettes*, the spiral-shaped letters in *art nouveau* scripts are intimately related to the contents of specific *art nouveau* motifs. Artistic motifs such as tendrils, the necks of swans and peacocks, in addition to flame-like, cloud-like, and wave-like forms, manifest the sense of a propagation of living things and organic growth.

A predilection for flowing, sinuous forms characterizes many *art nouveau* types, scripts, and illustrations. It is found to an equal degree in Henry van de Velde's woodcut for Max Elskamp's book *Dominical* (Pl. 24) and in the title page of Faulkner's *Marionettes* (Pl. 23).[36] Whereas Faulkner limits the curvilinear element in his title page to the shaping of individual letters, the entire page of his sketch for the Organizations section of *Ole Miss*, dating from the same period, is dominated by similar curves (Pl. 25). Wave form in the script of *The Marionettes* is particularly pronounced in the 'M' and the 'N,' but to a certain extent animates all letters. The sigma-like, serpentine 'S' is especially interesting. It resembles the initials designed by van de Velde (Pl. 26) and seems to spring from the same *art nouveau* sensibility which inspired woodcuts like Josef Váchal's *The Little Elf's*

THE MARIONETTES

A PLAY IN ONE ACT

BY

W. FAULKNER

23. Faulkner, title page of *The Marionettes*, 1920

DOMINICAL.

24. Henry van de Velde, title page of Max Elskamp's *Dominical*, 1892

OLE MISS

Organizations

25. Faulkner, drawing for *Ole Miss*, 24, 1919–20

26. Henry van de Velde, design for initials, from *Van Nu En Straks*, 1896

Pilgrimage (Pl. 27). While details such as the serpentine 'S,' the diagonal crossbars of the 'N' and the 'H,' with the former rising from left to right, the low-set bar of the 'E,' and the intersecting middle strokes of the 'M' and the 'W' produce an uneven, mannered effect, there is an equally apparent counter-tendency toward simplification. Examples of this within the text are the rectangular shapes of the 'u' and the 'n,' the omission of the dot over the 'i,' and the simplified verticals and semicircles of the letters 'p,' 'd,' and 'b.' The juxtaposition of simplified and ornate forms is quite common in *art nouveau* manuscripts, as calligraphic poems by Laurence Housman (Pl. 28) and the German poet Stefan George clearly show.

The lettering on the spine and on a white label affixed to the front of Faulkner's copy of the Imagist Anthology (1915) illustrates this very well (Pls. 29–31). Although the script is not sinuous and ornate as in *The Marionettes*, but of an angular and simplified Roman kind, the arrangement of the letters testifies to the same calligraphic care as Faulkner's own hand-crafted booklets. The initial letters of the three words of the title *Some Imagist Poets* are made to rise considerably above the rest. In addition to this ornamental effect, the lower curve of the *S* displays a characteristic *art nouveau* shape and is made more prominent by decorative barbs. The digits of the date (1915) placed underneath have an elegant flow and handwritten quality, and thus contrast with the lettering of the title.

The caption on the spine of the book is further proof of Faulkner's awareness of the Arts and Crafts ideals. Because of the limited space, the text is condensed further, and the two words *Some Imagists* are effectively related. The shape of the longer word *Imagists* placed underneath *Some* to resemble *Some* is made to look shorter through the close linkage of the decoratively elongated 'I' and 'T' with the neighboring letters. Faulkner's binding and hand-lettering of the *Imagist Anthology* as of his own booklets are contributions to that specific tradition of the "*Gesamtkunstwerk*", total work of art, initiated by William Blake.

The illuminated poems of William Blake are perhaps the best proof that simplified forms can be thoroughly reconciled with vigorous, sinuous lines. Blake's poems perfectly integrate script and ornament, picture and word, into a complete work of art. Artists like Rossetti, Crane, Beardsley, and Arthur Mackmurdo returned to Blake repeatedly to experience the vitality which expresses itself in his fluid spirals and floral shapes. They also found, already

27. Josef Váchal, *The Little Elf's Pilgrimage*, 1911

No long time after, Jane was seen
Directing jumps at Daddy Green;
And that old man, to watch her fly,
Had eyebrows made of arches high;
Till homeward he likewise did hop,
Oft calling on himself to stop!

9

28. Laurence Housman,
illustrated page, 1892

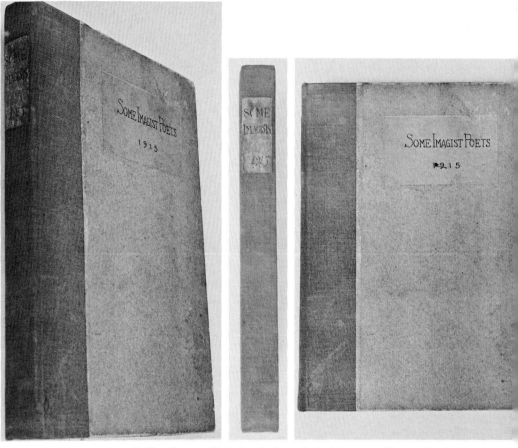

29–31. Faulkner's copy of *Some Imagist Poets: An Anthology*, 1915 (from the Louis Daniel Brodsky collection)

realized in Blake's work, that dissolution of three-dimensional forms and reduction to a flat surface which Oscar Wilde was later to prescribe as the necessary requirement of a good illustration.[37] It was following this prescription that Charles Ricketts was able to assimilate illustration and script in his sketches for Wilde's *A House of Pomegranates*. Similar efforts on Faulkner's part can easily be recognized in his "Nocturne" illustrations and in the *Dramatis Personae* for his play *The Marionettes*.

Faulkner's illustrated poem "Nocturne" (Pl. 32), published in the 1920–1 *Ole Miss*, is a variant of a part of the third poem of *Vision in Spring*, a lyric cycle written in the summer of 1920 and dedicated to Estelle Oldham, who was then married to Cornell Franklin. Like *The Marionettes*, *Vision in Spring* is a handmade, although not handwritten, volume and demonstrates the breadth of Faulkner's Arts and Crafts interests. Blotner describes the book as follows:

It was another carefully crafted gift volume. He had covered the thin 5½-by-8-inch boards with a brownish-green mottled paper. On a small square of white linen paper in the upper right-hand corner in India Ink he had lettered the title, *Vision in Spring*, and his name. He had pasted a strip of white parchment or vellum over the spine. The white pages within were stapled together.[38]

NOCTURNE.
Colombine leans above the taper flame:
Colombine flings a rose.
She flings a severed hand at Pierrot's feet.
Behind, a perpindicular wall of stars,
Below, a gleam of snows.
Pierrot spins and whirls, Pierrot is fleet;
He whirls his hands like birds upon the moon.
Pierrot spins and whirls . . . .
His eyes are filled with facets of many worlds
Of silver and blue and green,
And he would hide his head, yet the keen
blue darkness
Cuts his arms away from his face.
Listen! A violin
Freezes into a blade, so bright and thin
It pierces through his brain, into his heart,
And he is spitted by a pin of music on the dark.
Swift the wisps of motion blown across the moon;
Colombine flings a paper rose, —
Pierrot flits like a white moth on blue dark.
Black the taper, sharp their mouths in starlight,
The sky with icy rootless flowers gauntly glows.
They are stiffly frozen, bright and stark.

32. Faulkner, "Nocturne," 1920

It is obvious that Faulkner intended the layout of *Vision in Spring* to appeal to the same *art nouveau* taste as had *The Marionettes*, with its carefully contrived black-and-white effects. The figures and motifs central to the "Nocturne" poem (Pierrot, Columbine, dance, moon, and candles) also appear as the main graphic motifs in the illustration, which is in accordance with Wilde's call for two-dimensional representation: the graphic motifs do not disturb the effect of the script through excessive realism. The two blocks of text are integrated into the design by means of the supporting candlesticks and the outstretched arms of the two dancers, who themselves rise out of the candle flames like arabesques. Words, standing out against a white background, do not only impart subject matter but are just as important as decoration and have the same function as the irregularly placed stars in the background of the illustration. Faulkner's effective use of black–white mirroring is altogether worthy of attention.

In exploring the origins of Faulkner's early attempts in graphic art and his efforts to integrate illustration and text, ornament and script, it is useful to compare works like "Nocturne" to the main body of American *art nouveau*

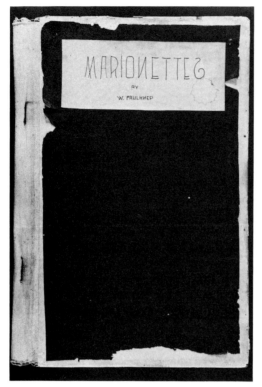

33. Faulkner, cover of *The Marionettes*, 1920

34. Faulkner, cover of *Vision in Spring*, 1920

UNLIKE are we, unlike, O princely Heart!
Unlike our uses and our destinies.
Our ministering two angels look surprise
On one another, as they strike athwart
Their wings in passing. Thou, bethink thee, art
A guest for queens to social pageantries,
With gages from a hundred brighter eyes
Than tears even can make mine, to play thy part
Of chief musician. What hast thou to do
With looking from the lattice-lights at me,
A poor, tired, wandering singer, singing through
The dark, and leaning up a cypress tree?
The chrism is on thine head,—on mine, the dew,—
And Death must dig the level where these agree.

THOU hast thy calling to some palace-floor,
Most gracious singer of high poems! where
The dancers will break footing, from the care
Of watching up thy pregnant lips for more.
And dost thou lift this house's latch too poor
for hand of thine? and canst thou think and bear
To let thy music drop here unaware
In folds of golden fulness at my door?
Look up and see the casement broken in,
The bats and owlets builders in the roof!
My cricket chirps against thy mandolin.
Hush, call no echo up in further proof
Of desolation! there's a voice within
That weeps . . . as thou must sing . . . alone, aloof.

35. Helen M. O'Kane, page from Elizabeth Barrett Browning's *Sonnets from the Portuguese*, 1900

VIII

AND you, great sculptor—so, you gave
A score of years to Art, her slave,
And that 's your Venus, whence we turn
To yonder girl that fords the burn!
You acquiesce, and shall I repine?
What, man of music, you grown gray
With notes & nothing else to say,
Is this your sole praise from a friend,
" Greatly his opera's strains intend,
But in music we know how fashions end ! "
I gave my youth ; but we ride, in fine.

IX

WHO knows what 's fit for us ? Had fate
Proposed bliss here should sublimate
My being—had I signed the bond—
Still one must lead some life beyond,
Have a bliss to die with, dim-descried.
This foot once planted on the goal,
This glory-garland round my soul,
Could I descry such ? Try & test !
I sink back shuddering from the quest.
Earth being so good, would heaven seem best ?
Now, heaven and she are beyond this ride.

36. Samuel Warner, page from Robert Browning's *The Last Ride*, 1900

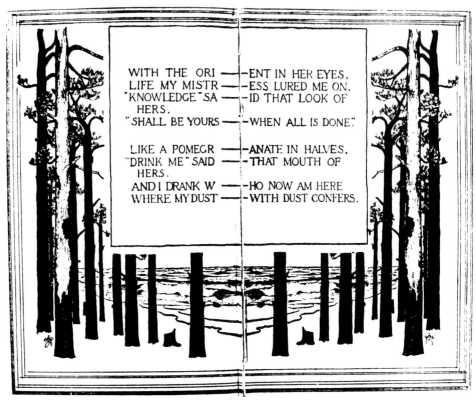

37. Tom B. Meteyard, endpaper from Bliss Carman and Richard Hovey's *Songs from Vagabondia* (1894)

illustration.[39] In his illustrations to Elizabeth Barrett Browning's *Sonnets from the Portuguese*, H. M. O'Kane establishes a relationship between the waterlily pattern of the illustrations and the Gothic script by repeating the motif in the initials and vignettes within the text blocks (Pl. 35). Samuel Warner, in his illustrated edition of Robert Browning's *The Last Ride*, links the ornamental background of the illustrations to the poem by varying the positions of a depicted figure in relation to the text (Pl. 36). In the endpaper of Bliss Carman and Richard Hovey's *Songs from Vagabondia*, Tom B. Meteyard achieves a similar unity of illustration and text by stressing the affinity between the typeface and the patterned trees; Meteyard also orders pattern and text along a central axis (Pl. 37).

The same principles of order found in illustrations by O'Kane, Warner, and Meteyard appear in Faulkner's "Nocturne." Here, symmetry results particularly from the moon, the central position of the candlesticks, and the parallel arrangement of the text blocks to the dancers and the candles, respectively. Faulkner's emphasis on silhouettes, a fascination he shares with Warner, corresponds to the *art nouveau* tendency toward two-dimensional ornamentation. As comparison with his professional predecessors shows, Faulkner made a very respectable contribution to the American *art nouveau* tradition with "Nocturne."

Alongside "Nocturne," a number of pages in *The Marionettes* set off by poetry and the two-paged illustration *Pierrot's Two Visions* (Pls. 38, 39) demonstrate Faulkner's conception of the page as a graphic unity. In *The Marionettes*, he observed the relationship of text to page only with regard to the regular spacing of lines and margins. "Lyrical" pages gave him the opportunity to bestow unity on two separate pages through the interaction of text and space.[40] *Pierrot's Two Visions* is the only illustration in *The Marionettes* to cover more than one page. This spatial expansion is justified by a thematic enlargement, since the illustration deals with two separate phases of Marietta's story: on the left side, Pierrot's courtship, and on the right, her solitude at the beginning as well as the end of the play. Taken separately, each of the pages has a vertical structure, but together they are structured horizontally. This horizontal effect is due to both the black background of the wall, which connects the bottom parts of the two pages, and to the two black poplars, which parallel one another on each of the pages and stand out against the upper part of the white background of the sky. Faulkner, who with this picture obviously shared the *art nouveau* predilection for symmetrical decoration, placed a classical portico behind the main figures and used it as the pictorial axis. In addition, he framed the illustration with the rosebushes behind the observing figures on the left, and the sleeping Pierrot on the right. A closer look at the illustration reveals that, despite Faulkner's efforts to unify the two sides, they are not placed exactly parallel: the right-hand side is slightly higher than the left. This elevation counterbalances Pierrot's protrusion from the bottom of the picture which would otherwise destroy the delicate relationship of the two pages. Pierrot's positioning is itself characteristic of the *art nouveau* tendency to flow beyond the frames and borders of pictures.

Although Faulkner's *art nouveau* calligraphy and Beardsleyesque illustration are clearly the experiments of a novice, this need not distract our attention from the young artist's deeply-felt urge to create graphic as well as poetic beauty. Obviously influenced by Beardsley, the illustrated *Dramatis Personae* of *The Marionettes* is indicative of Faulkner's approach to stylization (Pl. 41). His handling of the garlanded rose motif, with its emphasis on individual roses, recalls Beardsley's illustrations for the title page of *Salome* and its *Contents Border Design* (Pl. 40). Despite his amateurish simplification, Faulkner undoubtedly strove to give organic unity to picture and text. The extent of his effort is best demonstrated by the way he integrated the text into the main design: rose garlands enclose the white background of the text and connect it at the same time to the black background underneath. Apart from the structure of the illustration, the affinities between the letter forms and the roses contribute substantially to the fusion of picture and text. The rounded, spiral shapes of the letters, in particular the 'S' and the 'G,' mirror the spiral forms of the roses. The vertical quality of the letters 'F' and 't' reflects the vertical lines used in the shading of the garlands. Furthermore, even the upper white and lower black backgrounds correspond to

You are a trembling pool,
 Love!
A breathless shivering pool,
And I am a flame that only you can
 quench.

Then we shall be one in the silence,
 Love!
The pool and the flame,
Till I am dead, or you have become
 a flame.

Till you are a white delicate flame,

20

Love!
A little slender flame,
Drawing my hotter flame like will-o-
the-wisp in my garden.

But now you are white and narrow as
 a pool,
 Love!
And trembling cool.
Let me drown myself between your
breast points,
 Beloved!

21

38–9. Faulkner, "Lyrical pages" and *Pierrot's Two Visions*, from *The Marionettes*, 1920

40. Beardsley, design for the title page and *Contents Border Design*, from *Salome*, 1893

41. Faulkner, *Dramatis Personae*, from *The Marionettes*, 1920

each other by introducing the characters through different media. Above, the names of the characters are listed in the usual way, while below, the main characters are seen in an emblematic illustration (Pierrot proposing to Marietta). Those critics familiar with the central role mirroring plays in *The Marionettes*, both as motif and structural principle, will not overlook the cleverness of this correspondence.

In *art nouveau*, graphic motifs tend to ignore borders and frames, breaking out, so to speak, into more comprehensive decorative settings. This tendency can be explained as a predilection for ensemble effects, which it would not be exaggerated to see in terms of the profound aesthetic and philosophical uncertainties of the period. This same tendency exemplified by Otto Eckmann in his design for Hegeler's *Sonnige Tage* (Pl. 42) surfaces in Faulkner's *Dramatis Personae*, which is enclosed by floral borders. Like Eckmann, Faulkner avoids a hard-edged border at the top of the page by using asymmetrical, organic patterning. At the bottom of the page, the border's edge is broken by the protrusion of the depicted figures. On the sides, the two flanking figures create non-geometric boundaries in the same way as the flower stalks in Eckmann's design and in the 1916–17 cover vignette of *Ole Miss* (Pl. 8) or the *Ex Libris* from the 1920–1 volume of the yearbook (Pl. 9). The structural importance of these statuesque figures lies in the lateral support they give to the illustration and in the counterbalance their swinging verticals lend to the two rounded, garlanded backgrounds.

The flanking figures have two additional characteristics which merit attention: their symmetrical positioning and the dissolution of their corporeality into a pattern of vertical lines. This tendency towards symmetry, along with the transition from three dimensions to two-dimensional linear ornamentation and patterned surfaces, exemplifies the historical position of *art nouveau*, located midway between the representational art of the nineteenth century and the abstract art of the twentieth. One of the most important of these transitional figures was Beardsley, and much of what Faulkner took from *art nouveau* he easily could have found in Beardsley's *Salome* drawings. Behind the symmetry of the candlesticks in "Nocturne" lie symmetrical effects like those of the torches in Beardsley's *The Eyes of Herod* (Pl. 51). Illustrations like *The Woman in the Moon* (Pl. 50) or *John and Salome* (Pl. 43) are likely sources of inspiration for Faulkner's transformation of the symmetrical figures in his *Dramatis Personae* into linear ornaments and decorative patterns.

A discussion of the *Dramatis Personae* would not be complete without mention of the miniature portico. This structure makes the transition between the black background and the depicted figures Pierrot and Marietta, who, in introducing the marionette motif, use the bottom of the illustration as a proscenium. The classical portico is also important to the overall structure of the page, since its geometric, centered form counterbalances both the organic, rounded backgrounds and the swing of the vertical lines. At the same time, its horizontal, rectangular shape mirrors graphically the vertical columns of the text. Furthermore, the portico reappears throughout *The Marionettes* as a graphic leit-

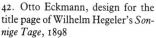

42. Otto Eckmann, design for the title page of Wilhelm Hegeler's *Sonnige Tage*, 1898

43. Beardsley, *John and Salome*, from *Salome*, 1893

motif. It corresponds to the metamorphosis of an image in the text of the play itself, the colonnade: "The twin poplars . . . are like two blind virgins swaying before a colonnade, and the nine white columns of the colonnade are nine muses standing like votive candles before a blue mountain" (*MAR*, 6–7).

In view of the Arts and Crafts, *art nouveau* affinities in Faulkner's graphic work and his interest in Swinburne and Wilde, his Beardsley imitations make sense. But the fact that Faulkner owned and used a copy of Oscar Wilde's *Salome* with Beardsley's illustrations is also in line with a more general interest of American artists and literati in the Aesthetic movement. (See Appendix 1). Against the background of the Beardsley interest visible in *The Chap-Book* and *The Double Dealer*, *The Nassau Literary Magazine* and *The Princeton Tiger*, *The Dial*, *The Smart Set*, and *Vanity Fair*, similarities between details in Faulkner's and Beardsley's drawings – cloud-like patterns (Pls. 49, 97), rose garlands (Pls. 39, 40, 41), and the trellis (Pls. 44, 93) – receive added significance.

What is more important than any coincidental influence is that a common tradition links the two artists. Faulkner takes the same figures (Pierrot) and the same motifs (the formal garden, mirroring, peacocks) from the same tradition as

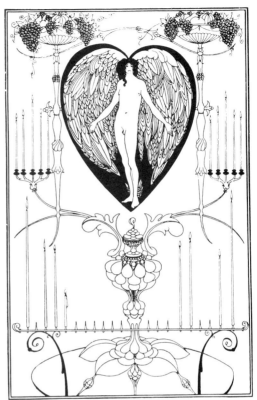

44. Beardsley, frontispiece for Ernest Dowson's *The Pierrot of the Minute*, 1897

45. Beardsley, *The Mirror of Love*, 1895

Beardsley. They approach problems of form in the same way, and Faulkner shares Beardsley's predilection for a sinuous, serpentine line. In his use of graphic motifs like candles and fountains (Pls. 32, 45, 46, 51), Faulkner exhibits a similar delight in variations of the wave form and the *art nouveau* arabesque. The chairs in *The Toilette of Salome II* (Pl. 47) and *Pierrot Sleeping* (Pl. 48) both consist of swinging *art nouveau* curves. The tables differ in style, but they share a decisive formal principle in design: as with the chairs, they are made light so that their material nature itself comes into question, and they almost dissolve into pure ornament. The great Austrian mediator between *fin de siècle* and Modernism, Hugo von Hofmannsthal, with his acute sensitivity for the relationship of particular forms to particular cultures, found this quality of lightness characteristic of contemporary English furniture, and his description holds equally true for Faulkner's and Beardsley's pieces:

It is the spirit of English life which removes the heaviness from furniture and replaces it with form: it is a furniture intended for the small, tentlike rooms of country houses and for the cabins of ships. The result is a unique slenderness and lightness of form.[41]

SOCIAL ACTIVITIES

46. Faulkner, drawing from *Ole Miss,*
24, 1919–20 (*Social Activities II*)
47. Beardsley, *The Toilette of Salome
II*, from *Salome*, 1893

48. Faulkner, *Pierrot Sleeping*, from
The Marionettes, 1920

Beardsley's and Faulkner's shared predilection for transforming furniture into ornament corresponds to their habit of treating pieces of clothing as abstract surfaces with sinuous lines as borders. Their figures retain their heads but lose their bodies to abstract systems of lines or to decorative patterns, a trait characteristic of *art nouveau* paintings like Gustav Klimt's *The Kiss* (Pl. 100). As a result of this kind of rudimentary abstraction, forms blend into what is traditionally background and become part of a new two-dimensional context.

In these "backgrounds" or "contrasting surfaces," it is not difficult to discern Beardsley's influence on the illustrations in *The Marionettes*. Like Beardsley in his *Stomach Dance* (Pl. 58), Faulkner uses a black band in the bottom half of *Pierrot's Two Visions* (Pl. 39) to turn about forty per cent of the page into a contrasting surface. In a variation in *Pierrot Sleeping* (Pl. 48), the band rises toward the upper right half of the page. In *Marietta by the Pool* (Pl. 94), black and white contrasting surfaces meet along a curved line. The effect is similar to that of the curve in Beardsley's *The Climax* (Pl. 49), which rises reversely from left to right. In *Marietta's Apotheosis* (Pl. 97), where black, spike-like segments intersect the white background, Faulkner seems to rely on Beardsley's *The Woman in the Moon* (Pl. 50). But while Beardsley alternates between black and white segments, and to

49–50. Beardsley, from *Salome*, 1893: *The Climax*; *The Woman in the Moon*

some extent gives them a natural cloud-like shape, Faulkner mechanically places abstract black segments within the white background. In contrast to Beardsley, who links the spike-like segments in the background to the predominant form of Salome's pointed dress by means of transitional wave and rounded forms, Faulkner does not relate the patterns in the background to the main motifs in the illustration.

Faulkner's use of patterned and shaded surfaces for the rosebushes in *Pierrot's Two Visions* and *The Kiss* (Pls. 39, 96) is another element that follows certain tendencies in a number of important *art nouveau* graphic works. The band which the lovers stand on in *The Kiss* is ornamented with spiraled roses and vertical shading and corresponds to the more strikingly placed rose ornamentation and diamond-shaped trellis in Beardsley's *The Eyes of Herod* (Pl. 51). There is no equivalent in the *Salome* cycle for the pool patterned with horizontal black and white lines and bands in *Marietta by the Pool* (Pl. 94), but certain parallels can be found in other works by Beardsley; in his rendering of waves in the vignettes for *Soleil Couchant* (Pl. 52), for instance, he also turns them into patterns.

Although Faulkner does not employ graphic motifs with Beardsley's

51. Beardsley, *The Eyes of Herod,*
from *Salome,* 1893

52. Beardsley, *Soleil Couchant,*
*c.*1892

cries of my peacocks have blighted

the ilex before the statue of Hermes.

Curtain

55

53. Faulkner, final vignette from *The Marionettes*, 1920

54. Tailpiece design, from *Salome*, 1893

virtuosity, the formal tendencies are the same for both. With every motif, whether it be the rose, the candle, or the peacock, Beardsley tries to reduce it to a decorative *chiffre*. Faulkner works along the same lines in utilizing poplars as a leitmotif throughout the illustrations (Pls. 39, 48, 93). To facilitate this effect, Faulkner simplifies the form of his trees to an even greater extent than Beardsley in his *The Eyes of Herod* (Pl. 51). The reduction of motifs like trees, peacocks, and roses to patterns is a logical consequence of the transition from representation to abstract ornamentation. In the composition of dual pages like "Nocturne" (Pl. 32) and *Pierrot's Two Visions* (Pl. 39), this tendency towards patterning accords with the *art nouveau* predilection for decorative symmetry. Similarities in form are not the only results of a comparison between Faulkner and Beardsley; differences in moral outlook and artistic attitude become equally apparent. In contrast to the intellectual brilliance and tragic irony of Beardsley's illustrations for *Salome*, the illustrations for *The Marionettes* are obviously the work of a melancholic, somewhat esoteric, but otherwise guileless young man.

As his model Beardsley did in *Salome*, Faulkner closes *The Marionettes* with a final vignette (Pl. 53). A horizontally and vertically well-balanced composition presents the narcissistic Pierrot standing in front of Marietta's bier and staring into a mirror. The thematic conception and design are equally effective: the mirror and the Chippendale couch upon which the dead Marietta lies enhance the scene. Yet a mere glance at Beardsley's tailpiece (Pl. 54) demonstrates that Faulkner's is no more than the work of a talented amateur. Beardsley's grotesque genius reveals itself in an elegant inspiration: a satyr and a degenerate Pierrot lift a hermaphroditic Salome into a rococo powder box. Neither the elegance nor the obscene and grotesque features of this art are to be found in Faulkner. But in some of the sketches for *Ole Miss* the spirit of the Jazz Age lets Faulkner come closer to his model's wit.

2

Faulkner as Cartoonist and Parodist of the Twenties

FAULKNER'S DRAWINGS for *Ole Miss*, which Carvel Collins has so attractively presented to a larger public in the collection *Early Prose and Poetry*, were originally intended not to stand alone but to illustrate and decorate the student yearbook. To explore their function in this 'subservient' capacity, I will attempt to reconstruct their original context. Obviously, a student yearbook does not provide the optimal conditions for creating an ensemble out of picture and text. When a sketch like Faulkner's "Jazz Musicians" (*Red and Blue III*) (Pl. 66) is enlarged and freed of "extraneous material," it inevitably takes on a more advantageous and important appearance than it initially possessed in *Ole Miss*.[1] In the yearbook it is squeezed in rather awkwardly between genteel photographs and the membership list of the dance club Red and Blue. Yet only by regarding it in context can we accurately compare it to similar examples of applied art by Faulkner's fellow students and see his early work against its cultural background.

Interest in these applied or "lesser" arts had greatly increased as a result of Ruskin's vision of a new humane and harmonious life and William Morris's creative craftsmanship.[2] William Bradley and countless other American and European *art nouveau* artists aligned themselves with this tradition and brought about an unprecedented flourishing of the applied and commercial arts. These artists also felt the need to beautify every aspect of printing, and nothing, be it esoteric books and magazines or cartoons and advertisements, was unworthy of their attention. They began an all-inclusive revolution designed to counteract the ugliness of industrial society and the banality of mass democracy with elegant posters, decorative bookplates, and elaborately designed calling cards and invitations. In addition, there were factors of an intrinsically artistic nature. Poster design and the decoration of title pages and tables of contents required a special interest in working with different media and a sensitivity for the problem of integrating illustration and script. The student annual *Ole Miss* proves that this fascination with the interaction of picture and text was not limited to professional artists: amateurs such as the students at the University of Mississippi were also caught up in the same general trend toward ensembles and ensemble-like effects.

In light of this background, Faulkner's contribution to the decoration of *Ole Miss* takes on a new perspective. Within the bounds of the annual format and his own talents, he made every effort to give his work the versatility of other *art*

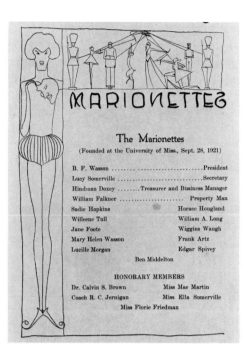

55. Faulkner, drawing for the theater group "The Marionettes," *Ole Miss*, 25, 1920–1

56. Beardsley, *Avenue Theatre* poster for John Todhunter's *A Comedy of Sighs* and W. B. Yeats's *The Land of Heart's Desire*, 1894

nouveau artists. A sketch like the one for his own theater group "The Marionettes" (Pl. 55), which is indebted to Beardsley (Pl. 56), strongly resembles *art
nouveau* poster art.[3] Other pieces suggest the influence of contemporary cartoonists like Richard Boix or John Held, Jr. Of particular interest is the way in which
Faulkner adapts Beardsley to the spirit of the Jazz Age and fuses his influence
with Modernist tendencies.

Faulkner's *Ole Miss* sketch for the theater group "The Marionettes," for
instance, shows unmistakable signs of Beardsley's influence, and the stylistic
affinities help explain Faulkner's attraction to Beardsley as an artistic model.
Faulkner combines the marionette motif with a particular character type that has
the facial features of Beardsley's *femmes fatales* and the slender body of his
hermaphrodites. Like Beardsley in his *Avenue Theatre* Poster (Pl. 56), Faulkner
places this full-length figure within a decorative border on the left side and
connects it with a horizontal border at the top, illustrating the caption "Marionettes." To counterbalance the space reserved for text material, both Faulkner and
Beardsley emphasize these inter-connecting, decorative borders. Faulkner,
moreover, unifies the two themes of his sketch with them: he relates the female
figure with mask in hand in the vertical border to the marionettes in the horizontal
decoration. In accord with *art nouveau* principles, both Beardsley and Faulkner
embellish the calligraphy and seek to integrate it into the illustration. Faulkner
even attempts a one-to-one correspondence between the individual letters and the
marionettes, but his inexperience in graphic design prevents an ideal solution.
Still, his attempt to create the effect of a carousel-like, rounded form among the
juxtaposed figures, by means of the marionettes' strings, is quite successful. The
second marionette from the left and the third from the right are reminiscent of the
stylized Pierrot and Columbine in Faulkner's "Nocturne" (Pl. 32). The device of
using two somewhat larger soldiers to flank the marionette group shows the care
taken with this sketch, despite its amateurishness. Although the marionettes are
the main subject of Faulkner's sketch for *Ole Miss*, there is no denying that the
stylized figure in the vertical border predominates. The sharp hairline and the cut
of her chin reveal her connections to Beardsley's *femmes fatales*, in drawings like
his title page for *Keynotes* (Pl. 57). Her odd pantaloons appear to be a variation on
Salome's in Beardsley's *The Stomach Dance* (Pl. 58). In the patterning of the
costume, the presentation of the feet as arabesques, and the framing of the
elongated hermaphroditic body, the figure in the sketch embodies the *art nouveau*
tendency to dissolve figures into ornament also evident in *The Marionettes*.
Overall, the sketch is a curious combination of theatrical and graphic elements
and provides artistic documentation of the way Faulkner's interests in modern
theater and *art nouveau* coincide.

Apart from various occasional pieces, Faulkner's known and available graphic
work comprises the illustration projects *The Marionettes, The Lilacs, Mayday,* and
Royal Street: New Orleans and the caricatures for the student yearbook *Ole Miss*
and the student magazine *The Scream*. While the *Marionettes* drawings and the
Mayday watercolors reveal a late Romantic, Symbolistic Faulkner fascinated by

Le grand   Americaine Parlee-vous Anglais, mam'zelle?
La petite Francaise — Mais oui, n'cœur, un peu; Do you love me? Kees me queek! Damn' 'ell!

57. Beardsley, design for the cover and
title page of *Keynotes*, 1893
58. Beardsley, *The Stomach Dance*, from
Salome, 1893
59. Faulkner, drawing from *Ole Miss*, 24,
1919–20

esoteric stylization, the *Ole Miss* and *The Scream* caricatures divulge a witty artist of the Jazz Age. In addition to Beardsley, critics have repeatedly named John Held, Jr as a major influence on Faulkner's graphic work, but Held's competitors like Fish, Ralph Barton, Herman Palmer, and L. Fellows, whose cartoons appeared in various magazines of the period like *Judge*, *Vanity Fair*, and *The Dial*, can be cited with equal right. The ironic treatment of such themes and motifs as the war (Pl. 59), automobiles and airplanes (Pls. 60, 61), the flirting flapper and jellybean (Pl. 62) is, like the geometrically patterned clothing in Faulkner's drawings for *The Scream*, far too widespread in the twenties to limit influences to John Held, Jr. Ilse Dusoir Lind, in her illuminating essay "The Effect of Painting on Faulkner's Poetic Form," has taken precisely the right approach by placing Faulkner's relationship to John Held, Jr in the larger historical context:

> The first two decades of the century were the golden age of cartooning. Faulkner was drawn to it and taught himself by means of imitation – of British cartoonists and of the whimsical satirist John Held, Jr who depicted jellybeans and flappers and their ways.[4]

More recently, M. Thomas Inge, besides confirming Faulkner's affinity with John Held, has also stressed his debt to the Funny Papers of the time.[5]

The uncertainty and self-consciousness of the "lost generation" as well as the new vitality of the Jazz Age made the "snappy" medium of the cartoon a characteristic genre for the twenties. The ironic drawings in *Ole Miss* and *The Scream*, which combine reminiscences from Beardsley, Held and other cartoonists besides inspirations from post-Armory Show art, seem to have been decisive for Faulkner's breakthrough to the ironic portrayals of characters like Cecily, George, and Januarius Jones in *Soldiers' Pay* and Mrs Maurier and Talliaferro in *Mosquitoes*. A good example of the fusion of these influences is Faulkner's AEF sketch for the 1919–20 issue of *Ole Miss* (Pl. 59). The situation, an encounter between an American officer and a French "mam'zelle," whose English is limited to "Do you love me? Kees me queek! Damn! 'ell," brings to mind the Held caricatures so typical of post-war America.[6] The formal elements, however, suggest two very different kinds of influence: Modernism and *art nouveau*. The bandlike street, swinging from the foreground to the background, anticipates a modern cartoon by Richard Boix, *Las Matemáticas no son siempre ciencias exactas: 3+3=2* (Pl. 63)[7], but the curve and the "meretricious" trees framing it also recall Beardsley. Similarly, Faulkner's sketch for the Organizations section in *Ole Miss* displays a modish mixture of Modernist and *art nouveau* elements (Pl. 25). While his ironic depiction of a windblown couple here and in Pl. 64 perfectly captures the flavor of the twenties, the wavy lines of the woman's dress bear the mark of *art nouveau*. By stressing the wave forms, he integrates the script into the overall design. The leaves dancing over the heads of the figures link them and their fluttering clothing to the script. By extending the curve of the letter 'n' and by adding a twist to the tails of 'g' and 's' and to the dash of the 't,' Faulkner sets the individual letters into motion, which catches them up and becomes the theme of the sketch.

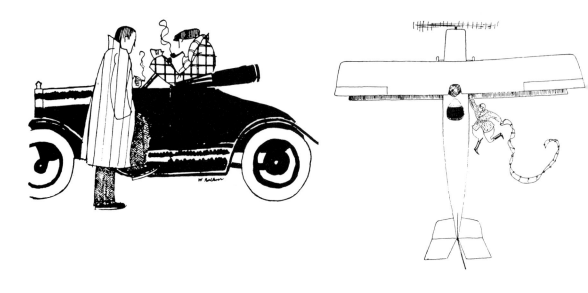

Lit—Aw, come on; aincher goin' to the show?
Law—Na-ah, what I wanta spend good money on a show for?

60–2. Faulkner, drawings from *The Scream*, 1925

Although there is no direct evidence that Faulkner knew such classic works of American poster art as William Bradley's bicycle advertisement (Pl. 16), certain stylistic affinities between contemporary posters and a number of his drawings, above all the close inter-relationship of graphic and script forms, are striking. Through their delineation, the figures in *Red and Blue II* (Pl. 82) dancing the jerky steps of the Charleston illustrate the text. Although Beardsley's influence lingers on in the neatly contrived contrast of the white dancer to her partner in black, their bodies are not stylized in the same manner as in *The Marionettes*. There the organic forms of *art nouveau* dominate; here in the *Ole Miss* sketch the arrangement of geometric segments stands out anticipating the Art Deco forms fashionable after the great Paris exhibition of *Arts décoratifs et industriels modernes* in 1925. The extremities of the dancers' bodies are made up of parallelograms and triangles and the dancers have only one head. Realism is obviously not the aim of this avant-garde sketch that contrasts with rather than embellishes the bourgeois photographs and membership list of the Red and Blue Club. In the drawing itself Faulkner surrounds the white form in the center with alternating black-and-white forms that project from it, suggesting the motion of the Charleston. This kind of geometrical stylization of figure and composition goes beyond Beardsley and signals before the actual Art Deco the new influence on Faulkner's art. Wherever Faulkner had encountered it – perhaps in the work of Richard Boix or other illustrators in *The Dial* – new possibilities for abstraction had been explored in America since the Armory Show in 1913.[8]

The rectangular lettering in *Red and Blue II* matches the content of the design, the diagonal, ornamentally elongated ampersand mirroring the abrupt and elongated movements of the dancers. Such clever correspondences help to unify script and sketch and, like the positioning of the script in the lower left-hand corner, capture the spirit of the Jazz Age. Faulkner had already inventively used a rectangular script in an earlier sketch, *Red and Blue I*, as background for a scene in which a flapper is courted by a baldheaded Prufrock-Talliaferro-Pierrot figure (Pl. 65). Interestingly enough, other *Ole Miss* illustrators experiment with the same kind of rectangular lettering. In contrast to rounded, serpentine *art nouveau* scripts, this angular lettering provides a distinctly modern touch.

Dancing appears as a major pastime and becomes a popular metaphor of the Jazz Age. *Ole Miss* sketches like Faulkner's *Red and Blue III* (Pl. 66) and M. B. Howorth's *Cotillion Club* (Pl. 67) testify to the fact that Oxford, Mississippi was no exception. Howorth's sketch is placed near the top of the page, above a long membership list and directly below an arabesque that combines neo-rococo and *art nouveau* tendencies and reappears throughout the volume; Faulkner's sketch is more advantageously positioned in the middle of the page. Both pieces depict a dancing couple in front of a jazz band, but Faulkner gives his sketch compositional momentum by moving his couple slightly left of center. The motion he suggests is fully developed in the dancer's dress, which extends from the left-hand side to the middle in long *art nouveau* curves, and the outstretched arms of the dancers carry the movement even further to the right. The musicians seem to

63. Richard Boix, *Las Matemáticas no son siempre ciencias exactas: 3+3=2*, from *The Dial*, July 1921

C'est horrible! – Quel donc? – Le mal de mer de ma fiancée.
La, pourquoi ne trouvez-vous pas une amie qui est orpheline?

64. Faulkner, drawing from *Ole Miss*, 25, 1920–1

65. Faulkner, drawing from *Ole Miss*, 22, 1917–18 (*Red and Blue I*)

66. Faulkner, drawing from *Ole Miss*, 25, 1920–1 (*Red and Blue III*)

67. M. B. Howorth, drawing from *Ole Miss*, 26, 1921–2

receive their animation from this dynamic focus. In contrast to Howorth, Faulkner brings his sketch alive through an astonishingly versatile depiction of the bearings and gestures of the individual musicians. The figure of the bass player, who physically embodies the vibrations of jazz, is especially original. The arrangement of the musicians plays a large role in creating motion in Faulkner's sketch. Unlike Howorth, who distributes his musicians evenly on both sides of the dancers, Faulkner avoids strict symmetry and places two on the left side and four on the right side. Their bouncing heads, placed at different levels and turned up, down, to the front, and to the side, add a final element of motion to the sketch. The effectiveness results largely from a subtle distribution of black and white derived from Beardsley. The black piano works as a contrasting background behind the dancers, counterbalances their motion, and provides structural support for the sketch as a whole. Furthermore, this larger black area gives the smaller black forms of heads and hands the necessary reinforcement to assert themselves within the composition. While Howorth reproduces tails and tie with pedantic realism, Faulkner deals with clothing in a much more abstract way, using stylized body proportions not mimetically but expressively. The faces of Howorth's musicians are comic and stereotypical "black minstrels"; when compared to the faces of the dancing whites, racial clichés become evident. For Faulkner, on the other hand, both the white dancers and the black musicians are objects of formalization. He utilizes the black faces and skullcap-like hairstyles of the dancers as rounded, contrasting forms and integrates them into the composition. The tendency here toward idealization, also apparent in the depiction of clothes and feet, is along the lines apparent in *The Marionettes*. It is possible, for instance, to associate Faulkner's striking treatment of the curving hem of the dancer's dress to that of the gown in Beardsley's *The Woman in the Moon* (Pl. 50). In both drawings, the swinging curves are more important than the clothing they define. Of course, there are significant differences as well. The dancer in the Faulkner sketch is not Salome and not a *femme fatale*, but a flapper of the twenties. The music playing is no longer Wagner's, which had cast its spell over Beardsley and the decadents, but that of the Jazz Age.[9] Above all, a new austerity of form replaces the Beardsleyesque delight in decoration still found in *The Marionettes*, revealing the influence of Modernism.

In several sketches the two elements even exist side by side. The symmetrical candelabra in Faulkner's *Social Activities II* (Pl. 46) are clearly related to Beardsley and *art nouveau*, but the checkerboard patterning here and in *Social Activities I* (Pl. 70) confirms Faulkner's Modernist tendencies. Checkerboard patterns play an important role in a number of paintings and are characteristic of American art after the Armory Show. In both Max Weber's *Chinese Restaurant* of 1915 (Pl. 68) and Marsden Hartley's *Painting, Number 5* of 1914–15 (Pl. 69), checkerboard sections are prominent. In Faulkner's illustrations, this motif is part of a system of abstractly patterned surfaces, marking the Modernist search for non-representational forms and decorative structures. The decorative quality is what provides the common element in Faulkner's *Social Activities II* (Pl. 46)

68. Max Weber, *Chinese Restaurant*, 1915.
Oil on canvas. 40 × 48 inches.

69. Marsden Hartley, *Painting, Number 5*.
1914–15. Oil on canvas 39½ × 31¾ inches.

1914–15. Oil on canvas. 39½ × 31¾ inches.

70. Faulkner, drawing from *Ole Miss*, 22, 1917–18 (*Social Activities I*)

and connects the Modernist, checkerboard patterns with the Beardsleyesque, *art nouveau* candelabra. Like other Faulkner drawings, two distinct influences are evident here, which the young artist fuses in quite a convincing manner. The figures themselves are indebted to the spirit of *fin de siècle* and are closely related to those in *The Marionettes*. The patterns of their clothing, however, the balloon-like circular forms to the left, together with the checkerboard floor in the foreground, signal the presence of a new tendency.

Strangely enough, these Modernist elements seem even stronger in a sketch done two years earlier, *Social Activities I* of 1917–18 (Pl. 70). The Beardsley influences which so dominate the illustrations for *The Marionettes* (1920) are found neither in the figures, two somewhat caricatured Jazz Age dandies and a flapper, nor in the strikingly designed checkerboard background. Like Weber and Hartley, Faulkner uses checkerboard patterning abstractly, as a decorative surface, and not as a means to achieve perspective. In this regard a glance at a Richard Boix cartoon proves illuminating. although *Dolcissimo* (Pl. 71) attests to the popularity of the checkerboard, the caricaturist employs it to enhance the illusion of three-dimensionality so necessary for the comic effect.

Checkerboard patterning is also evident in a number of sketches by other contributors in *Ole Miss*. It reappears as the design on a carpet and decorates the coat of a female golfer. In the illustration adorning the 1920–1 table of contents (Pl. 72), it takes the quite original form of a balloon-shaped dress juxtaposed against a black-and-white-striped ellipse. The immense popularity of the checkerboard motif signals the transition from representational to abstract art, and its pronounced use in *Ole Miss* is one of several indications that Faulkner and other Mississippi students kept in touch with the newest trends in contemporary American art.

In *Social Activities I* (Pl. 70) Faulkner's early acquaintance with modern painting is demonstrated not only by the checkerboard patterning, but also by a peculiar kind of drapery relating it to the figures in the center. It consists of a system of cubistically arranged surface segments resembling those encountered by an astonished American public in such Armory Show paintings as Francis Picabia's *Dances at the Spring* of 1912 (Pl. 73). At a time which saw American artists like Stanton Macdonald-Wright (*"Oriental." Synchromy in Blue-Green*, 1918, Pl. 74) working on the assimilation of Cubism, Faulkner, flirting with Modernist tendencies, interwove black, gray, and white triangular and trapezoidal forms to create Cubistic decoration. That Faulkner's experiments failed to go as deeply as those of Joseph Stella (*Brooklyn Bridge*, 1917–18) and Charles Demuth (*Incense of a New Church*, 1921) was due in part to the limitations of his abilities. On the other hand, it corresponds precisely to the general situation of the reception of Cubism in America:

For the majority of Americans who called themselves Cubists, Cubism meant little more than sharp lines and acute angles. Cubism was seen, not as a new attitude of mind, but in terms of its surface effects. Thus, many blithely set about superimposing directional lines and fragmented shapes on top of essentially realistic compositions.[10]

71. Richard Boix, *Dolcissimo*, from *The Dial*, July 1921

72. Table of contents, *Ole Miss*, 25, 1920–1

The last sentence could be applied *mutatis mutandis* to the young Faulkner, who did not hesitate to utilize Cubistic elements as the background for realistically conceived figures. Apparently, Cubistic forms appealed to him above all as a modish, graphically effective means of making the transition from geometric background to foreground figure. Faulkner's sketch *Social Activities I* of 1917–18 is thus important to the study of the early Faulkner for several reasons. It documents his experimentation with Modernist methods of representation contrary to mainstream developments in art history considerably *before* his Beardsleyesque, *art nouveau* studies. Apparently Faulkner did not view Beardsley's *art nouveau*, which he was to use two years later in *The Marionettes*, as superseded by Cubistic abstraction, but simply as another form of stylized art.

   The impact of Beardsley's art is still apparent in some features of Faulkner's cartoons for the student magazine *The Scream* (1925–7) as, for instance, in the graceful curves and clever positioning of a black dancer-like female shape in the center of a group of three flappers and two gentlemen (Pl. 62). But the realistically caught movements of the mini-skirted flapper boarding the streetcar or of the drunk whom his sober friend restrains from following the departing nymph are clearly more indebted to American cartoons in *Judge*, *Vanity Fair*, and *The Dial* than to Beardsley's *Salome* drawings. In another drawing (Pl. 60), the contrasting

73. Francis Picabia, *Dances at the Spring*, 1912

74. Stanton Macdonald-Wright, *"Oriental." Synchromy in Blue-Green*. 1918. Oil. 36 × 50 inches.

geometric patterns of the clothing and the worldly nonchalance with which the
gentleman in a striped mackintosh and herringbone trousers smokes his cigarette
and rests his foot on the running board of his friend's car also owe little to
Beardsley. In the *Scream* drawings we already encounter the spirit of the twenties
that informs the tennis party scenes in *Flags in the Dust* (1927). But before writing
his first real novel, the young writer apparently felt it necessary to undertake an
intensive learning process in parodic art, not only in *Soldiers' Pay* (1926) and
Mosquitoes (1927) but also in the cartoon-like drawings for *Ole Miss* (1917–22) and
The Scream (1925–7) and the mixed media work *Mayday* (1926). What is
particularly astounding is the stylistic scope of these parodic experiments ranging
from the ironic realism of contemporary cartoons to the parody of flowering
medieval language in *Mayday*. Faulkner's ability to capture details is quite
impressive in the drawing of the sagging drunk who collapses in the arms of a
friend (Pl. 75). Ironically, this scene takes place in front of a goddess or nymph-
like nude whose white form is thrown in bold relief by the black masses of
shrubbery in the background. Although this cartoon from *The Scream* (1925)
seems worlds apart from *Mayday* stylistically, it is close to the medieval romance
in its satire of a frustrated love experience.

Faulkner's prose romance *Mayday*, in which he parodies the quest of a quasi-
medieval hero, Galwyn of Arthgyl, breathes the spirit of both Beardsley and
James Branch Cabell. Like the graphic and literary persiflages of Beardsley's and
Cabell's medieval forms of idealism – *Le Morte Darthur* illustrations in 1893–4 and

75. Faulkner, drawing from *The Scream*, 1 May 1925

Jurgen in 1919 – *Mayday* reveals more about its own time than about the Middle Ages. In sharp contrast to Tennyson's and the Pre-Raphaelites' escapist versions of the Arthurian legends, Cabell's depiction of the medieval quester–hero in *Jurgen* and Faulkner's in *Mayday* are marked by a sceptical consciousness. Like Edwin Arlington Robinson's lyric trilogy (*Merlin*, 1917; *Lancelot*, 1920; *Tristram*, 1927), they demonstrate that a critical awareness of living in a utilitarian, materialistic age does not exclude the need for an idealistic view of the world and for stylization in art. Robinson's hero Miniver Cheevy, who was "born too late" and dreams of "Thebes and Camelot" in a miserable modern existence, is a characteristic embodiment of this spirit: "Miniver cursed the commonplace / And eyed a khaki suit with loathing; / He missed the medieval grace / Of iron clothing."[11] The ironic play with traditions of highly stylized lyricism in John Crowe Ransom's "The Equilibrists" or in the poetry and plays of Edna St Vincent Millay derives from the same historic situation.

The reappraisal of values during and after the First World War had intensified the longing of artists for ideal beauty but at the same time it revealed the knowledge of inevitable unfulfillment. The cynical view of the world with which Sir Galwyn's quest ends accords with the young Faulkner's deep immersion in the pessimistic poems of A. E. Housman.[12] Sir Galwyn and, after him, Quentin Compson welcome "little Sister Death" out of disappointed idealism. It is in this context that the text and illustrations of *Mayday* with its tension between idealistic stylization and ironic realism take on added significance. The sarcastic drawing of the artist–faun serenading a naked flapper in the first *Mayday* drawing (Pl. 80) is a characteristic product of the frivolous Jazz Age and prepares us for the parodic clash of the highly stylized medium and the straightforward message of the text:

Lady, though the sound of your voice is as that of lute strings touched sweetly among tapers in a windless dusk and therefore I will never tire of hearing it, and though your body is as a narrow pool of fair water in this twilight, do you not think – "diffidently" – that it would be wise to call your women and put something on it beside the green veils of this twilight? You know how difficult a spring cold can be.   (*MAY*, 68–9)

But the self-ironic persona of the artist–faun – who somewhat resembles Faulkner's well-known self-portrait in one of the letters from Paris – with the disdainful flapper (Helen Baird?) is the only comic element in the *Mayday* illustrations.[13] All the others are serious in intent and esoteric in form. Like *Royal Street: New Orleans* (Pl. 4),[14] *Mayday* has colored initial capital letters (Pl. 76) and, as a graphic work, also belongs with *The Marionettes* and the other handwritten and illuminated booklets, yet as a parody it reminds us more of the witty cartoons for *Ole Miss*. The fact that Faulkner maintained an interest in calligraphy and illustration for some time even after his start as a novelist shows what a deep impact the "art book" of the Morris tradition had on him.

From the perspective of *The Marionettes*, the most striking aspect of *Mayday* is its three watercolor illustrations (Pls. 77–9). While the two other black-and-white

76. Faulkner, text page with colored initial letter from *Mayday*, 1926

And the tale tells how at last one came to him. Dawn had already come without, flushing up the high small window so that this high small window which had been throughout the night only a frame for slow and scornful stars became now as a rose unfolding on the dark wall of the chapel. The song of birds came up on the dawn, and the young spring waking freshly, golden and white and troubling: flowers were birdcries about meadows unseen and birdcries were flowers necklaced about the trees. Then the sun like a sword-blade touched his own stainless long sword, his morion and hauberk and greaves, and his spurs like twin golden lightnings where they rested beneath the calm sorrowful gaze of the Young Compassionate One, touching his own young face where he had knelt all night on a stone floor, waiting for day.

And it was as though he had passed through a valley between shelving vague hills where the air was gray and smelled of spring, and had come at last upon a dark hurrying stream which, as he watched, became filled suddenly with atoms drawings frame the text (figures and motifs are introduced in them as in an overture or summarized as in an epilogue), the watercolors depict central scenes from the narrative. The first watercolor, *The Vision in the Chapel* (Pl. 77), illustrates the opening scene "in which Galwyn of Arthgyl kneels / all night on a stone floor waiting for day"[15] (*MAY*, 47–8). Such vigils by squires awaiting knighthood or by knights before their quest were customary in the Middle Ages and thus appear as motifs in *fin de siècle* medievalism with which Faulkner was familiar.[16] Galwyn is kneeling in front of a kind of altar, before which he has placed his sword and armor. A candle on a stand draped in purple, the most intense of the restrained colors in the illustration, directs attention to a madonna-like statuette, presumably the "Young Compassionate One" (p. 49). Modeled against the blue-gray background, Faulkner's skilled use of white contours and intensified colors enables her to emerge more clearly. At the center of the illustration, the figure of a woman appears in a visionary shaft of light, vaguely reminiscent of the Symbolist Félicien Rops's *The Temptation of Antony*. She is blonde and nude, the woman of Galwyn's dreams, who motivates his search for the "ideal beloved." In accord with *fin de siècle* disillusionment, expressed for instance by Dowson in his "Princess of Dreams," Galwyn's search will be in vain, despite tempting encounters with the princesses Yseult, Elys, and Aelia.[17] It is only by means of his union with the Franciscan angel of death, "Little Sister Death," that he is able to exorcise his vision of the ideal lady.

Although the quasi-medieval hairstyle and the cut of Galwyn's robe bring to mind the gray and lilac figures in *The Marionettes*, further treatment of the robe reveals that Faulkner had learned to accommodate his style somewhat to the medium of watercolor. The purple-gray brush strokes around the arm and shoulder to the front of the robe, which is drenched in white light, create a plastic effect. In contrast to the figures, the composition as a whole avoids plasticity and remains flat, dominated by the shaft of light enveloping the figure of the woman and Galwyn. The blank white area of the beam of light expanding from the top left is counterbalanced by the serpentine column of incense or sacrificial flame. Beginning at the bottom center, this characteristic *art nouveau* shape twists to the left, then swings through the light to end at the top right-hand corner of the illustration. The bottom part of the column is emphasized by the blue-gray tones of the background. The middle and upper parts consist of Cubistic forms, drawn in with pencil, some of which are lightly colored in yellow or purple.[18] It is apparently a rather half-hearted attempt on Faulkner's part to combine *art nouveau* with his Cubistic experiments from such *Ole Miss* sketches as *Social Activities I* (Pl. 70). The Cubistic contours are not strong enough in themselves, however, to give the serpentine column a powerful Cubistic structure. Even the shaft of light is more closely connected to the ornamental background surfaces in *The Marionettes* than to the Cubistic "lines of force" used by Demuth in *My Egypt* to draw buildings into a kind of magnetic field.

The second watercolor (Pl. 78) in *Mayday* illustrates in almost exact detail the scene in which Princess Aelia and Sir Galwyn return to earth after quarreling in

77. Faulkner, *The Vision in the Chapel*, from *Mayday*, 1926

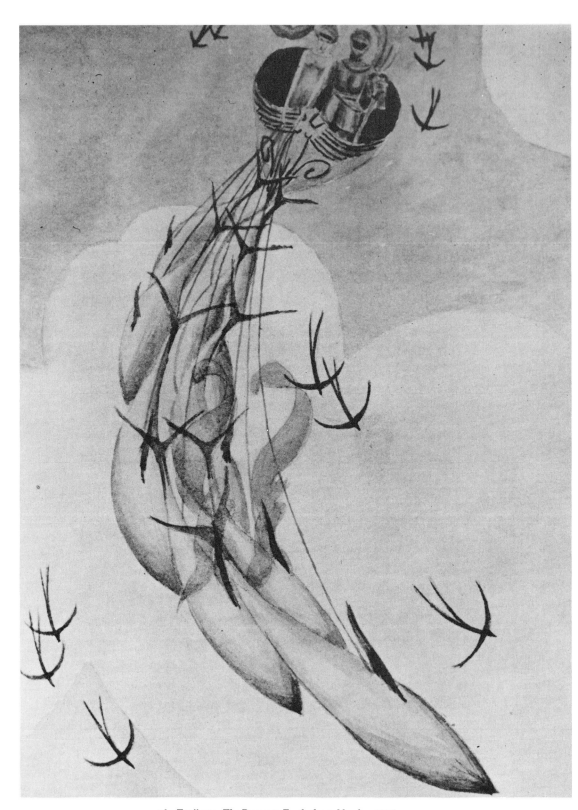

78. Faulkner, *The Return to Earth*, from *Mayday*, 1926

space: "She spoke to the nine white dolphins in a strange tongue, and they turned earthward and flew at a dizzying speed" (*MAY*, 78). Like the serpentine column in *The Vision in the Chapel*, the main graphic motif in *The Return to Earth*, the curve or chariot and dolphins swinging from the top to bottom right-hand corner, derives from *art nouveau*. But here, too, there is a trace of Cubism in the echeloning of the dolphins and the contouring of the bodies. By comparison, the white cloud pattern, set in relief against the pale green sky background, corresponds altogether to the *art nouveau* cloud-like patterns used by Beardsley in *The Climax* (Pl. 49) and by Faulkner himself in the stylization of peacocks in *Marietta's Apotheosis* (Pl. 97). Faulkner's sense of ornamental form, developed as a result of his exposure to Beardsley, reveals itself in the rendering of the falcons and in the arabesques and borders of the gondola-like chariot.[19] The depiction of the flight motif with two small figures is reminiscent of the enchanted *art nouveau* world of Winsor McCay's *Little Nemo in Slumberland*. By virtue of its clear-cut composition and dynamic motion, reinforced by the three pastel garlands waving in the wind, Faulkner's *Return to Earth* deserves recognition alongside illustrations in the better *art nouveau* children's books.

Unlike the first two watercolors, *The Final Vista* (Pl. 79) does not precisely follow the plot of Faulkner's text. It is possible to associate a number of passages near the conclusion of the narrative with this illustration. The scenery resembles the background of Galwyn's final encounter with St Francis (repeated from his initial vision): "a valley between shelving vague hills where the air was gray . . ." (*MAY*, 81). The lovers are most probably Sir Galwyn and "Little Sister Death" (p. 87).[20] The view from beneath the arch of a big tree onto the moonlit landscape evokes similar landscapes by Caspar David Friedrich and seems emblematic of the borderline experience between life and death: "Young Sir Galwyn looked upon this face and he was as one sinking from a fever into a soft and bottomless sleep; and he stepped forward into the water" (p. 87). In its generalized treatment of scenery, *The Final Vista* conveys the same impression as a quick sketch of stage scenery intended for a late Romantic opera. It has a spatial dimension which the other *Mayday* illustrations lack, the result of Faulkner's deft handling of lighting effects, and corresponds to his thematic intention of portraying a transitional stage between life and death. But even here Faulkner does not avoid the use of *art nouveau* silhouettes. Set against the nocturnal landscape, the two trees take on a vague symbolic suggestiveness and resemble the abstract shapes of the poplars or pines in the illustrations to *The Marionettes*.

The two black-and-white drawings which open and close the book differ markedly in theme and style from the three watercolors, yet because of distinct structural affinities they provide *Mayday* with a unified frame. The first drawing (Pl. 80), a kind of frontispiece for the book, is defined by three white bands of various sizes. All three enter the drawing at the upper right-hand corner, swing through the black background area in powerful curves and, after completing turns to the right, are cut off at their widest points by the three sides of the drawing. In the final drawing (Pl. 81), the three bands are not quite as wide nor

79. Faulkner, *The Final Vista*, from *Mayday*, 1926

their curves as dynamic. Here the compositional scheme is the reverse of the first: the bands begin on the left and diverge toward the top and the right. The motion of these bands seems to continue outside the drawings, forming spirals that in effect encircle the book. This circular, spiraling motion perfectly illustrates the experience of futility which brings Sir Galwyn's quest to an end:

And young Sir Galwyn stopped at the brink of the stream and Hunger and Pain paused obediently near him, and as he gazed into the dark hurrying waters he knew that he had stood here before, and he wondered if his restless seeking through the world had been only a devious unnecessary way of returning to a place he need never have left. (*MAY*, 82)

Faced with an endlessly recurring, frustrated search for an unattainable ideality, Faulkner formulates with youthful radicality a pessimistic vision of the world, from which the only deliverance is death: "and he stepped forward into the water and Hunger and Pain went away from him . . . " (p. 87).[21]

The allegorical figures Hunger and Pain, who according to the narrative withdraw upon the death of the hero, nevertheless appear in both drawings in *Mayday*. Their very presence helps establish the graphic unity of the frame, despite the fact that Faulkner uses them quite differently from drawing to drawing. In the first drawing, Hunger and Pain appear as linear ornaments superimposed on two of the white bands. Here the important factor is Faulkner's adherence to the overall design. He orders the lines defining the figures parallel to the motion of the bands and embellishes both figures with a three-lined arabesque. For the sake of decorative variation, the arabesque of Pain opens to the bottom of the page and the arabesque of Hunger to the top. The thoroughness with which Faulkner completes this design of black-and-white bands by means of spiraling arabesques demonstrates that, even as late as 1926, he remained under the influence of *art nouveau*. There is no need to look further than his own sketch for the AEF Club (Pl. 59) to find an immediate model for his use of the band motif in *Mayday*. The Boix caricature (Pl. 63), already compared to the AEF Club sketch, provides another interesting parallel. Apart from the main composition, three corners of Faulkner's first drawing contain somewhat extraneous material. In the upper left-hand corner Faulkner depicts the silhouette of two nymphs chased by a faun as variants of one graphic pattern. Less stylized is the nude on the lower edge of the picture, whose disdainful back may ironically refer to Helen Baird but who, despite her flapper hairstyle, is probably the Princess Yseult, whom Sir Galwyn happens upon while bathing, standing "like a young birch tree in the water" (p. 66). In positioning the nude with her back to the viewer, Faulkner seems to have modeled her after his own Marietta in *Marietta by the Fountain* and *Pierrot's Two Visions* (Pls. 95, 39). Unlike the depiction of Yseult, the flute-playing faun in the bottom right-hand corner, like the two nymphs, has no direct connection with the text; in fact, this Arcadian cast is something of an incongruity within the medieval context and not so much an illustration of the text as a recurring mask or *chiffre* of the author.[22]

Since both the first and the last drawings depart somewhat from the course of

80–1. Faulkner, initial drawing and Sir Galwyn's Grave, from *Mayday*, 1926

the narrative, it is difficult to determine who the figure is that stands over Sir Galwyn's grave flanked by Hunger and Pain. That it is Sir Galwyn himself, as Carvel Collins assumes, cannot be ruled out, although that would contradict the ending of the allegory: "and Hunger and Pain went away from him" (*MAY*, 87).[23] Another possibility is that it is Charon: "beyond the dark hurrying water a gray man in a gray boat" (p. 84). On the basis of the figure's outward appearance (he is dressed in a monk's robe) and the thematic development of the prose narrative, however, the figure in the middle is most probably "the good Saint Francis," whose reference to "Little Sister Death" brings the work to a close (p. 87). The uncertainty in the matter of identity is at least partly due to Faulkner's stylized depiction of the figures. Decorative symmetry and the impression of the figures' melancholic, solemn air must have struck the young artist as more important than specific details of appearance. The symmetrical arrangement of the figures, a stylistic characteristic of *art nouveau* discussed earlier in connection with the figures in the *Dramatis Personae* of *The Marionettes* (see p. 43), is enhanced by the cross, the plaque, and the ornamentally curved edges of the grave. That the same kind of Beardsley-inspired roses which decorate the *Dramatis Personae* are entwined around Sir Galwyn's gravestone is indicative of the stylistic continuity in Faulkner's graphic work.

To phrase this point rather more critically: the *Mayday* illustrations do not surpass Faulkner's earlier graphic work in *Ole Miss*, *The Scream*, and *The Marionettes* in quality. The kind of tentative experimentation with Cubism evident in a few of the *Ole Miss* sketches does not occur in *Mayday*, although Faulkner's earlier results were very possibly responsible for the impressive simplification and force of line in the first drawing. For an amateur, Faulkner's drawings are admirable, but for an artist who instinctively made the highest demands on himself, which he would later satisfy in his great novels, his talent as a graphic artist must have seemed unacceptable. The *Mayday* illustrations helped him finally to recognize his own limitations.

Since Faulkner, who around 1920 "was trying seriously to improve his graphic skill," by 1926 "was no longer expecting to give his professional artistic life to drawing and painting,"[24] is there reason to explore this apprentice work at all? If we continued to ignore it, we would probably fail to acknowledge and appreciate an essential dimension of his major works. The lasting effect of Faulkner's graphic apprenticeship does not, however, show itself in occasional later "art-work" such as the *risqué* drawings he did at the beginning of his affair with Meta Carpenter.[25] The real implications of the early illuminated booklets and drawings for his artistic genius become apparent in a letter to the editor Saxe Commins in 1955 about the illustrated edition of *Big Woods*. Here Faulkner expresses not merely the appreciation of a writer pleased with what the illustrator Shenton has done for his book; his suggestions to Edward Shenton show above all that the late Faulkner retained his sense of illustration as an artistic medium:

. . . would you risk suggesting Sam Fathers is an Indian to this extent? He is bare-headed, his hair a little long, a narrow band of cloth bound or twisted around his head? . . . Since

you are not *illustrating*, but *illuminating* (in the old sense) you could have any liberty you like. I realise the figures must be too small for much detail. Which gives an idea for story *THREE*.
(My italics, *SL*, 376–7)

Faulkner's knowledge and interest in art manifests itself in several ways and has been noted by his more perceptive readers. Guy Davenport, Ilse Dusoir Lind, and Jürgen Peper have all traced the influence of specific artistic movements on Faulkner's novelistic technique:

Cubists include visual information which would require several points of view. *The Sound and the Fury* is therefore a Cubist narrative . . . The architectonics of a narrative are emphasized and given a rôle to play in dramatic effect when novelists become Cubists . . .[26]

Other critics such as Kartiganer, Kinney, and Guerard have used the analogy of painting and music more generally as a metaphor to define the structural unconventionality of Faulkner's novels. Following the study of Faulkner's own graphic work we may perhaps point to another profound impact which art had on him.

Faulkner's painstaking efforts as a young craftsman to create a harmonious work of art in each multimedia booklet speak of a fascination with ideal beauty. This creative experience modified his sensibility and apparently was a prerequisite for his aesthetic transformation of the vast horrors of the Southern past and the inarticulate banality of his own time. Moreover, through his artwork Faulkner unconsciously became familiar with non-discursive aesthetic structures that evidently made it easier for him to organize his narrative without adherence to the conventional order of logic and time. Finally, exposure to and experiments with highly stylized art forms enabled him to develop that power of imaginative transfer which is the secret of his poetic prose. In this respect the early artwork probably had an impact on the style of his mature literary works similar to that of his early poetry.

How Faulkner's drawing specifically helped him to develop his writing can be illustrated by pointing out the connection between a dancing couple in the novel *Soldiers' Pay* (1926) and one among the earlier *Ole Miss* drawings of 1919 (Pl. 82). George Farr and later Mrs Powers and Gilligan each in turn see the same dance couple like a picture in which the two partners appear as related contours or complementary planes, a situation remarkably similar to the *Ole Miss* drawing:

watching her head beside another head . . . seeing the luminous plane of her arm across his black shoulders . . . (*SP*, 195)

The luminous plane of a bare arm upon conventional black. She saw two heads as one head . . . (*SP*, 198)

her arm crossing conventional black a slim warm plane . . . (*SP*, 200)

Apparently Faulkner could not have completely assimilated this painterly mode of perception without actually trying it out in his own artwork. Later, in his first Modernist novel it enabled him to produce that degree of Symbolist stylization

82. Faulkner, drawing from *Ole Miss*, 24, 1919–20 (*Red and Blue II*)

necessary to present the realistic surface of the scene side by side with the metaphoric revelation of its erotic tensions:

The couple slid and poised, losing the syncopation deliberately, seeking and finding it, losing it again . . . The syncopation pulsed about them, a reiteration of wind and strings warm and troubling as water.   (*SP*, 197)

In writing *Soldiers' Pay* he became aware that he could now do directly – and infinitely better – by literary means what he had been groping for in the other medium. But the experiences gathered from his artwork, like those gathered from his other auxiliary art, poetry, were vital to the development of his artistic genius. Considering the amount of work he put into both, he must have realized the importance of such training. Without it, his fate might have been similar to that of Dreiser, whom he refers to with some condescension in *Flags in the Dust*: "nobody ever had more to say and more trouble saying it than old Dreiser" (*FD*, 185).

PART II

"A Keats in Embryo."
On Faulkner's Poetry

3
Points of Departure: Faulkner's Pre-Raphaelite Poems

[*A Green Bough*] was written at the time when you write poetry, which is seventeen, eighteen, nineteen – when you write poetry just for the pleasure of writing poetry and you don't think of printing it until later. It may be – I've often thought that I wrote the novels because I found I couldn't write the poetry, that maybe I wanted to be a poet, maybe I think of myself as a poet, and I failed at that, I couldn't write poetry, so I did the next best thing.
Faulkner in the University, 4

MANY READERS of Faulkner praise him as a storyteller and creator of true-to-life characters, but then, backing off, admit that they find his style involved, overly poetic, and needlessly obscure. But ideal readers know that we must experience his "novels as poems," as a unique medium in which the narrative and the poetic elements blend and not as a substitute for the poetry he felt unable to write.[1] In this respect even the traditional poems of his early period are important because they mark the initial phase of a development leading through the transitional stages of the poetic prose in his one-act play and his prose poems to the richly imaginative prose of his great novels. Since the poems in the collections *The Marble Faun* and *A Green Bough* have already received considerable critical attention,[2] we will concentrate on those in *Early Prose and Poetry* and *Vision in Spring*, which, with their late Romantic and early Modernist motifs, their idealizing forms and language, constitute a striking parallel to the stylized artwork of the early Faulkner.

In his retrospective article "Verse Old and Nascent: A Pilgrimage" of 1925, Faulkner mentions several poets including Swinburne, Aiken, and Housman whose influence on his poems is indeed conspicuous. But the no less influential T.S. Eliot is noticeably absent from his list. In light of the strong Eliot influence on poems VI, IX, and XI of the cycle *Vision in Spring*, on "The Lilacs" as well as *Soldiers' Pay* and *Mosquitoes*, this is all the more puzzling. Was Faulkner attempting to cover his tracks to avoid charges of plagiarism? Perhaps. But the real reason is probably that reference to the rootless internationalism of the poet of *The Waste Land* would have conflicted with the new persona as the Southerner close to his native soil which he had just created for himself with the help of Sherwood Anderson. This new persona allows him – even after his Prufrock paraphrases – to find "the secret after which the moderns course howling like curs on a cold trail in a dark wood" (*EPP*, 117) in the simple and traditional verse of A.

81

E. Housman's *The Shropshire Lad*. Faulkner voices these new primitivist convictions firmly:

> that having fixed my roots in this soil all contact . . . with contemporary poets is impossible. That page is closed to me forever. I read Robinson and Frost with pleasure, and Aldington; Conrad Aiken's minor music still echoes in my heart; but beyond these, that period might have never been.   (*EPP*, 116–17)

This somewhat extreme statement has to be seen in the context of the New Orleans experience of 1925, but its reference extends beyond that situation and helps us to understand two distinctive features of Faulkner's poetics: his criticism of contemporary American poetry in his reviews "Books and Things" in *The Mississippian* between 1920 and 1922, and his extensive practice and advocacy of traditional forms:

> Occasionally I see modern verse in magazines. In four years I have found but one cause of interest; a tendency among them to revert to formal rhymes and conventional forms again. Have they, too, seen the writing on the wall?   (*EPP*, 117)

Some of the criticism which the young Faulkner levels against his fellow American poets is witty and even justified: "Mr Vachel Lindsay with his tin pan and iron spoon, Mr Kreymborg with his lithographic water coloring, and Mr Carl Sandburg with his sentimental Chicago propaganda"; "Ezra Pound furiously [toying] with spurious bronze in London" (*EPP*, 75, 94). But it hardly indicates a deep understanding of the key poetic issues of the times when, for instance, he refuses to see the essential affinity between Aiken's music poems and Amy Lowell's polyphonic prose (*EPP*, 76). That Aiken's glib blend of late Romanticism and cautious Modernism impresses Faulkner so much ("In the fog generated by the mental puberty of contemporary versifiers . . . appears one rift of heaven sent blue," *EPP*, 74) seems surprising when seen against the radically new poetic prose of the Benjy and Quentin sections of *The Sound and the Fury*, but it makes sense if related to the overall situation in which the young man from Mississippi found himself. Given his cultural surroundings, the pleasantly pagan sensuality of Swinburne and the accessible beauty of a Pre-Raphaelite-Keats naturally exercise a more powerful appeal, despite the obvious excitement over the daring new things Eliot and Aiken were doing with language: "Or is this age, this decade, impossible for the creation of Poetry? Is there nowhere among us a Keats in embryo, someone who will tune his lute to the beauty of the world?" (*EPP*, 118).

To visualize Faulkner's artistic beginnings better, it is essential to find a suitable frame of reference. Obviously, we should not measure Faulkner's juvenilia by T. S. Eliot's *The Waste Land* (1922), Wallace Stevens's "Sunday Morning" (1923), or other literary landmarks which have since been established, but by the poetic fashion around 1920 as it manifests itself in contemporary magazines and anthologies. On January 5, 1921, the same year in which the cycle *Vision in Spring* was written, Ben Wasson gave Faulkner a copy of William Stanley Braithwaite's *Anthology of Magazine Verse for 1920 and Yearbook of*

American Poetry.[3] A few years later in 1925, Braithwaite included Faulkner's own poem "The Lilacs."[4] While Braithwaite's anthology by no means offered the historically most important poems from the period 1913–26, his yearly selection of poems from magazines like *Poetry*, *The Dial*, and *The New Republic*, as well as *Harper's*, *Yale Review*, *Contemporary Verse*, *The Bookman*, and *The Granite Monthly* provides considerable insight into the tastes of the times.[5] Among the authors are unknown or forgotten names such as Sara Teasdale and William Alexander Percy.[6] At the same time, however, in the three volumes of 1919, 1920, and 1921 given special emphasis in this study as a basis for comparison with Faulkner's poetry, poems appeared by Edna St Vincent Millay, Edgar Lee Masters, John Gould Fletcher, Amy Lowell, Maxwell Bodenheim, Alfred Kreymborg, Conrad Aiken, and Elinor Wylie.

The first impression made by the poems as a whole is the altogether competent handling of form and style as demanded by Faulkner (*EPP*, 117) and the indebtedness of their content to late Romanticism. A prime example is Babette Deutsch's sonnet "Lacrimae Rerum." The title corresponds to the *fin de siècle* fashion of giving poems Latin inscriptions and thereby creating ritual overtones. The poem itself evokes Rossetti and the Pre-Raphaelite melancholy of his "Woodspurge": "Rossetti walked his sorrow to a field, / Lay in the grass, and watched the woodspurge flower."[7] Similarly, Millay reworked Pre-Raphaelite material (the Arthurian legends, for example) and used correspondingly medieval stylistic elements in "Elaine" and "To a Poet that Died Young": "Minstrel, by whose singing / Beauty walked."[8] This general tendency toward literary anti-quarianism is also notable in the collection (Sara Teasdale's "Effigy of a Nun" set in the sixteenth century, for instance).[9] The "orchards" connoting shelter and sensuality so common in Pre-Raphaelite poetry maintained their popularity in the poetic America of 1920: "Women and Orchards";[10] "So still the orchard, Lancelot."[11] The large number of poems which turn "spring" and "April" into poetry in the "wistful" style of the late Romantics ("The wistfulness that April keeps") helps to explain the young Faulkner's liking for such touches.[12]

Braithwaite's selection reveals that even the Jazz Age was attracted by the disturbing ambiguity of diverse *femme fatale* images. Models such as Swinburne's "Implacable Aphrodite" in "Sapphics" and the erotic quality which accompanies them fascinated not only epigonic imitators like John Hall Wheelock ("Implacable Beauty"), but besides Faulkner authors like Fitzgerald in *This Side of Paradise* (1920) and Dos Passos in *Three Soldiers* (1921):

The Queen of Sheba . . . white and flaming with worlds of desire, as the great implacable Aphrodite, stood with her hand on his shoulder . . . [13]

Just as in Swinburne's "Masque of Queen Bersabe," a cluster of *femmes fatales* appear in Walter Adolphe Robert's "Ave" ("old pageantries arise / Of queens and splendid courtesans"), among them a Semiramis.[14] As an integral part of this setting, we find the same rabbinic Lilith ("Lilith, Lilith wept for the moon") whom Rossetti had fashioned into a prototype of fatal sensuality ("Lilith" (For a picture): "Body's Beauty").[15] It is first in connection with this modish continuation of late Romantic tradition in the twenties that poems like Faulkner's sonnet XXXVII in *A Green Bough*, originally entitled "Cleopatra," take their place within literary history: "Ay, Lilith she is dead and she is wombed . . ." (*MF & GB*, 60). When keeping the affiliation of Faulkner's early work with such artistic tendencies in mind, it becomes clear to what extent he draws on *fin de siècle* material, giving it new functions in such late works as *The Town* (1957):

> The quiver borne on Manfred de Spain's back, but the arrows drawn in turn by that hand, that damned incredible woman, that Frenchman's Bend Helen Semiramis – no: not Helen nor Semiramis:Lilith: the one before Eve herself whom earth's Creator had perforce in desperate and amazed alarm in person to efface, remove, obliterate, that Adam might create a progeny to populate it; and we were in my office now . . . (*TWN*, 44)

Braithwaite's anthology provides further convincing evidence that the surfacing of *fin de siècle* attitudes, motifs, and stylistic devices in Faulkner's work is not out of the ordinary. The poems in the anthology contain fountains and naiads, Pierrots and decadent ladies with "languid eyelids," "who droop from weariness."[16] As in Rossetti's "Blessed Damozel," women are treated as cult figures, extravagantly adorned with religious imagery: "The crucifix of her mind," "Her body gleams like an altar candle," ". . . confessed/Upon the altar of your breast."[17] The manneristic distortion and the ingenious combination of precious images present in many poems indicate that the image structures in Faulkner's *Marionettes* and *Vision in Spring* are clearly in accord with historical tendencies:

> The voices are as white
> As altar candles.
> Their voices are as gold as wheat . . .   (Hildegarde Flanner)[18]

> Red small leaves of the maple
> Are clenched like a hand
> Like girls . . .   (Sara Teasdale)[19]

Such Symbolist elements as the massing of synesthesia appear in connection with corresponding motifs in modern American poetry around 1920 (for example, "ancient city," "memories," "precious things"). In view of a poem in the Braithwaite anthology like Charles Wharton Stark's "Beauty's Burden," the striking use of synesthesia in Faulkner's early works becomes perfectly understandable:

> I am weighed down beneath a clustering load of fragrances, rich sounds and
>   lovely shapes . . .
> I seem to stagger from an ancient city
> With golden armor, swords, fierce jewels, rings
> Treasure that stirs deep memories with the pity
> Of fate-foiled heroes and forgotten kings.[20]

In late Romanticism, the fascination for the substitution of senses which takes place in synesthesia corresponds to the blurring of the distinctions separating the different arts. Entirely in accord with this, poems about painting ("After

Whistler"), poems with musical titles ("Gavotte in D Minor," "Nocturne"), and even combinations of the two ("In the Key of Blue") surface during this time in Braithwaite's anthology.[21] Marjorie Allen Seiffert's title of the poem "Nocturne" is an indication that titles like Aiken's "Nocturne of Remembered Spring" and Faulkner's "The World and Pierrot: A Nocturne" have their origins in widespread literary trends and fashions. When Faulkner's poetry is approached from the perspective of his realistic short stories or novels, late Romantic motifs and stylistic elements seem inexplicable, irritating relics. When seen within the historical context of their origin, however, not only the poems themselves, but also their manifold and long-lasting effects on major works like *Absalom, Absalom!*, *The Hamlet*, and *The Town* take on new meaning.

Faulkner's early poems are so literary that the biographical element is not immediately apparent, but there is little doubt that the traditional lover's lament in "A Song," the first of a group of three short poems, was occasioned by Estelle Oldham's marriage to Cornell Sidney Franklin (1918).[22] What is of particular interest here is the fact that the young Mississippian feels the urge to transform his painful experience in a rather sophisticated if traditional manner. Like Joyce in *Chamber Music* and so many great artists before them, Faulkner, by trying to master established literary conventions, is initiating the arduous process of finding a poetic voice of his own. The literary motifs, the polished form, and the stylized phrasing are perfectly in line with the outward appearance of this miniature cycle of three poems as a calligraphic and illuminated multimedia work of art (Pls. 83–5).

Apart from minor deviations, in this early cycle Faulkner has already developed that artistic script which he was to employ with such remarkable consistency in all known copies of *The Marionettes*, *Helen*, and *Mayday*. In "A Song," as the script of the title shows, Faulkner was already caught up in the spirit of *art nouveau* calligraphy; he conceives the 'g' at the end as a symmetrical complement to the initial 'S' (Pl. 83). In the raised position of her head and the rendering of her mouth and eyes, the nymph dominating the illustration closely resembles the just as scantily clothed Marietta in the *Apotheosis* illustration of *The Marionettes* (Pl. 97). The short skirt is torn, undoubtedly a result of the inescapable fate shared by all nymphs of being chased through "a brake." The somewhat exaggerated pose of the nymph and the bearded, masked Mephisto head isolated in the upper left-hand corner create an ironic, parodic atmosphere; this effect is perfectly in keeping with the positioning of the illustration on the back of the serious poems. The illustration is obviously more closely related to the irony of the cartoons in *Ole Miss* than to the more somber illustrations in *The Marionettes*. The pictorial element and the calligraphic form of the three poems are not the only homogeneous factors in this cycle: above all, the poems share a delicately contrived if song-like simplicity. But their sequence in Faulkner's cycle is in accordance with a carefully developed plan. "A Song" takes the direct, confessional form of a lover's lament. Following this "complaint," "Dawn" is dedicated to fulfillment and, on the basis of another poem with the title "Aubade" among the Virginia manuscript poems, may be read in the sense of the French *l'aube*, as an allusion to *aubade*, the morning song.[23]

The eight lines of "Dawn," like those in the first poem, are cross-rhymed: a-b-a-b-c-d-c-d. In contrast to "A Song" and despite the change in the rhyme pattern after the fourth line, however, "Dawn" is made up of one and not two stanzas. In "A Song," the division of the stanzas accentuates the thematic tension ("Even though she chose to ignore me"); the continuous use of the identical rhyme word "me" points toward the steadfastness of the suffering lover.[24] In "Dawn," the single stanza underlines the unity of the love experience, while the change from the first to the second set of cross rhymes intimates that the poem expresses two phases within a single relationship. The imagery is of that clichéd decorative, allegorical nature ("Love's altar," "cup Delight," "feet of the night") already identified above as typical of the literary fashion of the time. A striking feature in view of the sound effects in Faulkner's mature prose is that the thematic change in line 5 is ingeniously accompanied by the transition from 'l' to 'd' alliteration:

> Lithe lips that clung now falter
> . . .
> Lovers dream, pale on Love's altar
> . . .
> Then limb from limb dividing
> Drained dry the cup Delight
> Desire goes . . .

With its intensive Swinburnian sound and late Romantic motifs and techniques, the poem is hardly a personal statement. The subtle construction, however, with the conclusion ("From the feet of the night") almost imperceptibly referring back to the title "Dawn" gives some indication of the consciousness of form which the young Faulkner commanded.

The last poem in the group, "An Orchid," is the shortest, but in the development of motifs and metaphors, artistically the most successful. The love theme convincingly finds its most sublime expression at the end of this cycle of poems. Although the material remains conventional, Faulkner's handling of it is successful within the framework of the late Romantic tradition. Light and breeze are images embodying the lovers: "The light lay soft upon the breeze –/ Yielding its sweet caress." The "light," accentuated alliteratively in the first line, and the "breeze" return in the fourth line in the form of their "offspring": "the flower of light and air." By way of this repetition and modification, the structure of the five-line poem is given both tension and compactness. That the flower growing from this conjunction is a mystery (". . . from that kiss, a mystery thing . . . did spring") corresponds to one of the basic tendencies of Symbolism. As in the poem "Dawn," in "An Orchid" there is a subtle relationship between title and poem. It is no coincidence that the product of the union is an orchid. Due to their exotic beauty and the artificial cultivation necessary in northern climates, orchids enjoyed great popularity as a *fin de siècle* motif. Writers in America were well acquainted with this tradition: "Gatsby indicated a gorgeous, scarcely human

A SONG

It is all in vain to implore me,
　　To let not her image beguile,
For her face is ever before me —
　　And her smile.

Even though she choose to ignore me,
　　And all love of me to deny,
There is nought then behind or before me —
　　I can die. .

p. 2

DAWN

Lithe lips that clung now falter,
　　And the hands no longer cling,
Lovers dream, pale on Love's altar
　　In the sleep stilled passions bring.
Then limb from limb dividing,
　　Drained dry the cup Delight,
Desire goes like the tide subsiding
　　From the feet of the night.

p. 3

AN ORCHID

The light lay soft upon the breeze —
　　Yielding its sweet caress,
Lo! from that kiss, a mystery thing,
The flower of light and air did spring
　　Trembling with lovliness

83–5. Faulkner, "A Song," "Dawn," "An
Orchid," 1918

orchid of a woman who sat in state under a white-plum-tree."[25] There is an orchid in Faulkner's prose poem "Hong Li" and in *Soldiers' Pay* the description of Cecily's face while dancing discloses his own awareness of the *fin de siècle* and Symbolist connotations of this flower: "Her face was smooth, as skillfully done and as artificial – as an orchid" (*SP*, 165–6).

The question is, of course, how much Faulkner really knew about Symbolism, whether we understand it as the actual Symbolist school, the French Symbolist tradition since Baudelaire, or the international Symbolist movement manifest in several arts since the nineteenth century. Since Martin Kreiswirth has shown that Faulkner used Symons's Verlaine translations in composing his own, we can assume that Faulkner's knowledge of French language and literature was relatively modest.[26] But with Symons's *The Symbolist Movement* (1893), he had access to one of the most significant documents of the movement. As regards Faulkner's poem "L'Après-midi d'un faune," whose title seems to point to Mallarmé's great eclogue known to many in Debussy's musical rendering, considerable surprise lies in store: close examination of Faulkner's "translation" and Mallarmé's eclogue shows that, with the exception of the faun, a figure typical of the imagery of the time, the two poems have very little in common. The depiction of motifs and the use of language in the two works are so different that not even a comparative contrast is particularly relevant. Apparently, a number of scholars have been misled by the French title; by way of consolation, something similar to this must have been Faulkner's intention.[27] The use of a French title for a poem firmly implanted in the English tradition is intended to suggest familiarity with the work of the most difficult French Symbolists. Like the title of "Une Ballade des femmes perdues," which resembles a quotation, and the retention of the original titles of the Verlaine translations, the borrowing of Mallarmé's title "L'Après-midi d'un faune" reflects the desire of the young Count No 'Count to adopt the role of a sophisticated author and to dissociate himself from banal everyday existence. Besides these French titles, inscriptions such as "Sapphics," "Naiads' Song," and "Cathay," itself a title reminiscent of Pound's translations from the Chinese (1915), must have seemed provocatively exotic to many of Faulkner's fellow students in Oxford, Mississippi.

Ironically, the literary debt in "L'Après-midi d'un faune" is not to the great Mallarmé, but to the little remembered Robert Nichols and his poem "The Faun's Holiday" in his collection *Ardours and Endurance* (1917), as Martin Kreiswirth, working from Michael Millgate's discovery of the connection, has demonstrated.[28] Since Robert Nichols is a characteristic epigone of nineteenth-century Romanticism, it is not surprising that his poems, like so many in Braithwaite's anthology, are informed in motif and style by the Pre-Raphaelite tradition. Interestingly, Faulkner, working with Nichols's material in both "L'Après-midi d'un faune" and "Naiads' Song" shows a similar predilection for Pre-Raphaelite features.[29] As the comparison of the variants illustrates, Faulkner was not concerned with a vitalistic pursuit of the nymph by the faun, but rather, like the Pre-Raphaelites, with the metaphoric embroidering of a state of erotic yearning ("Her streaming clouded hair . . . Like gleaming water from some place/ Of sleeping streams").[30] In the typescript, this condition is appropriately designated by the corresponding *terminus technicus*, "languorous." The adjective is hardly appropriate in regard to "knees," however, and Faulkner most likely replaced it for that reason with a word from his Swinburne vocabulary, "lascivious." While the addition of "dreaming" undermines the phrase "lascivious dreaming knees," it conveys a state of erotic wistfulness, strengthens the internal rhyme chain ("streaming – dreaming – gleaming"), and with its 'i' assonance contributes to a Swinburnian sensuousness of the language:

> I follow through the singing trees
> Her streaming clouded hair and face
> And lascivious dreaming knees
> Like gleaming water from some place
> Of sleeping streams . . .

The presence of the adjective "love-wearied" also demonstrates Faulkner's familiarity with Pre-Raphaelite diction. Not only the content, a specific blending of human and natural phenomena ("singing trees"), of eroticism and languor ("of autumn leaves/Slow shed through still, love-wearied air"), but also the compound form itself is of interest. Like the Pre-Raphaelites, Faulkner found compound forms fascinating both for the possibility of fusing content and for the somewhat bizarre stylistic effects they have in English. Equally characteristic are the "unrealistic" comparisons ("hair," "face," "knees," and "gleaming water") and the suggestive vagueness of the setting. And like the Pre-Raphaelites, the young Faulkner in both "L'Après-midi d'un faune" and "Naiads' Song" conveys his thematic implications through a peculiar kind of Symbolism combining images of beauty ("green," "silver") with images of death ("night," "west," "pale") and in both poems utilizes imaginary creatures and their worlds to give poetic expression to a pessimistic sense of life and the escapist eroticism pervading it.

From Heine's "Lorelei" to Eliot's "Prufrock" ("I have heard the mermaids singing, each to each"), the song of the naiads appears as a persistent motif in the Romantic tradition. Faulkner's "Naiads' Song" is related to images like the one in Edward Burne-Jones's *The Depths of the Sea* (1886; Pl. 86). In the center of this painting, a naiad has entwined herself around a handsome youth and glides with him into the depths of an underwater landscape. No less striking than the Pre-Raphaelite motifs in "Naiads' Song" are the *art nouveau* forms (wave and hair motifs, the glittering effect of sun and gold):

> And shaken ripples cover us,
> . . .
> In undulations dim and deep;
> Where sunlight spreads and quivering lies
> To draw in golden reveries
> Its fingers through our glistered hair . . .   (*EPP*, 55)

With manneristic ingenuity, Faulkner varies the immersion in water and the

union with the naiads in the first stanza by the image of a bee plunging into a rose
in the second stanza:

> . . . come and steep
> Yourselves in us *as does the bee*
> Plunge in the rose that, singing, he
> Has opened . . .   (my italics; *EPP*, 55)

Characteristic features of Pre-Raphaelite style, such as archaizing allegorical
expressions ("in a garment clad/of sorrow") and intentionally awkward rhymes
("lies" – "reveries"; "trees" – "forgetfulness") are also evident. Keywords
("sleep," "dream," "soft," "sad," "dim and deep," "twilit streams") evoke a
peculiar Pre-Raphaelite sensitivity. It manifests itself most clearly in motifs
suggesting the union of Eros and Thanatos.

What Faulkner attempted to articulate in "L'Après-midi d'un faune" and
"Naiads' Song," two poems modeled after late Romantic motifs, must have
arisen from subconscious experiences which moved him profoundly. These
experiences and motifs surface again and again in the course of his artistic
development, assuming diverse forms and taking on a different quality. In

86. Edward Burne-Jones, *The Depths of the
Sea*, 1886

Soldiers' Pay, Faulkner will treat the underlying erotic frustration of the faun–nymph motif ironically (Jones – Cecily) as well as tragically (Donald – Emmy). At the close of the pseudo-medieval prose romance *Mayday*, following Cabell's parodies, the death wish is expressed in the form of a ritualistic tableau. Ultimately, in *The Sound and the Fury*, Faulkner will find the authentic expression of that "nameless wish to travel to some midnight land of lonely rivers" with the death of Quentin.[31]

Despite its French title, "Une Ballade des femmes perdues" has as little to do with Villon as "L'Après-midi d'un faune" has with Mallarmé. Clearly, though, Faulkner wanted to arouse precisely such associations, an idea demonstrated by his use of the famous refrain "Mais où sont les neiges d'antan" from Villon's "Ballade des dames du temps jadis" (or, more likely, from the Villon epigraph in Swinburne's "Felise"). Combining repetition and variation, some other French fragments (not from Villon) ("vraiment, charmant") in the framing stanzas become part of a rudimentary refrain ("I sing in the green dusk/ . . . Of . . . ladies"). The French refrain components in "Une Ballade des femmes perdues" fuse with the title and epigraph to create a stylized and distancing effect and, as in Eliot's "Prufrock," provide the element of coherence necessary in the irregular and rhymeless verse of the period. "Une Ballade des femmes perdues," where Pre-Raphaelite themes are given expression in a kind of Modernist *vers libre*, should be seen beside such exercises in regular meter and rhythm as "Naiads' Song."

"Une Ballade des femmes perdues" is a graceful poem, not the lyrical outpouring of a young man close to the Mississippi soil, and shows the same awareness of form seen in "Naiads' Song." Stanzas one and four create a unified frame; the poet refers to himself as a "singer," suggesting the image of a medieval troubadour:

> I sing in the green dusk
> Fatuously
> Of ladies that I have loved
> . . .
> I am old, and alone
> . . .
> I sing in the green dusk
> Of lost ladies . . .   (*EPP*, 54)

The striking association of color with the time of day ("green dusk") corresponds to Pre-Raphaelite models ("as some green afternoon/Turns toward sunset"),[32] and the repetition of this expressive phrase conveys the same rondeau-like return of the poem to its beginning as in "Naiads' Song." The initial situation is transformed – the singer is old and lonely at the end, his earlier loves are now "lost ladies" – by the vision of the "femmes perdues" described in the middle stanzas.

The encounter with a lost love, or more generally, with a guilt-ridden or squandered past, is a central theme of Pre-Raphaelitism (for example, Rossetti's "Lost Days" and "A Superscription").[33] In "Une Ballade des femmes perdues" it is presented in an elegant manner. The "lost ladies" here have the character of charming, rococo-like sprites rather than "gothic" ghosts: "gay little ghosts of loves in silver sandals." The author was obviously familiar not only with the melancholic eroticism of Pre-Raphaelitism ("L'Après-midi d'un faune," "Naiads' Song"), but also with the movement's other side manifest in the playfulness of Swinburne's "Madonna Mia" and "A Match." To appreciate Faulkner's accomplishment in "Une Ballade des femmes perdues" it is necessary to recognize that young writers with such a subject do not usually achieve a light, stylized tone, but more often fall into sentimentalized eroticism or tragic postures. Faulkner is able to maintain his tone, a delicate balance between a delight in play and a touch of melancholy, from beginning to end in the poem. Irony and daring imagination speak from his combination of Pre-Raphaelite images with modern phrasing: "*gay little* ghosts"; "with the *ab*andon of *b*oarding school virgins"; "*moths*/Amorous of my *white seraglio*"; "A *s*ort of ethereal seduction."[34] The result is an accomplished poem which parallels Austin Dobson's and Andrew Long's revival of old forms, Joyce's *Chamber Music*, and Edna St Vincent Millay's Elizabethan experiments.

Unfortunately, the irony and lightness of touch in "Une Ballade des femmes perdues" is rare among Faulkner's poems in the Pre-Raphaelite mode. It is nevertheless important to note that Faulkner was still attracted by the Pre-Raphaelite style which dominated so many of his early poems, though he was already assimilating Aiken and Eliot in *Vision in Spring*. Despite unifying elements in this cycle of fourteen poems, the young poet quite obviously struggles with heterogeneous stylistic traditions.[35] The late Romantic features, contrasting with the strong Modernist elements in the other poems, are markedly noticeable in poems I ("Vision in Spring"), II ("Interlude"), XIII ("Philosophy"), dominate poems X ("The Dancer") and XIV ("April"), and, most interestingly, merge with characteristics of Eliot in poem XI ("Laxly reclining").[36]

Vision in Spring is not a collection of nature poems on spring, although both the opening title poem and the concluding poem "April" contain stylized nature descriptions. Instead, the cycle emphasizes a special quality of the springtime experience, best illustrated by poem XI ("Laxly reclining") in which an interior scene with a piano, obviously indebted to Eliot's "Portrait of a Lady," imaginatively expands into a Pre-Raphaelite landscape. In the process, the woman assumes characteristics of Tennyson's Lady of Shalott or of the Ophelia in Millais's Shakespeare painting: "She is a flower lightly cast/Upon a river flowing, dimly going/Between two silent shores where willows lean . . ." (*VS*, 71). In this melancholy scene, spring loses its usual positive connotations. It is no longer a matter of an immediate experience of spring, but rather a nostalgic remembrance of a spring long past:

> Could she but stay here forever, where slow rain slants above them,
> With starlight soft as rain upon her breast;
> Could she but dream forever on this river
> Through springs and springs, back to a certain spring
> That blossomed in shattering slow fixations, cruel in beauty
> Of nights and days   (*VS*, 72)

Spring in Faulkner's cycle resembles the season in Aiken's *Nocturne of Remem-bered Spring*.[37] But Aiken in turn has taken up the theme of lost spring from the Pre-Raphaelite tradition which Beardsley, for example, evokes in *Withered Spring* (Pl. 87). Faulkner uses this theme in both *Vision in Spring* ("beyond these ghostly springs in which she strayed," 73) and *The Marionettes* ("Hither come the ghosts of stripped springs," 39). It is no surprise then that the spring month in the final poem "April" has none of the vitality commonly associated with this season:

> . . . In dim-lit ways
> A sighing wind shakes in its grasp
> A straight resilient poplar in the mist,
> Until its reaching hands unclasp,
> And then the wind and sky bend down, and kiss
> Its simple, cool whitely breathless face.   (*VS*, 88)

It is not only the melancholy scenery and its peculiar Pre-Raphaelite eroticism in which the ideal and the sensual fuse which appealed to Faulkner, but also the simplicity and quietness that the Pre-Raphaelites saw in the paintings and poems of Giotto, Dante, and the other early Italians.

In "April" the hazels appear in a Symbolist scene (pool – mirror) and are anthropomorphized in Pre-Raphaelite fashion: "And ruffling the pool's face quietly below/Where each clump of hazel stands,/Clad in its own simply parted

87. Beardsley, *Withered Spring*, *c*.1892

hair . . . " (*VS*, 86). In connection with this stylized vocabulary, "delicate" appears as a key word, as for instance in "Delicately swung the narrow moon above him" (p. 3) and "a delicate violet thins the rose" (p. 38). The ideal of beauty is derived by *art nouveau* from Pre-Raphaelitism. Correspondingly, in poem X, youth is personified as a dancer in *art nouveau* style: "I am Youth, so swift, so white and slim" (p. 65). But lassitude and melancholy are just as characteristic of this ideal of beauty. "Peace" is sought with "weary feet" (p. 2) and the experience of beauty itself is accompanied by "quietness" and a peculiar exhaustion: "this beauty touched him, quiet, weary" (p. 3). The fact that the word "peace," whose key role in Pre-Raphaelitism reflects the sense of crisis of the late Victorians, appealed to artistically inclined young people of the "lost generation" like the young Yeats and the young Faulkner is not surprising. Related to this quietistic notion is a wide range of interconnected vocabulary and imagery. "Soft," for instance, appears in *Vision in Spring* in many variations: "soft hands of skies," p. 3; "softly clad in grey," p. 60, and the words "quiet," "still," and "calm" are used just as often. Characteristically, the depiction of peace is frequently

88. Pierre Puvis de Chavannes, *Ste Geneviève veillant Paris*, 1898

combined with sadness or pain: "Your face, grown calm and sad"; "in quiet pain" (p. 9). In determining the stylistic effect of these recurring mood words, it is important to note that they repeatedly appear in unusual combinations, for example, "in the autumned stillness of their hair" (p. 3). The symbolic intention remains perfectly clear: the Pre-Raphaelite and *art nouveau* hair motif, with its sensual implications, is given a quietist touch and takes on the melancholy of the season of decay. Faulkner seems to have found the esoteric effect of extravagant phrasing ("clothed in quiet sound for my delight," *VS*, 37) just as important as the thematic content.

The need for "peace" and "stillness" is closely related to the tendency to create indefinite, shadowy, or dream-like states. In both *Vision in Spring* and the tradition which influenced the cycle, spatial experience ("Vague dim wall[s]," p. 36) and inner feelings ("A sudden vagueness of pain," p. 1) remain vague and often blend. Twilight and evening are the favorite times of the day. Faulkner apparently found this unrealistic world in late Romantic poetry and in the paintings of Puvis de Chavannes attractive and worth assimilating because it enabled him to establish the distance of a "beautiful" style between himself and his immediate environment (see Pl. 88).[38]

4

From Swinburne to Eliot

THE POEMS "Aubade" and "Sapphics" were both influenced by Swinburne, but they originated during different phases of Faulkner's development and represent two different levels of impact. The poem "Aubade," first published by Joan St C. Crane, probably dates from 1916, whereas "Sapphics" is among the poems of the *Lilacs* cycle; it was also published as a separate poem in *The Mississippian* and suggests that Faulkner was by that time (1919) an advanced student of Swinburne.[1] Beyond this difference, the two poems return to stylistically opposed models: "Aubade" imitates Swinburne's "Before Dawn," a poem in the medieval style of the Pre-Raphaelites, while "Sapphics" follows Swinburne's attempts in the classical Greek manner.

Swinburne's poem "Before Dawn" describes, at the central point of its ten stanzas, lovers waking and parting before dawn, a situation treated by the medieval troubadours in a fixed genre (*alba*: *l'aube*: "before dawn").[2] Most modern readers are more familiar with the theme from Shakespeare's *Romeo and Juliet*, and Faulkner was probably no exception. Although the subtitle of his poem "Aubade" attributes troubadour poetry to the sixth century ("Provence. Sixth Century"), it does not indicate any real knowledge of the flowering of Provençal poetry from the eleventh to the thirteenth century. There is no denying that Swinburne's "Before Dawn" served as the model for "Aubade."[3] Far from being a mere imitation, however, Faulkner's poem represents a quite original variation. The most striking difference is undoubtedly Faulkner's condensation: instead of the ten stanzas in "Before Dawn," "Aubade" has only four. The closest affinity exists between Swinburne's eighth and Faulkner's third stanzas, demonstrating Faulkner's sure grasp of literary structures and their thematic centers:

> As, when late larks give warning
> Of dying lights and dawning,
> Night murmurs to the morning,
>   "Lie still, O love, lie still;"
> And half her dark limbs cover
> The white limbs of her lover,
> With amorous plumes that hover
>   And fervent lips that chill.

(Swinburne)

> When dawning warns of changes
> The promised morn estranges
> The mouth that mouthward ranges
>   And Love his throne descends;
> A lady and her lover
> Whose breast her own did cover
> Find, now his reign is over,
>   No lovers are, nor friends.   (Faulkner)

Faulkner prepares for the depiction of love in the third stanza by introducing the reader to a peculiar brand of neo-paganism in the second. The model for stanza two is another Swinburne poem, "Hymn to Proserpine," and not "Before Dawn."[4] In the same way in which the older, vital gods are contrasted with the "pale Galilean" in Swinburne's "Hymn," Faulkner sets the "bandit Love" against the "cold Christ." Stanza two also alludes to Kipling, indicating the extent of the young Faulkner's involvement with the art of quotation and montage practiced by Pound and Eliot.[5] The reference here is to the poetic epigraph ("The Convert") which heads the first of Kipling's *Plain Tales from the Hills* (1880). The theme of "Lispeth" is the repressive effect of Christianity on the spontaneous love of a girl from the Himalayas:

> Look, you have cast out Love! What Gods are these
>   You bid me please?
> The Three in One, the One in Three? Not so!
>   To my own gods I go.
> It may be they shall give me greater ease
> Than your *cold Christ* and *tangled trinities*.   (Kipling)

> The *Christ* is cold they leave us
> With the bandit, Love, to rieve us
> Of ease, while they deceive us
>   With *tangled trinities*.
> Who is he but will rue him
> Who sought for Love and knew him,
> And finding him so slew him,
>   Nor found there any ease?   (my italics; Faulkner)

Faulkner disassembles the Kipling lines and rearranges the phrases which he finds of thematic and verbal interest – "cold Christ" and "tangled trinities" – as part of a new, Swinburnian context: the diction of "sought for Love . . . slew him." Through the Swinburne–Kipling montage in stanza two, the love theme takes on a deeper, more philosophical meaning. The clear contours of the center in "Aubade" are effectively framed by stanzas one and four, both of which refer generally to the transitoriness of love. This symmetrical arrangement receives full expression in the final lines of these stanzas: "Ah, Love! he flies so soon!" (stanza one); "Ah, God, to flee so soon!" (stanza four).

Condensation and structural clarity also characterize the six-stanza poem "Sapphics" that Faulkner carved out of Swinburne's twenty stanzas.[6] Like

Swinburne, Faulkner places the tension between love and art at the middle of the poem. The figure of Sappho, however, no longer appears in Faulkner's poem although it dominates Swinburne's original. Sappho personifies the tragic conflict between art and life in Swinburne's "Sapphics." What makes Sappho's song at once "perfect" and "terrible" is that it can only come into being through a renunciation of heterosexual love, in a sterile land of art forsaken by Aphrodite: ". . . and the land was barren,/Full of fruitless women and music only."[7] In his identification of sterility with art, Swinburne was moved less by a coincidental, individual form of perversion than by a central experience evolving from the complex relationship between artist and society during the nineteenth century. Great predecessors in this tradition were Baudelaire ("Lesbos"; "Femmes damnées: A la pâle clarté"; "Femmes damnées: Comme un bétail pensif") and Mallarmé, whose "Hérodiade" is considered one of the sources for Faulkner's play *The Marionettes*.[8]

To reconstruct Faulkner's development as an artist, it is important to note that his adaptation of Swinburne's "Sapphics" clearly reveals his familiarity with its theme and the tradition behind it. He concentrates on the departure of Aphrodite, the goddess of happy and fruitful love from the seat of art, depicting it in the present tense as a visionary experience. This concentration produces an intensity, which together with its shortening gives the poem an inner power. Faulkner further enhances this effect by presenting the departure of Aphrodite from Lesbos in a decorative, mythological tableau:

> In the purple beaks of the doves that draw her,
> Beaks straight without desire, necks bent backward
> Toward Lesbos and the flying act of Loves
> Weeping behind her.

After establishing a visionary frame – "A vision from the full smooth brow of sleep" – and the departure of Aphrodite in the first three stanzas, the second part of the poem is dedicated to Lesbos, the center of the arts where "The nine crowned muses about Apollo/Stand like nine Corinthian columns singing in a clear evening." Faulkner emphasizes the depiction of the nine muses taken from Swinburne by comparing them with nine Corinthian columns; in the process, he makes use of parallelisms, word repetitions, and alliteration. With the allusion to the iconographical tradition of Memnon's columns, Faulkner effectively draws a connection between the visual arts, music, and poetry. The Lesbians whose "fruitless love" has been an image for the socially ineffective and sacrificial role of the artist since the nineteenth century appear in stanzas five and six. Here Faulkner adopts and cleverly varies an image from Swinburne associating Lesbian love and art:

> [Sappho] Saw the Lesbians kissing across their smitten
>   Lutes with lips more sweet than the sound of lute-strings
>   (Swinburne)
>   [Aphrodite] She sees not the Lesbians kissing mouth
>   To mouth across lute strings, drunken with singing   (Faulkner)

How clearly the young poet has the art theme and its structural demands in mind can be seen by the fact that he continues the music motif from stanza four – "nine Corinthian columns singing/In the clear evening" – in stanza five in the image of the "dancing Oceanides." Images of artistic fulfillment in stanza five ("the Lesbians kissing mouth/To mouth across lute strings, drunken with singing") give way to the metaphorical depiction of the artists' sterility, loneliness, and suffering in stanza six, the concluding stanza of the poem:

> Before her go crying and lamentations
> Of barren women, a thunder of wings,
> While ghosts of outcast Lethean women, lamenting,
>   Stiffen the twilight.

The statue-like appearance of the nine muses in "Sapphics" reminds us that Faulkner, like many writers of the period between *fin de siècle* and Modernism, also saw sculpture as an image of the shaping aspect of literary art. In keeping with this tendency, a close relationship exists between his "Marble Faun" mask and his interest in Swinburne's group of sonnets on the "Hermaphrodite" in the Louvre as well as between his use of the Grecian urn as leitmotif in *Sartoris* and his return to Gautier's Parnassian ideal in *Mosquitoes*. In his Hergesheimer review of 1922 Faulkner makes a significant comparison of literary figures with those on a frieze: "unforgettable figures in silent arrested motion . . . troubling the heart like music" (*EPP*, 101). A number of different image clusters belong to this "statuary" iconography in Faulkner. At the end of *Soldiers' Pay* there is the description of a "monument to Donald Mahon, with effigies of Margaret Mahon-Powers and Joe Gilligan for caryatides" (p. 300). In the short story "There Was a Queen," Faulkner expresses the tension between degradation and dignity through the repeated use of caryatid images:

She wore white: a large woman in her thirties, within the twilight something about her of that heroic quality of statuary. "Do you want the light?" she said. "No," the old woman said. "No. Not yet." She sat erect in the wheel chair, motionless, watching the young woman cross the room, her white dress flowing slowly, heroic, like a caryatid from a temple façade come to life.   (*CS*, 738)

Faulkner had already begun to experiment with the stylizing quality of the sculpture metaphor that he put to such impressive use in this mature story (1929), in his early poetry ("Sapphics"), his *fin de siècle* play *The Marionettes*, and his post-war novel *Soldiers' Pay*:[9]

> The nine crowned muses about Apollo
> Stand like nine Corinthian columns singing . . .   (*EPP*, 51)

. . . and the nine white columns of the colonnade are nine muses standing like votive candles before a blue mountain . . .   (*MAR*, 7)

. . . against a wall of poplars in a restless formal row were columns of a Greek temple, yet the poplars themselves in slim, vague green were poised and vain as girls in a frieze. Against a privet hedge would soon be lilies like nuns in a cloister and blue hyacinths swung soundless bells, dreaming of Lesbos.   (*SP*, 55)

These variants of the sculpture metaphor emphasize slightly different aspects and have different connotations, yet they also retain a major similarity: each variation expresses oppositions or symbolic metamorphoses such as music/sculpture, sound/silence, motion/rest, living being/artwork. They involve the key issue of mimetic representation and stylization and ultimately embody two tragic polarities: the fulfillment but transitoriness of life as well as the permanence but sterility of art:

> Bold Lover, never, never canst thou kiss
> Though winning near the goal – yet, do not grieve;
> She cannot fade, though thou hast not thy bliss,
> For ever wilt thou love, and she be fair![10]

Horace Benbow in *Sartoris* applies Keats's apostrophe to the Grecian urn to both his self-made glass vase and his sister Narcissa; this leitmotif, characterizing Horace's amateurish glass art and his sterile relationship with his sister, represents the problematic relationship of art to life reflected in the imagery of caryatides and frieze figures:

apostrophizing both of them impartially in his moments of rhapsody over the realization of the meaning of peace and the unblemished attainment of it, as "Thou still unravished bride of quietness."

(*SAR*, 182)[11]

The complement of Horace's desire for the stillness of art and the sterility of his sister's love is the marble faun's desire for the animation of life, these two contrary drives representing in Faulkner's work two possible resolutions of a single polarity. In *Mosquitoes* the sculpture being created by Gordon suggests motion ("expecting motion . . . that sense of swiftness"), but at the same time appears

motionless and passionately eternal – the virginal breastless torso of a girl, headless, armless, legless, in marble temporarily caught and hushed yet passionate still for escape, passionate and simple and eternal in the equivocal derisive darkness of the world.

(*MOS*, 11)[12]

Patricia Robyn, the niece of the art patron Mrs Maurier, is aware of her affinity with the statue as is the sculptor:

Gordon examined with growing interest her flat breast and belly, her boy's body with the poise of it and the thinness her arms belied. Sexless, yet somehow vaguely troubling.

(*MOS*, 24)

Sexual ambivalance, or that "vaguely disturbing" sexlessness of Gordon's sculpture is, of course, central to the hermaphrodite motif, a traditional figure in art and literature discussed in another passage of the same novel. Previously it had appeared in important late Romantic works like Gautier's "Contralto" and *Mademoiselle de Maupin* or Pater's Platonistic essay "Diaphaneité" ("The beauty of the Greek statues was a sexless beauty"), mirroring the specific philosophical, sociological, and artistic problems of the period.[13] The same applies *mutatis mutandis* to *Mosquitoes*, where the hermaphrodite motif gives expression to literary as well as human ambivalence of the twenties. Fairchild, in line with

Sherwood Anderson's ideals of healthiness, simplicity, and naturalness, refers disapprovingly to it:

" 'Hermaphroditus,' " he read. "That's what it's about. It's a kind of dark perversion. Like a fire that don't need any fuel, that lives on its own heat. I mean, all modern verse is a kind of perversion. Like the day for healthy poetry is over and done with, that modern people were not born to write poetry any more . . . Kind of like men nowadays are not masculine and lusty enough to tamper with something that borders so close to the unnatural. A kind of sterile race: women too masculine to conceive, men too feminine to beget . . . "   (*MOS*, 252)

Another example of this motif is the Hermaphroditus sonnet ("Lips that of thy weary all seem weariest") which remained important enough for Faulkner to include in *A Green Bough* (poem XXXVIII) and is related to Swinburne's "Hermaphroditus" cycle inspired by the famous "Hermaphrodite" sculpture in the Louvre. Faulkner's variation on Swinburne is of interest with respect to both the theme of ambivalence and the sculpture motif. Swinburne's cycle, inscribed "Au Musée du Louvre, Mars 1883," must be seen as linked to Gautier's hermaphrodite poem "Contralto." Here these connections come full circle, since in *Mosquitoes* and *New Orleans Sketches* Faulkner had explored the ideals expressed by Gautier in *Mademoiselle de Maupin* and *Emaux et camées*: "I love three things: gold, marble and purple . . . form solidity colour . . . splendor, solidity, color" (*MOS*, 340; *NOS*, 3–4).

The quotation from *Mosquitoes*, together with variants in the opening piece of *New Orleans Sketches*, place Faulkner's striking interest in sculpture in line with a specific tradition of the analogy between literature and the visual arts that began with Gautier. The conception of the poet as an enameler and jeweler (*Emaux et camées*) or goldsmith and sculptor fostered a new sensuality of language and an emphasis on its plasticity and color. The increasing number of metaphors from the visual arts with entire poems being written about actual or imaginary paintings and sculptures is another result of this fashion. Like the hermaphrodite poems of Swinburne and Gautier, Faulkner's portrait sonnet "Lips that of thy weary all seems weariest" stands in the tradition of these painting and sculpture poems. In this poem Faulkner only returns to Swinburne's language in the opening lines, but throughout, Faulkner's hermaphrodite undoubtedly suffers from the same "strong desire begot on great despair" as Swinburne's.[14] This hermaphroditic despair – "thy twinned heart's grief," as Faulkner puts it – results from the double nature which both Faulkner and his admired predecessor found so fascinating: "The double blossom of two fruitless flowers? . . . To thee that art a thing of barren hours?"[15] The tension and ambivalence implied in the hermaphrodite motif let it become, like the other motifs expressing "impossible loves" (Lesbos, nymph, Narcissus, sibling), a central image of the frustrated idealistic yearnings for many artists of that sceptical era. It appealed to some of them all the more since its sexual dimension also allowed them to incorporate their personal psychological dilemmas into it.

The examination of Faulkner's various Swinburne studies shows that these works were not simply the result of youthful enthusiasm and emotional empathy, but represent professional and deliberate stylistic exercises. The transition from Swinburne to the Modernists appears unusual to us, since we lack an adequate picture of Swinburne's importance for the early Modernists. We immediately recognize the break between early Modernism and late Romanticism, but we fail to see the connections. Under the sway of Eliot's and Pound's influence, we tend to regard Swinburne as another imprecise Romanticist, or even as an outdated Victorian bard.[16] Many early Modernists, however, saw Swinburne in a very different light. For them, Swinburne was the author of *Poems and Ballads* (1866), a provocative volume of poetry in which the forbidden themes of blasphemy and perversion were expressed in the images and sounds of a new enchanting sensuality. In Pound's view, Swinburne merits respect as someone "who kept alive some spirit of paganism and of revolt in a papier-maché era."[17] A similar response to Swinburne is reflected in both the literary reminiscences that have gone into O'Neill's *Long Day's Journey into Night* and Dos Passos's war novel *Three Soldiers*. The formative effect of Swinburne's influence can also be detected in the "Villanelle of the Temptress" passage from Joyce's *A Portrait of the Artist as a Young Man* (1916) and in Fitzgerald's *This Side of Paradise* (1920). Poems such as Pound's "Simulacra" – "Why does the horse-faced lady of just the unmentionable age/Walk down Longacre reciting Swinburne to herself, inaudibly?" – demonstrate how Swinburne's literary heritage was ironically transformed into Modernist writing.[18] Pound's Imagist poem "Shop Girl" also embodies this reception of Swinburne; the modern heroine of the title is brought into poetic focus by the contrast with the stylized women from Swinburne, Guido, and Baudelaire. Another example illustrating the bridge between late Romanticism and Modernism can be seen in the poems "Yeux Glauques" and " 'Siena Mi Fe; Disfecemi Maremma,' " where Pound dedicates an ironic tombeau to the Pre-Raphaelite, Decadent tradition.

It is within this historical context that Faulkner's Swinburne paraphrases and his combination of Modernist elements and Swinburne material in "The Lilacs" can best be understood. Not only did Swinburne enable the young Faulkner to break out of a narrow-minded moralistic world, he also inspired him to develop a language of exotic richness. Thus it is not surprising that this "infatuation with words" (*MOS*, 248) draws so much attention in *Mosquitoes*. The language of this new sensuality, with its wealth of alliteration and assonances, of unusual vocabulary and manneristic imagery, also requires a strong organizing principle, and precisely this realization is most striking in Faulkner's Swinburne exercises. The poetic intelligence displayed by Faulkner in handling and controlling the sensuality of the material from Swinburne proves him to be a contemporary of both Pound and Eliot. In his Swinburne paraphrases, the young Faulkner tries his hand at associating sensuous and reflective elements, and in light of these attempts, his transition from Swinburne to Eliot no longer appears as an inexplicable leap. His experiments combining Swinburnian diction with avant-garde elements from Eliot are brought to a logical conclusion in "The Lilacs," which had been the title poem of the calligraphic *Lilacs* booklet and was to become the opening poem of *A Green Bough*.

The title of the poem "The Lilacs" is related to its lilac décor, which in all likelihood was inspired by Eliot's ironic "Now that the lilacs are in bloom/She has a bowl of lilacs in her room" in "Portrait of a Lady."[19] Lilacs appear as the framework at the beginning and end of Faulkner's poem "Beneath the lilacs . . . The pale lilacs stirring against the lilac-pale sky" (*MF & GB*, 7, 10). At the outset, the lilacs form part of the setting, and at the end this motif reflects the internal situation of the wounded soldier: "I no longer see/The pale lilacs . . . ," 10). The ingenious combination of the color of natural lilacs with the metaphorical coloring of the sky as well as the carefully contrived symmetry between pale lilacs and lilac-pale sky clearly demonstrate the poem's Symbolist quality. The poem is especially helpful for our understanding of Faulkner's literary development; it indicates how early he assimilated Modernistic elements and makes clear that this process of assimilation did not immediately result in a loss of interest in late Romantic material. "The Lilacs" may be characterized as a war poem, since it includes an account of a dogfight in the skies over Mannheim. It also resembles *Soldiers' Pay*, *Sartoris*, and Hemingway's *Soldiers' Home* with its theme of a soldier's alienation from the civilian world. The hero's injury, however, like Donald Mahon's wound or Bayard's psychological trauma, is not simply a war injury, but symbolic like that of the Fisher King in Eliot's *The Waste Land* and reflects the deep-lying insecurity of the roaring twenties.

It is largely through a specific use of late Romantic material that "The Lilacs," in form and content a Modernist poem, takes on its Symbolist dimension. Eliot's work had an impact here as well: "mermaids" and "nymphs" also appear in the shabby cityscape of "The Love Song of J. Alfred Prufrock" and *The Waste Land*. What justifies Eliot's introduction of the mermaids, however, is his use of irony; Faulkner, unfortunately, seems to overlook this, and his association of the fighter pilot and the nymph remains unrelieved by irony:

> – It was a morning in late May:
> A white woman, a white wanton near a brake,
> A rising whiteness mirrored in a lake;
> And I, old chap, was out before the day
> In my little pointed-eared machine,
> Stalking her through the shimmering reaches of the sky.
> I knew that I could catch her when I liked
> For no nymph ran as swiftly as she could.   (*MF & GB*, 8)

More important than the question of poetic success is what Faulkner actually set out to do here. He is obviously interested in combining the theme of the aerial dogfight with the time-honored literary motif of the pursuit of the nymph. Recurring in different variations in Faulkner's early work, this motif is developed from "L'Après-midi d'un faune" through "Nympholepsy" to the Cecily episodes in *Soldiers' Pay*. As the overall structure of "The Lilacs" shows, the young poet clearly realized that the effectiveness of combining different motifs depends on a careful adjustment of stylistic techniques. The poem's realistic quality is transmitted by the RAF jargon, which Faulkner picked up in Toronto and enthusiastically used in his early short story "Landing in Luck" (1919). The Symbolist dimension is added by the return to Swinburne ("The white wealth of thy body made whiter"),[20] who emphasized the white form of the *femme fatale* in several poems and often intensified that effect by means of alliteration: "A white woman, a white wanton near a brake,/A rising whiteness mirrored in a lake" (Faulkner). The nymph in "The Lilacs" embodies a kind of sterile yearning, but her behavior does not exactly fulfill the requirements of iconographical tradition. She flees, of course, but then, like the naiads in Faulkner's poem "Naiads' Song," changes into a *femme fatale*. In an ambiguous encounter with her, the fighter pilot feels the cold touch of death: "I felt her arms and her cool breath./The bullet struck me here . . . " (*MF & GB*, 8). Characteristic of the young Faulkner's psychology (cf. "Nympholepsy," *Mayday*, and *The Sound and the Fury*), here the themes of erotic longing, inhibition, and death are brought together.

In view of the young writer's close affinity to the spirit of late Romanticism, his appreciation of Eliot's inventive use of small talk and ironic rhymes ("Comfortably, at our ease/With fresh linen on our knees," *MF & GB*, 7) is quite remarkable. Imitating Eliot's use of the German place names "Starnbergersee" and "Hofgarten" in *The Waste Land*, Faulkner unexpectedly sets the name of the German city Mannheim in an English context: "We had been/raiding over Mannheim. You've seen/the place?" p. 9). This Modernistic effect is similar to the appearance of letters and numbers in Cubist collages. Like Eliot in "Prufrock," Faulkner also experiments with stanzas of various lengths and with the leitmotif repetition of such single lines as "One should not die like this" (pp. 8, 9, 10). The repetition of this particular phrase highlights the concern with death as a central theme in the poem. But despite the wartime setting, death appears unrelated to the political and moral implications of war; instead, it is connected with erotic frustration and manifests itself, as it will again in *Sartoris* and *The Sound and the Fury*, as a problem of the individual psyche. In conjunction with "Sapphics" and the various other statuary images in Faulkner's work, it is interesting to note that the hollow man in "The Lilacs" also attempts to transcend death through an aesthetic metamorphosis:

> One should fall, I think, to some Etruscan dart
> In meadows where the Oceanides
> Flower the wanton grass with dancing,
> And, on such a day as this
> Become a tall wreathed column: I should like to be
> An ilex on an isle in purple seas.
> Instead, I had a bullet through my heart –   (*MF & GB*, 9)

The influence of Eliot is also strong in the second poem of *A Green Bough*. This poem (II) which opens with the lines "Laxly reclining, he watches the firelight going" (*MF & GB*, 12) originally belonged to a group of Eliot *études* in *Vision in Spring*.[21] Details like the lilacs, the music imagery, and especially the lovers' frustrated eroticism recall Faulkner's model, Eliot's "Portrait of a Lady." But very little is taken directly from Eliot. The poem is a typical example of Faulkner's eclectic style; it deserves just as much attention for its Modernistic distortions as for its peculiar Pre-Raphaelite landscape descriptions. What is modern about the poem, besides its frankness in the treatment of eroticism, is that the perception of the outer world (the pianist–beloved) is interrupted again and again by the inner experience of the Prufrock-like hero. Later, in the piano scene of *Flags in the Dust* and in the portrayal of Quentin Compson whose perceptions of the outer world are profoundly affected by his trauma, the novelist was to profit from the experiments of the poet. Here in these early verses the firelight illuminating the pianist seems like "a golden river" to the protagonist, but also "like music dying down a monstrous brain," the latter comparison producing the leitmotif of the "deforming" brain. In the course of the poem, the protagonist experiences the schizophrenic effect of the music played by the *femme fatale*:

> Play something else.
>   And laxly sees his brain
> Whirl to infinite fragments, like brittle sparks,
> Vortex together again, and whirl again.
> . . .
> Play something else, he says.
>   And on the dark
> His brain floats like a moon behind his eyes,
> Swelling, retreating enormously. He shuts them
> As one concealed suppresses two loud cries
> And on the troubled lids a vision sees:
> . . .
> A bursting moon: wheels spin in his brain,
> And whirl in a vortex of sparks together again.   (*MF & GB*, 13–15)[22]

Eliot's interest in clinical descriptions ("the sky/Like a patient etherised upon a table," p. 13) and Faulkner's use of the "deforming" brain as a poetic leitmotif are unthinkable outside the framework of early Modernism. Given models or parallels like Eliot's "Rhapsody on a Windy Night," Faulkner's penchant for distortive imagery can be better understood.

In this context, distortion refers to a particular use of imaginative and intensified similes, as for instance in Eliot's famous lines "And through the spaces of the dark/Midnight shakes the memory/As a madman shakes a dead geranium" (Eliot, p. 24, lines 10–13). This technique was imitated and practiced by the young Faulkner in *Vision in Spring* and was later to give the daring touch to the poetic prose of the great novels. In the "Pierrot" poem (III, viii) in *Vision in Spring*, Faulkner cleverly combines a Prufrock-like identity crisis with a mannerist image from Eliot's "Preludes" IV, the notion of a soul stretched out across the sky:

> Who am I, thinks Pierrot, who am I
> To stretch my soul out rigid across the sky?   (Faulkner, p. 25)

> His soul stretched tight across the skies
> That fade beyond a city block.   (Eliot, p. 23)

While the Prufrock situation dominates "Pierrot" (III, viii), the borrowed "Preludes" metaphor is followed by some quite original imagery of the kind distinguishing Faulkner's mature style:

> Who am I to chip the silence with footsteps,
> Then see the silence fill my steps again?   (p. 26)

What is effective in this example is the concretization ("to chip . . . footsteps;" "see . . . fill . . . steps again") of abstractions like silence.

Distortion is not primarily a process that leads to destruction; on the contrary, it implies a metaphoric dynamization of realistic modes of perception: "Watching the streaming stars in a narrow pathway/Between rooftops grown snatching and shrill in darkness" (p. 21). Pierrot, the persona of the late Romantic artist as sufferer and scapegoat, is paralyzed by an oppressive exposure to cosmic and imaginary forces and feels that "the keen blue darkness/Cuts his arms away from his face" (p. 13) and that "the sky swims down into his eyes" (p. 20). As part of this metaphoric dimension, the violin literally becomes an instrument of torture. The cosmic dance in which the artist participates contains both his fate and his martyrdom:

> Listen! A violin
> Freezes into a blade so bright and thin,
> It pierces through his brain, into his heart,
> And he is spitted by a pin of music on the dark.   (p. 13)

Given the close relationship of Pierrot to the protagonists in *Vision in Spring* I and II, it is not surprising to find the same dynamization of the world of things:

> . . . Around him
> Spread widening circles of a bell.
>
> And then another bell slid star-like down the silence
> Stagnant around him, and awoke
> A sudden vagueness of pain . . .   (p. 1)

In its combination of acoustic phenomenon with imagery of motion ("bell slid . . . down the silence"), this last example illustrates the inner connection between distortion and the Symbolist forms of oxymoron and synesthesia.

Distorting effects are particularly evident in the description of spatial dimensions. The view of nature which mirrors Pierrot's vision of the world, for example, takes on the attributes of a nightmare: "The dark sea on a dark cliff silverly hurls/And freezes like teeth laid on the throat of the sky" (p. 12). "Deforming" metaphoric content is not the only technique that creates distortions; they are also produced by the seamless interweaving of "real" with allegorical landscapes, of external and internal worlds: "And Pierrot watches the shadows scurry across the street of stone/While above him, crouching, looms the shadow of his heart" (p. 23). In another poem in the *Vision in Spring* cycle entitled "After the Concert" (IV), an impressionistic setting – "The music falls, the light goes up the walls," (p. 30) – serves as the basis for unusual combinations of concrete and abstract language similar to those found in "Portrait of a Lady" and other Eliot poems:

> In a haze of trivialities
> We walk, and pause, and walk
>
> In a spring of certainties whitely shattered about us . . . .   (Faulkner, p. 32)

> – And so the conversation slips
> Among velleities and carefully caught regrets
> Through attenuated tones of violins.   (Eliot, p. 18)

The Symbolist striving for the dissolution of boundaries and the transcendence of everyday reality reveals itself just as often in synesthesia as in distortion. By providing the artist and seer in poem II ("Interlude") of *Vision in Spring* with powers of optical–acoustical synesthesia ("I will watch them through clear glass/ Of star-white silence," p. 7), Faulkner elevates the visionary dance beyond superficial reality. Particularly in the description of the vision itself, he employs synesthesia to stress the imaginary quality of the event, using for example the *art nouveau* image "Pass/In the vagrant music of their hair" (p. 7). The transformation of the harp music into blood in the poem "Pierrot" (III, v) results from more than a manneristic conceit:

> Pierrot bows his head above his harp
> And lets the notes fall slowly through his fingers
> Like drops of blood, crimson and sharp:
> He shatters a crimson rose of sound on a carpet of upturned faces.   (p. 19)

This unusual comparison of music to blood announces a major theme in late Romanticism and early Modernism: the idea of the suffering artist. It is characteristic of the structure of Faulkner's synesthetic imagery that he ingeniously expands it here. The "crimson" of the blood, for instance, becomes the "crimson" of the rose. At the same time, the original music motif ("harp"; "notes") is taken up and combined in a fugal pattern. The synesthetic image "crimson rose of sound" brings together and transcends the larger image cluster. In early works like *Vision in Spring* and *The Marionettes* Faulkner's predilection for intensified language, a phenomenon that later marks the prose of *Absalom, Absalom!* and of the Ike Snopes episode in *The Hamlet*, is not yet counterbalanced by more profound thematic objectives. In this particular example, however, the young writer manages to give the optical–acoustical image "crimson rose of sound" a further, spatial dimension by shattering the "tonal" rose onto "a/carpet of upturned faces."

What the Eliot *études* in *Vision in Spring* teach us about Faulkner is above all his obsessive desire to learn about language. The distinctive features of his experiments are reuse, transfer, and variation. Sometimes the imitations are so close to the originals (for instance, in "Love Song" (IX) of *Vision in Spring*) that they could be mistaken for parody if it were not for the unmitigated seriousness of the young writer who does not even notice how ludicrous it is to transform Prufrock's mermaids into "garden maidens dancing, white/And dim, across the flower beds" (*VS*, 62). At other times, the material is taken out of context and put to very different use as in the case of the famous invitation of Eliot's "The Love Song of J. Alfred Prufrock." The lines "Let us go then, you and I" (p. 13) do not come up in Faulkner's "Love Song" (IX) but instead are transferred to poem VI, a poem which with its impressionistic light effects and musical metaphors is otherwise more closely connected to Aiken. It may come as a surprise that on this occasion Faulkner misses the opportunity to reuse and perhaps improve on Eliot's well-known clinical image of evening. Faulkner's evening does not lie "like a patient etherised upon a table" but rather "grows/And a delicate violet thins the rose/That stains the sky;/We will go alone there, you and I" (p. 38). This departure from Eliot is probably motivated less by any fear of plagiarism than from the conviction that in his love poem "a violet rose" is more in place than an "etherised patient." Not only the beginning, but also the conclusion of Eliot's "Prufrock" must have fascinated Faulkner. This becomes apparent in the conclusion of his own "Love Song" and its variants among the manuscript fragments as well as in the additional use of another variation on Eliot's final line in a previous stanza:

> By sea-girls wreathed with seaweed red and brown
> Till human voices *wake us*, and *we drown*.   (Eliot, p. 17)
>
> I sit, watching the restless shadows, red and brown,
> Float there till *I disturb them*, then *they drown*.   (Faulkner, pp. 62–3)
>
> . . . to *wake him*, and *he dies*.
>
> (Faulkner, p. 64;
my italics)

Faulkner's variations clearly demonstrate his attempt to attune his ear to the subtleties of Eliot's verse and his compulsive desire to develop his own verbal skill. They also point forward, in an uncanny way, to Quentin Compson's "Death by Water."

Among the Modernist poets Faulkner's other great inspiration besides Eliot is Conrad Aiken. Judith Sensibar has made the influence of the cyclical structure of his music poems on Faulkner the focus of her book.[23] Since the emphasis of the present study is on the role of stylization in the development of Faulkner's poetic prose, we will concentrate on the imagery and the relation of *Vision in Spring* to the tradition of the music poem. Faulkner imitated Aiken's music poems ("Nocturne of Remembered Spring," "White Nocturne," "A Nocturne in a Minor Key," "Sonata in Pathos") for the reason that both authors were trying, as many other poets tried between late Romanticism and Modernism, to break away from the Victorian poetry of ideas. Faulkner's and Aiken's music poems belong to a literary tradition that begins with Gautier's "Symphonie en Blanc Majeur," develops through O'Shaughnessy's cycle *Music and Moonlight* and J. A. Symonds's cycle *In the Key of Blue*, to John Gould Fletcher's "White Symphony" and Amy Lowell's color symphonies "Town in Color" and *Can Grande's Castle*, reaching its conclusion in Wallace Stevens's *Harmonium* (1923) and Eliot's *Four Quartets*. The contributions to this tradition are often disparate in nature: there are mood poems related to music, color symphonies, Impressionist prose poems, or often only "musical" titles, but there are also musical forms and structures. Despite the differences within the genre, the following elements are essential and also characterize Faulkner's *Vision in Spring*: the description of sensual–spiritual moods producing a kind of Symbolist suggestiveness as opposed to the discursive logic of Victorian poems of ideas; the development of musical leitmotif structures that often extend beyond single poems to encourage arrangements in groups or cycles; and the tendency of poetry to regenerate itself through analogy to other arts or in connection with them (multimedia artworks).

In connection with the central motif cluster music–dance–vortex in *Vision in Spring*, Faulkner's review of Aiken's *Turns and Movies* is particularly revealing, since he deals explicitly with Aiken's principle of musical composition: "he has written with certain musical forms in mind" (*EPP*, 75). But when considering the transferability of musical structures, Aiken's moderate view – "I do not wish to press the musical analogies too closely" – should also be recalled.[24] In "Pierrot" III, i and III, ii, Pierrot himself takes part in the whirling dance. In "Pierrot" III, iv, the dance of the artist and the cosmos are placed together in a pattern of symbolic correspondence:

> Pierrot spins and whirls . . . [sic]
> Cities beat like surf below him in the dark.
> The darkness is a world of lesser worlds
> Swiftly spinning soundless rings of light. (p. 21)

In the course of *Vision in Spring*, this fundamental relationship undergoes a subtle process of repetition, variation, and mirroring. But the romantic conception of correspondences between the self and the cosmos can no longer be sustained in Aiken's and Faulkner's days, and so the artist appears thrown back upon himself after brief moments of visionary ecstasy. The cosmic harmony is reduced in the cycle to the aesthetic harmony between artist and work: "I am alone in a forest of sound around me/Woven with all beauty that I have felt and seen" (p. 27). Faulkner introduces the music theme in *Vision in Spring* with a variety of eclectic elements, a typical tendency in the early works of many writers. In "The Dancer" (X), youth appears as a dancer in a dialogue with the protagonist surrounded by typical *art nouveau* decoration. In the Modernistic poem XI, the music–dance–vortex motif aids the transition from an impressionistic exterior to a Symbolist dreamscape. Faulkner, like Aiken in his music poems, uses the word vortex and the image of dynamic whirling intentionally as part of the music-dance leitmotif in *Vision in Spring*.[25] The music–dance–vortex motif, however, does not occur in systematic musical patterns. The motif is present in all the poems in the cycle in some form, but the individual music poems still retain their own distinctive qualities. Detailed and systematic musical analogies are built into an instrumental poem like "A Symphony" (VII). Other poems like "After the Concert" (IV) and

XI have a personal touch and seem based on the memory of an actual love scene after a concert. The portraits of the allegorical figure of youth in "The Dancer" (X) and the singer in "Orpheus" (XII) have completely different thematic aims. "Philosophy" (XIII) is even "bare of sound" (p. 85) and consists entirely of "haunted silence" (p. 83). Like Eliot, Faulkner uses the title of "Love Song" ironically. Here the music motif so prominent in *Vision in Spring* is inverted into emptied sound: "We will go alone, my soul and I,/To a hollow cadence down this neutral street" (p. 58).

The music–dance–vortex leitmotif is also interwoven with minor motifs such as trees and flowers: "The trees tossed silver arms in sleeves of green,/And lustrous limbs and boughs/Moved in a hushed measure to an ancient music" (p. 2). Set against these images of beauty in a kind of polyphonic counterpoint are images of darkness, sea, and frost, suggesting violence and paralysis: "The dark sea on a dark cliff silverly hurls/And freezes like teeth laid on the throat of the sky" (p. 12). The Pierrot artist, embodying stasis in motion and the art theme, appears not only as vitalizing Orpheus and dancer, but with his face frozen into a mask ("feeling his face freeze into a mask of calmness," p. 20) and as a columned and sculptured figure:

> Pierrot would stand beside a night like a column of blue and silver.
> The column scintillates with orange and green,
> The column is dusty with facets of worlds that he has seen,
> The column is frozen with stars of white and blue.   (p. 10)

The frost imagery in the Pierrot poems indicates Faulkner's awareness of the Symbolist tension between beauty and paralysis, art and sterility already observed in "Sapphics" and "Hermaphroditus." Moon and star imagery provide further proof of the strong affinities between the *Vision in Spring* cycle and the Symbolist tendency within the late Romantic tradition. It is particularly revealing that the moon, which is part of the fixed iconography of "Pierrot lunaire," appears in *Vision in Spring* in image structures marked by the same Symbolist ingenuity which we will also encounter in *The Marionettes*: "The moon is a luminous bird" (p. 10); "The wasted moon silently combs his hair" (p. 11); and "The moon is a spider" (p. 11).

The most pronounced signs of Symbolist affinities in *Vision in Spring* are those images which, showing the correspondence of various spheres in the universe ("Stars swing back across the empty street,/And ghostly faces are blown like stars across his heart," p. 25), set the eternal world of the stars in relationship to the earthly, transitory world and juxtapose outer and inner experience. Here and in the several complicated similes where "stars are blown across the sky like candlelight, become confetti, and finally turn into leaves above and within a coffin," that peculiar kind of manneristic intelligence seems to be at work which characterized Renaissance sonneteers or the Metaphysicals "canonized" by Faulkner's master Eliot in the same year that the young poet gave *Vision in Spring* to Estelle (1921).

Estelle is also the subject of a poetry fragment with lofty language obviously inspired by the "Villanelle of the Temptress" in James Joyce's *A Portrait of the Artist as a Young Man* (1916):

> Estelle
> Ah, and sweet her mouth and cold:
> She is long weary of ardent ways,
> The burning vase and gilt and gold.
>
> Yet, cooler shapes the vase's rim
> In kissing, drank sup her mouth's suspire:
> Man's broken song she's had of him;
> And choired arisen Cherubim
> Are ghosts of agonies and fire
> Her graven music still betrays
> Though and sweet her mouth and cold
> And she is wearied of ardent ways.   (Faulkner[26])
>
> Are you not weary of ardent ways
> Lure of the fallen seraphim?
> Tell no more of enchanted days.
>
> Your eyes have set man's heart ablaze
> And you have had your will of him.
> Are you not weary of ardent ways?   (Joyce[27])

The expression "weary of ardent ways" is extravagant enough to exclude the possibility of an accidental parallel. Under Faulkner's pen, Joyce's phrase "fallen seraphim" is transformed into "choired arisen Cherubim." Joyce's "chalice flowing to the brim" is replaced by "vase's rim." The vase calls to mind not only Horace Benbow's glassblowing and his relationship to his sister, but Faulkner's own remark concerning his relationship to Caddy.[28] And Faulkner's line "Man's broken song she's had of him" probably refers back to Joyce's "had your will of him." In both poems there are images of fire and in both the traits of the *femme fatale* are drawn in the Swinburnian mode. What is of interest here is that the young poet transforms Estelle Oldham, the sexually attractive flapper from Oxford, Mississippi, into a mythic personage and that to do so he draws on literary precedent and, foreshadowing his practice in later novels, creates a stylized portrait. Faulkner's manly struggle with the refined and difficult form of the villanelle is completely in keeping with Millay's and other contemporary efforts including his own lyric cycle *Helen: A Courtship*. He had acclaimed precisely this tendency in "Verse Old and Nascent": "to revert to formal rhymes and conventional forms again" (*EPP*, 117). What reads like the poetics of a reactionary in this essay ceases to appear so when we become aware of Faulkner's own painstaking and extensive modification of traditional stanza, verse, and rhyme forms in *Vision in Spring* (see Appendix II) and recognize them as related to efforts by Eliot in the *Prufrock* volume (1917) and *Poems* (1920) to make "fragments of old forms" amenable to a new sensibility.

Faulkner also attempts to do the same in the Aelia fragments now located in the University of Texas Collection. Aelia, the name of the heroine from the two sonnets, already has a familiar ring for the reader of Faulkner's *Mayday* (*MAY*, 73). In the parodic prose romance modeled after Cabell, there appears a "Princess Aelia, daughter of Aelius the Merovingian," with whom Sir Galwyn of Arthgyl has one of his many affairs. The name Aelia, moreover, appears in *Soldiers' Pay*, and characteristically, in a passage which seems to be indebted to the montage art of the time. There Faulkner combines the Laforgue quotation ("*La lune . . .*") from his own "Fantoches" translation with the original quotation from Verlaine's "Fantoches" ("*Noir sur la lune*"), which he had ignored in his translation, and the material from the Aelia sonnets:

"My name is Emmy," she told him icily. "That's right," he agreed equably, "so it is Emmy, Emmeline, Emmylune, Lune – '*La lune en grade* [sic] *aucune rancune.*' But does it? Or perhaps you prefer '*Noir sur la lune*?' Or do you make finer or less fine distinctions than this? It might be jazzed a bit, you know. Aelia thought so, quite successfully, but then she had a casement in which to lean at dusk and harp her sorrow on her golden hair. You don't seem to have any golden hair, but, then, you might jazz your hair up a little, too. Ah, this restless young generation! Wanting to jazz up everything, not only their complexes, but the shapes of their behinds as well."
(*SP*, 130)

Like Stephen Dedalus in Joyce's *Portrait*, Januarius Jones attempts to prove his "consciousness of language" by means of an "exercise" in etymology which in his case unfortunately lapses into forced witticism. After he links the name of the poor Emmy with the word "lune" from the misquoted Laforgue verse in "Fantoches," the ironic comparison of the Cinderella-like heroine with the beautiful Aelia follows.

In the preserved quartet of the sonnet fragment "Aelia, at the casement of despair," the heroine assumes a pose of inconsolable sorrow for Ferdinand. The idealistic wish to be united with the loved one in death is cleverly parodied by Faulkner with the traditional image of twin stars: "To be, with Ferdinand, twin stars above." With the closing question – "But where's his grave, whom love has ever slain?" – Faulkner playfully drives the death wish theme so frequently found in poetry *ad absurdum*. In the other typescript sonnet "You see here in this leaden tenement," we encounter an Aelia buried in the Merovingian tomb. Her father does not bear the name Aelius like the one in *Mayday*, but rather Aelian, which may go back to "leech Aelian" in Cabell's The *Line of Love* (1905). What is certain, in any case, is that the names Aelia, Aelian, and Aelius are not to be found in the history of the Merovingians.[29] Aelia is most probably a fictitious character inspired by Cabell's medievalizing parodies and then fashioned by Faulkner into several variants. With regard to her origin, the ironic remark of the "genealogist" in Cabell's *The Rivet in Grandfather's Neck* ought to be kept in mind:

And when you are establishing a royal descent, and tracing it back to czars and Plantagenets and Merovingians, and making it all seem perfectly plausible, the thing is sheer impudent, flagrant art, and *you* are the artist.[30]

This irony and that in the Aelia sonnet is closely related to that of Eliot's earlier poetry: "Burbank with a Baedecker: Bleistein with a Cigar"; "Sweeney Erect"; "A Cooking Egg." In "Burbank with a Baedeker: Bleistein with a Cigar," the two themes of Venice's magnificent past and the *nouveaux riches* tourists are subtly played off against each other. In "Sweeney Erect," a literary backdrop is created, "Paint me . . . Cyclades . . . Aeolus . . . Ariadne's hair . . . Nausicaa and Polypheme" (p. 42), for the brothel scene with Sweeney, Doris and other "ladies." Faulkner makes use of the tourist motif in "You see here in this leaden tenement" in a manner similar to that of Eliot in "Burbank with a Baedeker: Bleistein with a Cigar." His juxtaposition of Aelia, or respectively Ophelia, and T. Coffey from New York corresponds with Eliot's "Sweeney Erect," where Nausicaa and Polypheme, and Doris and Sweeney are set off against each other:

> You see here in this leaden tenement
> The skull of Aelian's daughter, Aelia,
> A crumbled thing _ _ _ you know the sentiment:
> Alas, poor Yorick! Ah, Ophelia!
>
> This young dead Aelia had friends, suppose,
> To write her epitaph – but not content
> With mere eulogy, they must expose
> (One franc and tip) her broken monument.
>
> Hither came one who had no friends at all
> And left no bones: T. Coffey, from New York
> And still alive, who scribbled on the wall
> Where Aelia and the Merovingians slumber
> His own base epitaph in cheap red chalk –
> "Astoria Avenue", and gave the number.[31]

Even the names in the first quatrain of the sonnet, "Aelian's daughter, Aelia," transmit the dignity and dimension of a great past. The inclusion of the *Hamlet* allusion supports this effect by establishing a parallel between Ophelia and Aelia. The deliberateness with which Faulkner works here can be seen in the way he associates Aelia's destiny with a traditional "literary sentiment": "you know the sentiment:/Alas, poor Yorick! Ah, Ophelia." The ironic transition to the trivial world of modern tourism occurs subtly and almost imperceptibly in the second quatrain. In their eagerness to pay tribute to her, Aelia's friends are not satisfied with a traditional eulogy; instead, and here follows the comical twist, they exhibit her dilapidated monument for "One franc and tip." It is ironically noted that the modern-day tourist, T. Coffey, contrary to Aelia, does not have any friends and does not leave any relics behind. Continuing his trivial existence, he composes an epitaph by scrawling his own banal name on the monument. The sonnet is brought to a close with a sharp contrast between a glorious past ("Where Aelia and the Merovingians slumber") and a mediocre, banal present ("His own base epitaph in cheap red chalk –/'Astoria Avenue', and gave the number") and can be counted among the best of Faulkner's early exercises.

5
A Theater of Masks and Marionettes

THE TITLE of Faulkner's one-act play *The Marionettes* suggests the new concept of drama being evolved at the time by serious dramatists and producers both in Europe and the USA. The term "marionettes" implies not real characters in the Ibsen tradition but figures of art, masked players, ritualized action, or to name classic examples, Gordon Craig's Symbolist productions, Yeats's study of Noh plays, and O'Neill's concern with masks. That Faulkner contributed to this literary movement is not surprising in view of the nature of his artwork and his poetry. His dramatic ventures as well as his *art nouveau* booklets and Beardsleyesque drawings, his late Romantic "Sapphics" and his early Modernist Aelia sonnets, despite their diversity, have one striking feature in common: they are all attempts to create a highly stylized form of art. Apparently Faulkner first had to join that great international movement which Baudelaire and others had initiated to check the monopoly of the Realist–Naturalist tradition. As we shall see, the exercises in these non-Realist art forms enabled the young writer to develop the sensitivity and verbal strategies that would give his Realist perception a Symbolist dimension.

In connection with the uniqueness of the *Dramatis Personae* of *The Marionettes* and the use of masks in the anti-Realist theater of the early twentieth century, Faulkner's use of sculpture imagery in his poetry and his Hergesheimer review are again worthy of mention. Despite his rejection of Hergesheimer's characters as individuals in a realistic novel, he also shows appreciation and praise for them as artistic figures in a work *sui generis*: "It [*Linda Condon*] is more like a lovely Byzantine frieze: a few unforgettable figures in silent arrested motion, forever beyond the reach of time and troubling the heart like music" (*EPP*, 101).[1] What obviously fascinated Faulkner, and what perfectly illustrates his conception of the marionette, is the specific form of stylization which he projects onto Hergesheimer's characters. They appear to him to be frozen or figures arrested in motion. Like the sculpture, the marionette is a figure of art, freed from the laws of reality, from temporality, as well as from psychological motivation.

No less relevant here is the association of the term "marionettes" with the stereotyped rococo figures and sceneries for which the twenties continued to show the same enthusiasm as the *fin de siècle* that had rediscovered them. The strong Beardsley influence in *The Marionettes* immediately brings to mind Beardsley's own marionette cycle, *The Comedy Ballet of Marionettes*, which first appeared in *The Yellow Book* in 1894 bearing the parodic note "as performed by the troupe of the Théâtre-Impossible, posed in three drawings" (Pls. 89–91). Like Wilde's and Beardsley's Salome (in *The Stomach Dance*, Pl. 58) and the dancing Pierrot in both Faulkner's illustrated poem "Nocturne" (Pl. 32) and *The Marionettes*, the heroine in *The Comedy Ballet of Marionettes III* exemplifies the popularity of the dance motif around the turn of the century. The dancing harlequin-like figure, the satyr, and the grotesque rococo orchestra show that Beardsley treated marionettes not as dolls moved by strings but as eighteenth-century figurines (Pl. 91).

This also holds true for Verlaine, who designated the figures adapted by eighteenth-century French comedy from the *commedia dell'arte* as *fantoches*. Since "Fantoches" is among the four Verlaine poems translated and published by Faulkner in *The Mississippian*, Verlaine's title is very likely one source for the title of Faulkner's play. For Verlaine, as for Faulkner, who retained the French title in his translation, Scaramouche and Pulcinella, the Bolognese "doctor," his daughter and her handsome pirate are undoubtedly all *fantoches*, marionettes. The same applies to other characters from poems in Verlaine's *Fêtes galantes*: Pierrot, Arlequin, and Columbine in "Pantomime" or the rococo shepherds and shepherdesses Tircis, Aminte, Clitandre, and Damis in "Mandoline." Verlaine's influence was that of a comprehensive mode of artistic stylization rather than the mere transmission of isolated motifs such as Pierrot and Columbine, fountains, and garden sculpture.

But Faulkner's familiarity with this world of marionettes does not exclusively derive from the French world of *Fêtes galantes*; his awareness of the wider implications of the motif is indicated by the reference to Millay's *Aria Da Capo* in his 1922 review, where he admires the "surprising freshness of the idea" of combining a "pastoral tragedy" with a "thoroughly artificial Pierrot and Columbine suite" (*EPP*, 84). Moreover, he had met with the *fin de siècle* penchant for the rococo in George Moore's *Confessions of a Young Man* (1886)[2] and experienced its continuing popularity in the American twenties not only in Paul Eldridge's *The Carnival* (1923), a one-act comedy with Pierrot and Columbine in *The Double Dealer*, and in John Peale Bishop's *Fêtes galantes* in *Vanity Fair* in 1920,[3] but also, as we have seen in the yearbook *Ole Miss*, in his immediate environment.

The effect of the neo-rococo on the work of Wallace Stevens demonstrates perhaps most clearly its importance for the development of the new twentieth-century artistic consciousness. Stevens's interest in *Fêtes Galantes* and in the paintings of Watteau and Fragonard was obviously not just a superficial interest in the elegance of the *ancien régime*. Robert Buttel has developed an explanation which could be applied to any number of writers at the outset of Modernism: "The *fêtes galantes*, rococo world had a further advantage for Stevens in that it contained some of the qualities Romanticism tended to reject: a highly civilized, aristocratic order and a different sort of union of man and nature; that is, nature ordered and refined by the imposition of man's imagination."[4] The appeal of a neo-rococo park with avenues of trimmed trees, fountains, basins, little temples,

89–91. Beardsley, *The Comedy Ballet of Marionettes I, II* and *III* from *The Yellow Book*, 2, July 1894

and garden sculptures stems from the artifice imposed on nature. It is the intention to "give nature a lesson" which dominates the treatment of the park settings and garden scenes in these plays. Faulkner's conscious effort to stylize the natural world is not only evident in the scenery descriptions in *The Marionettes*, but also in the "meretricious trees and impossible marble fountains" with which he has Beardsley surround Margaret Powers in *Soldiers' Pay* (*SP*, 26).

The stylization of nature as a formal garden corresponds precisely to the treatment of characters as marionettes. The theoretical foundations for these developments in motifs and styles are found in such texts as Baudelaire's "Eloge du maquillage" (*Curiosités esthétiques*) and, deriving from it, in Oscar Wilde's "The Decay of Lying" (1889) as well as in Max Beerbohm's essay "A Defense of Cosmetics" (1894) and in the Luxembourg Gardens scene in Faulkner's novel *Sanctuary* which places the tragic realities of Mississippi at epic distance. As a result of Wilde's use of an ironic persona in "The Decay of Lying," many critics have missed the point of his attack on nature: "art is our spirited protest, our gallant attempt to teach nature her proper place."[5] This statement is not so much a decadent caprice as a reaction to the collapse, with the advent of Darwin, of the religious view of nature held by the Romanticists. The stylistic transformation of nature into neo-rococo and other types of artificial landscapes reflects this shift in sensibility. Wilde's criticism of nineteenth-century Realist and Naturalist literature also amounts to more than a frivolous exercise of wit. It is a manifestation of the same anti-Realist trend which was to play an important role in the development of the peculiar Symbolist distortion of reality practiced by Faulkner and many of his contemporaries.

There is a direct line from Wilde's regrets over "the decay of lying" to Beerbohm's praise of make-up and masks. Their interest in the concept of the mask laid the groundwork for the experiments with masks and marionettes through which Yeats, Maeterlinck, Craig, and the Provincetown Players contributed to the founding of modern theater. "A Defense of Cosmetics" contains a number of points directly programmatic for these experiments – "wise were the Greeks in making plain masks for their mummers to play in . . . why do we not have masks upon the stage?"[6] – and helps to explain why masks and marionettes were so fascinating to artists in the transitional period between 1880 and 1920. Like Verlaine and Beardsley, Beerbohm found the eighteenth century congenial to his taste because it struck him as an artificial age:

when life was lived by candle light, and ethics was but etiquette, and even art a question of punctilio, women . . . gave the best hours of the day to the crafty farding of their faces . . . in our fancy we see them . . . masked all of them, "lest the countenance should betray feeling," in quinze masks through whose eyelids they set peeping . . . [7]

These remarks reveal a perception of reality which has direct consequences for technique and expression. In acknowledging the dichotomy between inner life and external appearance, Beerbohm shows a distinct preference for the lovely surface, and in this signals the demise of the Romantic ideals of self-expression and sincerity in art.

An important characteristic links the rococo marionettes of Beardsley and Beerbohm with those Pierrots, Columbines, and shepherds of Verlaine, Laurence Housman, Millay, and Faulkner. In terms of Romantic and Victorian aesthetic theories, the appearance of these marionettes does not grow organically out of their inner essence. Instead, they express "soulless" beauty created by art. The mask and marionette motifs are undoubtedly projections and objectifications of an identity crisis felt by artists caught in an age of transition. Faulkner, in his continuance of this tradition in his play *The Marionettes*, gives clear expression to the split personality in his depiction of the dichotomy between an active and a passive Pierrot. This concern with split and multiple identities remains central throughout his work; in the novels from *Sartoris* and *Light in August* to *Go Down, Moses* he carries the theme over into the motif of twinship, miscegenation, and the relations between blacks and whites descended from the same father.[8]

The Modernist sense of life, which between 1880 and 1920 found artistic expression in the mask and marionette motifs, was given its definitive theoretical form by T. S. Eliot in his famous essay "Tradition and the Individual Talent" (1919). After historical ruptures had made the Romantic belief in the individual ego and the sincerity of its expression no longer appear a meaningful category, Eliot dismisses personality altogether and postulates the ideal of poetry's impersonality: "poetry . . . is not the expression of personality, but an escape from personality . . . the emotion of art is impersonal . . . "[9] Faulkner's review of Conrad Aiken's *Turns and Movies* demonstrates that he too was aware of contemporary theories of impersonality. One quality which Faulkner stresses is Aiken's "clear impersonality," regarding it as the factor which will never permit Aiken "to write poor verse" (*EPP*, 75). Although the passage which Faulkner cites is hardly a convincing example of impersonality, the phrasing of his appreciation for Aiken's qualities ("This is one of the most beautifully, impersonally sincere poems of all time," *EPP*, 76) leaves little doubt how well acquainted he was with the new literary ideal behind such motifs as masks and marionettes.

For Faulkner, the implications of the marionette motif are not limited to his early work. The marionette-mask phenomenon had a lasting effect on such questions of characterization as how and why realistic figures acquire mythic generality or symbolic importance. In the development of stylized methods of character portrayal, the Symbolist theater of Maeterlinck, Yeats, Craig, and Provincetown playwrights like O'Neill and Kreymborg is of major significance. The stylization of setting, figure, action, and speech in Faulkner's *Marionettes* and related plays of the period, like those by Millay, coincides with Craig's prescriptions for theater practice, particularly with his intention to replace actors with an "Über-marionette." Scorning the "clamouring of 'Life! Life! Life' which the realists keep up," Craig values Egyptian art "so silent that it is death-like" and "all passionless works of art." He finds the same quality in them which fascinates him in marionettes: "their power to retain the beautiful and remote expressions in form and face when subjected to a patter of praise, a torrent of applause."[10] The distance from life which Craig sees in primitive sculpture and Egyptian art, Yeats finds in Japanese Noh plays.[11] It is undoubtedly these same qualities which attract Faulkner to the "silent arrested motion" of the sculptures in *Mosquitoes* and the figures on Keats's "Grecian Urn" in *Sartoris*.[12] However, to do full justice to Faulkner's one-act play we should not only relate *The Marionettes* to the stylized features of the characters or poetic prose in his later novels, but to other contemporary and comparable plays.

The decades from 1910 to 1929 constitute a period of varied and fruitful experimentation in the history of the American theater.[13] America was also receptive to European influences, as the guest appearances of Max Reinhardt, Granville-Barker, and the Abbey Theatre in 1911 and 1915 demonstrate, and journals such as the *Theater Arts Magazine* attest. Ilse Dusoir Lind mentions the "dynamism of the new drama movement in Europe" as one of the inspiring forces of the "university theater movement" in America, which she sees as the context for Faulkner's *Marionettes*. As for the European models, she is thinking of Ibsen, Strindberg, and Shaw as well as of Symbolist and Expressionist drama.[14] American theater itself began to win worldwide acclaim with the dramas of Eugene O'Neill. New theater organizations such as the Little Theater Movement, Mackaye's Amateur Players, Professor George Pierce Baker's 47 Workshop at Harvard, the Carolina Playmakers in Chapel Hill, and the Theater Guild flourished in the wake of a new public consciousness of theater represented, for example, by the Drama League of America.

This new theater movement particularly favored Symbolist and Expressionist short dramas or one-act plays. Such Symbolist pieces as Maeterlinck's works and especially Oscar Wilde's *Salome*, which must be considered one of the sources of Faulkner's *The Marionettes*, are of considerable interest. The general cultural milieu, which partially explains Faulkner's fascination with Wilde's ostentatious, poetic one-act play, is clearly evident in *Vanity Fair*. Written for the upper middle class and using cultural snob appeal, the magazine includes in its June 1918 issue the picture of Madame Yorska as Salome (Pl. 1). The picture and its caption – "The heroine of Oscar Wilde's sinister tragedy which has recently been produced with success by the Washington Square Players" – show that it was not terribly unusual for Faulkner to possess a 1912 edition of Wilde's *Salome* with Beardsley's illustrations and to draw upon it for *The Marionettes* (1920).[15]

Productions in the new theater movement, which extended far beyond New York, were for the most part marked by anti-illusionistic tendencies, a reaction against commercial Broadway theater dominated by a superficial realism and exclusively oriented toward entertainment and profit. The forms and contents of the works in the Little Theater Movement were remarkably varied; the Provincetown Players' repertoire had room enough for both Millay's *Aria Da Capo* (1919 and 1920) and O'Neill's *Hairy Ape* (1922). What unifies such diverse directions in the theater reform movement are its reflections on the innate possibilities of theater and a renewed awareness of the necessity of stylization.

One important link between the Symbolist drama of Maeterlinck or Yeats and the Expressionistic drama of O'Neill, for example, *The Great God Brown* and *Lazarus Laughed*, is the concept of the mask.

While Faulkner did not have immediate contact with avant-garde theater, evidence indicates that he was more aware of its existence than has previously been assumed in Faulkner criticism.[16] His first opportunity to acquaint himself with the new theater was during his visit to New York and New Haven in April of 1918. Phil Stone and his friends at Yale could hardly have failed to enlighten the country boy in regard to the latest dramatic works and theories. Although there was little actual theater at Yale, the situation was naturally different in New York. But the similarities between Symbolist drama and *The Marionettes* seem to be due more to instinctive affinities than to direct influences. Faulkner's ability to capture the spirit of plays like Millay's *Aria Da Capo* and Wilde's *Salome* probably without ever seeing a performance is no more surprising than his assimilation of the essence of *art nouveau* from little more than his copy of Wilde's *Salome* and its Beardsley illustrations. In any case, after returning to his hometown Oxford in 1918, "he was," in Lucy Somerville's words, "reading plays and he was interested in the drama as an art form and in all phases of the theatre."[17] His particular liking for Shaw's *Candida* can be explained by its parody of Marchbanks's idealistic women cult. In 1920 Faulkner joined the student theater group "The Marionettes" at the University of Mississippi. Although the majority of the members of this drama club most likely did not realize the full implications of the name they chose for themselves, it was no mere coincidence that they did so at precisely this point in time. Ilse Dusoir Lind conducted several conversations with Ella Somerville in 1965 which confirm the impression that the Oxford drama club "The Marionettes" is to be seen in the context of the Little Theater Movement.[18] Ella Somerville had been recruited for the drama club by her relative Lucy, who was instrumental in founding "The Marionettes" and seems to have been just as literarily and artistically receptive as Ben Wasson and the young Faulkner. One indication of her artistic responsiveness is her immediate recognition of Helen Haiman Joseph's *A Book of Marionettes* (1920). As Blotner notes, Lucy Somerville passed this book around for Faulkner and other friends in their group to read. What makes Helen Joseph's book important is that it demonstrates a full awareness of the relationship between the Little Theater Movement, marionette shows, and Symbolist drama. More than a theater historian, Helen Joseph was herself the director of one of the puppet groups popular at the time. In 1918 she produced important marionette versions of Yeats's *The Shadowy Waters* and Yehring's *The Soul of Chopin*. Through her book the members of the Oxford student theater had access not only to the history of the puppet show, but, more importantly, to the new concepts of the marionette theater and Craig's avant-garde ideas and, by virtue of numerous photographs, to current productions. Helen Haiman Joseph's *A Book of Marionettes*, the name of the Oxford student theater group, the title of Faulkner's one-act play, and his Beardsleyesque drawing for the drama club (Pl. 55) are four details that together help us to envision the context in which Faulkner's studies of stylized character depiction take place.

Faulkner most probably saw, or at least read about, a number of productions by the Provincetown Players during his second stay in New York in the fall of 1921. As a clerk in a New York bookstore, he may have been aware of the publication of *Provincetown Plays* and *Best Plays* of 1919, 1920. Stark Young, the friend who had invited Faulkner to New York and with whom he initially stayed, had undoubtedly told him about the new theater in the preceding summer, and now Young became a direct mediator. As of 1917, Young was the theater columnist for *The New Republic*; he later became associate editor of *Theatre Arts Magazine* and a drama critic for the *New York Times*. Young was a friend of O'Neill's as well; in 1922 he wrote a critique of his *Hairy Ape* which influenced Faulkner's own view of the play, and in 1924 he staged O'Neill's *Welded*. Indeed, without his friendship with Young and the New York theater experience as a whole, Faulkner's interest in the modern theater and his articles in *The Mississippian* (1922) on O'Neill, American drama, and Millay's *Aria Da Capo* are hardly conceivable. Lind has strongly emphasized Stark Young's role as a cultural intermediary: "Maintaining his ties to his Mississippi birthplace and to his Oxford friends, Young acclimated them to innovative developments in the little theaters of New York."[19]

There is, of course, as little reason to exaggerate as to ignore Faulkner's relationship with contemporary theater, and his reviews certainly do not represent a deep or detailed understanding of the implications of the newly created American and international theaters. But the fact remains that Faulkner wrote a one-act play that has much in common with those by Symbolist playwrights. Aligned with poetic and Symbolist drama, as opposed to action-oriented, Realist plays, *The Marionettes* is closely related to a number of works from the Little Theater Movement. The affinities between Faulkner's *The Marionettes* and Millay's *Aria Da Capo* do not suggest that Faulkner read or saw her play, but it is true that the two plays have important features in common which could be accounted for simply by Stark Young's conversations with Faulkner in the summer of 1920. Nothing is more conceivable than that an experienced theater critic, home on vacation, would talk with a curious young writer about premieres and new developments in the art and theater world of New York. Edna St Vincent Millay, herself a part of the Provincetown circle, became as a result of the "gay and reckless verses" in her *A Few Figs from Thistles* (1920), "the unrivaled embodiment of sex appeal, the It-girl of the hour."[20] In 1918 the Playwright's Theater had performed her *The Princess Marries a Page*. *Aria Da Capo* was performed a year later on December 5, 1919 and again on March 3, 1920.[21] It is unlikely that Young did not know of the play and its performances; as a proficient, avant-garde work by a well-known writer, it could hardly have missed the attention of such a well-informed theater critic.

Millay's play is particularly interesting for its combination of two strands of action: the blasé and ironic Pierrot–Columbine scenes are interrupted by another plot, Arcadian in flavor, but containing undertones of the pessimism typical of the "lost generation." This crossing of plot lines combined with the interventions of a "play director" (Cothurnus) and with the repetition of the beginning at the end of the play bring *Aria Da Capo* into line with the contemporary, anti-illusionist spirit of Pirandello (*Sei personaggi in cerca d'autore*, 1921) and Piermaria Rosso di San Secondo (*Marionette, che passione!*, 1918). In light of the audacious handling of plot lines in Faulkner's later novels, it is interesting that in the review of *Aria Da Capo* he distinctly emphasizes the disruption of plot lines: ". . . the surprising freshness of the idea of a pastoral tragedy enacted and concluded by interlopers . . . in the midst of a thoroughly artificial Pierrot and Columbine suite alone makes it worth a second glance" (*EPP*, 84). In *The Marionettes*, Faulkner's extensive stage directions call for the sleeping Pierrot to be on stage as long as his "Shade" is acting. His strategy is clear, if somewhat amateurish: the two Pierrots not only personify the theme of split personality, but are also a step in the direction of the play-within-a-play structure of *Aria Da Capo*.

Apart from these structural features and the stylization of figures and settings, *Aria Da Capo* and *The Marionettes* are alike in that both are one-act plays. One-act plays were characteristic of the Little Theater Movement; the Washington Square Players, for example, had performed sixty-two one-act plays by 1918 but only six full-length dramas.[22] The one-act play was one of the more obvious ways for the new theater to distance itself from conventional theater. The Broadway public demanded an extended illusionary experience as its evening entertainment and would have rejected the neo-Naturalist, Symbolist, and Expressionist one-act plays produced by Baker's 47 Workshop and the Washington Square or Provincetown Players on the basis of their brevity alone. The one-act structure of Faulkner's *The Marionettes* parallels other models like Dowson's *Pierrot of the Minute* and above all, Wilde's *Salome*. There are, of course, several reasons for the popularity of the one-act play: it not only enabled these theatrical avant-gardists to experiment with minimal risk and less expense but also made it easier for them to realize the ideals of a poetic drama. As a review of an anthology of one-act plays in *The Mississippian* in 1921 shows, even students at Faulkner's hometown university were well aware of the importance of the Little Theater Movement:

The art of the one-act play has been realized, and a movement for the production of them has swept throughout the country, causing a revolution and many changes from the old set ways of the theater. With the little play has come the little theater, and the little theater has brought new art with it . . . We welcome the new idea.[23]

The scenery and costuming ("a stage set for a Harlequinade, a merry black-and-white interior")[24] provide further points of similarity between *Aria Da Capo* and *The Marionettes*. Millay's positioning of a table ("Directly behind the footlights, and running parallel with them") for Pierrot and Columbine resembles Faulkner's own stage direction: "Pierrot is seated at right front in a fragile black chair beside a delicate table" (*MAR*, 2). Finally, Millay's Pierrot does not wear the traditional white, but is dressed conspicuously "in lilac," which recalls the "Lilac Figure" in *The Marionettes*.

In interpreting Faulkner's *The Marionettes* it is just as important to note its differences from Millay's play as to emphasize the similarities. As might be expected, not only the themes and plots but also the tone in the two plays differ considerably. Millay's dialogue is a good example of the way Jazz Age conversation both imitated and parodied Wildean comedy dialogues. The difference between the quick, ironic repartee of Millay's marionettes and the solemn exchange of prose poetry between Faulkner's First and Second Figures could not be greater. While the Pierrot–Columbine scenes in *Aria Da Capo* are stylistically related to Wilde's comedies, the richly poetic language of *The Marionettes*, as we shall see, derives from a radically different play by the same author: Wilde's Symbolist tragedy *Salome*. Although *Aria Da Capo* and *The Marionettes* are in many ways similar, it should not be overlooked that Millay was a much more mature artist in the handling of tragic elements. She skillfully uses the Arcadian masks of Thrysis and Corydon and the wit of Pierrot and Columbine to intensify the bestiality with which the shepherds murder each other. Such a mixture of irony and horror is an appropriate expression of the post-war sense of life.

At the heart of *The Marionettes* lies a far different theme, Faulkner's unhappy love affair of 1918.[25] To be sure, he too had dealt with the war theme in lyrical experiments ("Lilacs") and especially in real life in the role of war returnee, but not until *Soldiers' Pay* (1926) and *Sartoris* (1929) did he begin to deal seriously with the aftermath of wartime and "wasteland" experiences. His innermost concern in 1920 was his relationship with Estelle Oldham, Mrs Cornell Franklin since 1918, and how to transform the accompanying wishful and retaliatory fantasies convincingly into literature. This problem proved to be difficult enough: while the ending to Millay's *Aria Da Capo* expresses the central tragic and ironic tendencies of the period, the corresponding end of the first part of *The Marionettes* is markedly subjective in nature. Marietta has been seduced and remains behind; Pierrot leaves, superior and in some undetermined sense heroic, only to subsequently, and with startling rapidity, be ruined. Using marionettes, Faulkner inversely revises the real situation before him and compensates for life's lack of generosity in 1918. The result is that, although "Fate and the gods" look on, the parting of Pierrot and Marietta is not tragic but sentimental.

Laurence Housman and Granville-Barker's *Prunella, or Love in a Dutch Garden* (1906) can be more closely related to *The Marionettes* than Millay's *Aria Da Capo*. Noel Polk has examined some of the striking common features and justly concludes that "*Prunella* stands significantly in the background of Faulkner's play" (*MAR*, xiii). But *Prunella* is a didactic play and the garden that serves as Symbolist scenery in *The Marionettes* appears as subject of a moral fable in Housman's play. The affinities between *Prunella* and *The Marionettes* are limited to certain themes which attracted Faulkner for biographical reasons: Pierrot courts, seduces, and then leaves his Prunella or Marietta. The regret and eventual return of Pierrot and the ultimate union of the lovers as seen in Housman are both missing in Faulkner. Instead, *The Marionettes* ends with the apotheosis of Marietta as a figure of art and in the vignette (Pl. 53) with a melancholy and narcissistic portrait of Pierrot. Judging by this conclusion, Faulkner's play appears much closer to the Aesthetic movement than *Prunella*. From a comparison with *Prunella* it becomes obvious that the young Faulkner was already surprisingly clear about his artistic intentions. He obviously did not want a theater-oriented, full-length amateur play with a large cast of characters, but a highly organized drama, which would derive its concentration and impact, in the manner of such Symbolist works as Wilde's *Salome*, from subtly handled iconography, language, and stylized movement.

6

The Iconography of Faulkner's *Marionettes*

GEORGE MOORE'S description of Pierrot in *Confessions of a Young Man* (1886) suggests the background tradition associated with the hero of *The Marionettes*: "And there is the Pierrot, that marvellous white animal, sensual and witty and glad, the soul of the century."[1] Moore's phrase "white . . . sensual . . . animal" may well be the source for Faulkner's own characterization of Pierrot: "Why do we fly to do his bidding, we who know him for the white sensual animal he is? For where goes Pierrot, also goes unhappiness for someone" (*MAR*, 43). More importantly, Moore's book would have exposed Faulkner to the many-sided figure of Pierrot from the *fin de siècle* reception of rococo art: "See the Fragonards . . . In the Watteaus the note is more pensive; there is satin and sunset, plausive gestures and reluctance – false reluctance; the guitar is tinkling, and exquisite are the notes in the languid evening . . ."[2] Moore, however, represents only one in a series of reference points, since Faulkner's Pierrot in *The Marionettes* reflects the assimilation of a wide variety of philosophical and aesthetic implications surrounding this figure. The character type of Pierrot derives from a rich literary and artistic tradition, which began with *commedia dell'arte* and reached its full development in eighteenth-century French comedy.[3] With subtle variations, Pierrot became one of the most important symbolic figures of the Romantic period and the *fin de siècle*: Banville, Baudelaire, Gautier, Flaubert, Verlaine, Huysmans, and Jules Laforgue all created their own Pierrots or elaborated on other versions. A common prototype for many of these romantic and modern embodiments of the figure is Watteau's clown portrait, *Gilles* (Pl. 92). In 1897 the French author Catulle Mendès sceptically described the process of fusing the comic Pierrot with the poetic Gilles:

Because Pierrot is white . . . like the melancholy wanness of the moon, we have, little by little, made of him an elegiac guitarist who gives aubades to the closed windows of a beloved, a poet in love with dreams . . . We are mistaken; deceived by the same lunar snow, we have transformed the popular Pierrot, the true Pierrot, into the poetic, subtle, and even perverse Gilles of Wateau [sic].[4]

It is difficult to envision the authentic Pierrot amid the confusion of his many forms, and since Mendès's time additional versions have been created by such diverse artistic talents as Picasso and Klee, Wallace Stevens and Schoenberg. The differences between several variants in the history of the type are considerable:

128

the moonstruck and idealistic Pierrot in Dowson's *Pierrot of the Minute*, for example, has little in common with the dandy in Millay's *Aria Da Capo*, and both differ from the seductive rogue in Housman's *Prunella*. Similar differences can also be identified between the Pierrot in Faulkner's poem "Nocturne" and his play *The Marionettes*. Despite such varying manifestations, Pierrot retains an unmistakable iconographical stability. For the most part, the traditional external appearance of the figure is maintained: Pierrot appears in whiteface, wearing a white blouson and loose white pants and adorned with black skullcap and ruff. Beardsley and *art nouveau* artists, followed by Faulkner and other imitators, often exploited the graphic possibilities of this costume for their own purposes. In *Pierrot Sleeping* in *The Marionettes* (Pl. 48), the wide costume of the seated Pierrot gives Faulkner the opportunity to experiment with sinuous, *art nouveau* lines; the cloud-like, rounded shapes produced by these lines are dissected by the arms' slender swinging motion and contrasted with the furniture, which in its delicateness resembles abstract décor. As in Faulkner's *Pierrot Standing* (Pl. 93), a tendency toward stylization is visible in the simplification of facial features and in the dissolution of the costume into ornamental lines.

The symbolic function of Pierrot's costume provides the key to interpretation, since its unusual appearance suggests his position outside society and reality. Pierrot is a figure of art existing within an artistic tradition and thus does not

92. Antoine   Watteau, *Gilles*, *c*.1717–19

descend from a mimetic representation of life. In a period characterized by the rise of a theory of masks and an ideal of impersonality in poetry, artists naturally gravitated to a stylized persona like Pierrot, because it enabled them to express their sense of philosophical and social disorientation. Hugo von Hofmannsthal, the great Austrian poet and playwright whose work marks the transition between *fin de siècle* and Modernism, emphasizes the central dichotomy of Pierrot – the combination of the stylized type with the modern self behind a mask – in 1893:

> The moonstruck Pierrot. Simply the old figure out of pantomine with chalk white face and widespread sleeves . . . Once again a long existent, long stylized creation of past art, a creature like a faun or an angel or like death itself. Filled again with the most modern of feelings and sufferings and peculiarities. This Pierrot is afflicted by the somnambulism and hysteria of the modern artist, he has his sensitivity for Chopin-like music and his martyr complex, his vibrant feel for the violin, for shrill reds and for hallowed, softened whites. He sits in cafés and daydreams from poisonous, green yellow clouds of absinth . . . But his loose white costume and white powdered cheeks give to all his melancholy phantasies something of the essence of tragicomedy, bringing on an ineffable sadness.[5]

And Arthur Symons, an English contemporary of Hofmannsthal, also sees the Pierrot as embodying the tensions and discrepancies characteristic of that era:

> Pierrot is one of the types of our century, of the moment in which we live, or of the moment, perhaps, out of which we are just passing. Pierrot is passionate; but he does not believe in great passions. He feels himself to be sickening with a fever, or else perilously convalescent; for love is a disease, which he is too weak to resist or endure. He has worn his heart on his sleeve so long, that it has hardened in the cold air. He knows that his face is powdered, and if he sobs, it is without tears; and it is hard to distinguish, under the chalk, if the grimace which twists his mouth awry is more laughter or mockery. He knows that he is condemned to be always in public, that emotion would be supremely out of keeping with his costume, that he must remember to be fantastic if he would not be merely ridiculous. And so he becomes exquisitely false, dreading above all things that "one touch of nature" which would ruffle his disguise, and leave him defenceless. Simplicity, in him, being the most laughable thing in the world, he becomes learned, perverse, intellectualising his pleasure, brutalising his intellect; his mournful contemplation of things becoming a kind of grotesque joy, which he expresses in the only symbols at his command, tracing his Giotto's O with the elegance of his pirouette.[6]

In addition to Pierrot's costume and his mask-like make-up, a recurrent feature of the type is his favorite setting, a rococo park. Neo-rococo artists of the *fin de siècle* like Dowson and Beardsley as well as the moderns Wallace Stevens, John Peale Bishop, and Faulkner seem to have been inspired by the setting of Watteau's *Gilles* and of other pictures in the *fêtes galantes* tradition. This artificial scenery, which corresponds to Pierrot's artificial nature, even appears in the work of such an apparently unrelated author as William Carlos Williams, who refers to both Watteau and Fragonard in "Portrait of a Lady."

Among the other common iconographical elements, Pierrot's pose is especially important, as a comparison of Watteau's *Gilles* (Pl. 92), Beardsley's frontispiece to Dowson's *Pierrot of the Minute* (Pl. 44), and Faulkner's *Pierrot Standing* in *The Marionettes* (Pl. 93) reveals. Beardsley's illustration is quite close to Watteau's

93. Faulkner, *Pierrot Standing*, from *The Marionettes*, 1920

painting in the depiction of costume, the placement of Pierrot's feet, and the park setting. Judging from the spiraled roses and the use of a trellis as a backdrop for Pierrot, Faulkner must have been acquainted with the Beardsley illustration, but the similarities of the positions suggest more than mere influence. What Richard Hamann says of Watteau's *Gilles* also applies to the Pierrots of Beardsley and Faulkner: "the Comedian stands before us, rigid and solemn, like a caryatid."[7] The statue-like posture conveys an impression of Pierrot's solitude. To emphasize his isolation and loneliness, Watteau draws him disproportionately large, and Faulkner, in an *art nouveau* manner, allows Pierrot's head and feet to project through the border of the picture. Beardsley leaves Pierrot within the edges of the illustration, but stresses verticality in quite a subtle way: above Pierrot's head, in sharp contrast to the white background, the black form of a pine serves as an extension of the figure. Faulkner achieves a similar vertical effect by placing the poplar or pine tree parallel to the trellis, which is enhanced by Pierrot's superior height. In *Gilles*, Watteau emphasizes vertical dominance by contrasting a group of figures in the middle ground with the background vegetation towering above. Beardsley manages a similar contrast by juxtaposing the white Pierrot against the background: supported by the white garden sculpture placed diagonally in the scene, he stands out against the complex black and gray patterns of the park.

In all three cases, Pierrot's solitary position is combined with a quiet, vacant, melancholy facial expression.

Faulkner's version gives a particular character to Pierrot's face through the downcast eyes mirrored by the eyebrows, the angle of the mouth, and the slight forward thrust of the face sharply framed by the black ruff. The crossed hands of the simplified linear figure further accentuate his expression. This drawing from *The Marionettes* underlines the relation of the artist to his subject; suffering from the disorientation of a "lost generation," out of place in his own hometown, and unhappily, seemingly hopelessly in love, the sensitive young Faulkner evidently thought he had found in Pierrot an appropriate persona to reflect his own melancholy.[8]

Faulkner's strong interest in the figure of Pierrot and its accompanying iconography was no doubt fostered by Beardsley's influence as an intermediary and model. With an obsession which foreshadows Picasso's fascination with harlequins, Beardsley repeatedly returned to the motif. A certain similarity between Beardsley's *Self-Portrait* and his *Death of Pierrot* reveals the extent to which Beardsley, like so many of his contemporaries, saw the suffering Pierrot as a symbol for the artist. In both works the figure is reduced to a tiny face nearly engulfed by the rest of the drawing, exemplifying the problematic relationship of the artist to society and social reality. Faulkner's early poem "Nocturne" (Pl. 32) depicts the situation of the artist in an even more radical position than either in his own *Marionettes* or Beardsley's earlier drawings.[9] The dance of the two *fantoches*, Pierrot and Columbine, becomes an overwhelming cosmic experience. For the Pierrot–artist, contact with the world is painful: "A violin/Freezes into a blade, so bright and thin,/It pierces through his brain, into his heart" (*EPP*, 83). In synesthetic imagery, music becomes an instrument of torture: "And he is spitted by a pin of music on the dark" (*EPP*, 83). Faulkner's Pierrot in "Nocturne," as a persona of the tortured artist, is hardly an isolated case in American avant-garde poetry. Amy Lowell makes similar use of synesthetic music imagery in her verses on the second piece of Stravinsky's *Grotesques for String Quartet*. Here, too, the imagery envelops and overwhelms the suffering Pierrot:

> Pale violin music whiffs across the moon,
> A pale smoke of violin music blows over the moon,
> Cherry petals fall and flutter,
> And the white Pierrot,
> Wreathed in the smoke of the violins,
> Splashed with the cherry petals falling, falling,
> Claws a grave for himself in the fresh earth
> With his finger-nails.[10]

It is hardly surprising that the Pierrot in Faulkner's "Nocturne" differs from the Pierrot in *The Marionettes*, since even there he is not a homogeneous figure. A comparison of the text and the illustrations makes clear that there is no basis for speaking of Pierrot's personality. Instead, we find a series of traditional Pierrot attitudes, which the young Faulkner ascribes to his marionettes in an attempt to articulate his slightly innocent theme. There are several different Pierrots: the kneeling lover (*Pierrot devoué*) adorning the *Dramatis Personae* (Pl. 41) and the melancholy Pierrot of *Pierrot Standing* (Pl. 93). And in *Pierrot Sleeping* (Pl. 48), there is the drunken, sleeping Pierrot of Dowson's *Pierrot of the Minute*: "he appears to be in a drunken sleep, there is a bottle and an overturned wine glass upon the table, a mandolin and a woman's slipper lie at his feet" (*MAR*, 2). The pose is characteristic of the loose relationship between the play's action and its illustrations and accordingly does not represent a specific phase of the dramatic action, but rather a variation of the Pierrot manner important to Faulkner, the *post festum* attitude equally visible in Ernest Dowson's poems "Beyond" and "Dregs" and Fitzgerald's *The Great Gatsby*.

Faulkner adds another thematic function to the motifs of dream and sleep by transforming Pierrot's visionary sleep, derived from Dowson's version of the traditional literary figure, into a decadent slumber. While in Pierrot's vision of the "moon maiden," Dowson presents the dreamer's destructive encounter with his ideal, Faulkner has Pierrot's "Shade" realize the sleeper's wishful fantasy, the seduction of Marietta. On the right half of *Pierrot's Two Visions* (Pl. 39), Faulkner reiterates his depiction of the sleeping Pierrot (cf. Pl. 48) to bring attention to the figure's constant presence on stage, while on the left half, Pierrot's "Shade" dances with Columbine–Marietta. This dancing couple resembles the couple in the "Nocturne" illustration (Pl. 32), but since the poses differ, it is obvious that Faulkner has taken the entirely different graphic requirements of a two-paged illustration into consideration. The couple returns in *The Kiss* (Pl. 96), where a silhouetted Pierrot waits for a kiss from Marietta in a scene indebted but not identical to the one in Faulkner's translation of "Fantoches."[11]

Pierrot, on the other hand, disappears in the middle of the play, which leads to the surprise of encountering him again in a vignette following the final curtain (Pl. 53). Caught staring at his own reflection in a mirror, he brings to mind the type *Pierrot narcisse*. For another late Romantic author, Gautier, the modern Pierrot is "profondément égoïste" in all his variants.[12] The final vignette with its juxtaposition of Pierrot gazing in a mirror and Marietta lying on her bier expresses a theme overshadowed in the text itself by the apotheosis of the heroine: Marietta as the victim of the narcissistic Pierrot's egotism. In other words, at first glance the vignette appears to be better suited for the theme of Housman's *Prunella* than *The Marionettes*. At issue in *Prunella* are the effects of egotism and the problem of sublimating them, with the end result meant to be true love. Faulkner, however, is interested in the aesthetic and not the moral aspects of narcissism. It cannot be denied that *The Marionettes* suffers from a certain thematic indecisiveness that makes the final vignette difficult to interpret. But in placing the dead Marietta and the narcissistic Pierrot side by side, Faulkner seems to have had more in mind than a moral lesson on the consequences of egotism. The final vignette depicts a tragic dilemma: Pierrot's self-reflection and fragmentation make any immediate relationship with other human beings and the world impossible.

The discrepancy between the representation of Pierrot in the illustrations and in the text of *The Marionettes* becomes evident long before the final vignette. While the proposal scene depicted in *Dramatis Personae* (Pl. 41) is related to the scene in the play itself, the sleeping and the melancholy Pierrot (Pls. 48, 93) have little in common with the singing, dancing seducer encountered in the text. As in *Prunella*, Pierrot forces his way into Marietta's world, lures her out of her garden, seduces and then deserts her. Noel Polk quite appropriately makes a connection between the implications of such a plot and Pierrot's birthplace, Paris, the "Western symbol for all that is voluptuous and sensual and unrestrained"(*MAR*, xvii). At the same time, Faulkner's reference to "Paris town" indicates his familiarity with the literary background, since Pierrot, the *fin de siècle*, and early Modernism all have their roots in Paris. That so many artists of such diverse artistic persuasions chose a figure from French comedy as a persona demonstrates the crucial role French literature played in the development of Modernism. Seen against the perspective of the generation of American artists and writers who took up residence in Paris, Faulkner's trip there in 1925 can be understood at least in part as an attempt to experience directly the French heritage central to his early poetry and *The Marionettes*.

Although *The Marionettes* is indebted to *Prunella* for the overt action of the seduction scene, its tone could not be further from the burlesque quality of the proposal scene in Housman's play. Faulkner's Pierrot proposes with ingenious Symbolist imagery, not with wit and wordplay:

> Your little feet have crossed my
> heart,
> Love!
> . . .
> And now I am a garden sprung
> beneath your footsteps.   (*MAR*, 19)

Due to the elimination of the comic element in this scene in *The Marionettes*, the seduction of Marietta takes on a certain resemblance to Gretchen's seduction in *Faust*. Moreover, Pierrot acquires Faustian overtones through Faulkner's emphasis on an unaccountable, but nonetheless definite urge to press forward in the parting scene:

. . . Fate and the gods stand aloof, watching him, his destiny waits wordless on either hand. Will he turn back where she awaits him in her rose bower, or will he go on? Ah, he goes on, his young eyes ever before him, looking into the implacable future. (*MAR*, 34)

There is not only a Faustian aspect in Faulkner's Pierrot, but also something of Don Juan.[13] After describing Pierrot as a "white sensual animal," the First Figure despairs, "for where goes Pierrot, also goes unhappiness for someone" (p. 43). The attribution of characteristic traits from both Faust and Don Juan to Pierrot is a good example of an author's impressing circumstances from his own life on a persona. It is possible to see a kind of wish fulfillment involved here through which Faulkner transforms and escapes the consequences of his unhappy love affair with Estelle Oldham. As a traditional literary figure, Pierrot has the function of a marionette or a mask, which permits the adoption of poses or the elaboration of situations in a way that is, in effect, a sublimation of biographical impulses. How much Faulkner himself understood of this is uncertain.

In the French variations of the *commedia dell'arte* tradition, Pierrot frequently appears with a female counterpart, Columbine. Although this precedent is followed in "Nocturne," Faulkner deviates from it in *The Marionettes*. He no doubt found the attributes generally associated with Columbine, a mischievous servant girl quick at repartee, inappropriate for the heroine of his Symbolist play. He proceeds to invert the tradition and the autobiographical facts: the hopeless lover, Pierrot, becomes successful, while the supercilious chambermaid is transformed into the "seduced innocent."[14] The model for these changes is probably Housman's *Prunella*, and the motivation was most likely Faulkner's personal life. It is important to recognize, however, that Marietta represents the Gretchen type, the "seduced innocent," in the first half of the play only. In the second half, Pierrot, the persona of the artist, has disappeared from the stage, and Marietta is the focus of attention. Here she undergoes a startling metamorphosis and joins the ranks of *fin de siècle* heroines like Mallarmé's Hérodiade, Pater's Mona Lisa, and Wilde's Salome.

Intriguingly, both hero and heroine in *The Marionettes* have curious split personalities: alongside the vital *Pierrot rusé* of the text derived from *Prunella* stands the melancholy and narcissistic Pierrot of the illustrations. Similarly, the heroine awakened to sexuality at the outset is transformed in the course of the play to a figure of art. Both characters exhibit essentially the same dichotomy. In Marietta, as in Pierrot, a sensual active side and a readiness to participate in life are juxtaposed against a contemplative, narcissistic posture emblematic of the stillness of art. Despite all appearances, these active and passive selves are not mutually exclusive in a narrow moralistic sense. Both sides – the narcissistic no less than the vitalistic – constitute essential components of the theme of *The Marionettes* and the direct expression of Faulkner's particular artistic dialectic: motion and stasis, life and art.

Marietta, as a figure of art, is closely related to the marble faun in Faulkner's first book of poems; both embody the tensions between art and life. They differ, however, in that the end of *The Marionettes* shows the idealized Marietta accepting her existence in art, while the sculptured faun continues to yearn for life. His vitalist urge by no means implies a one-sided decision on Faulkner's part in favor of life, nor does this urge proclaim the faun as a moral improvement over and beyond Marietta and her stylized beauty. On the contrary, the faun merely signifies another aspect of the same thematic continuum: as the faun attempts to move from art to life, Marietta moves from life to art.

In our discussion of the Pierrot figure, it proved useful to distinguish between his portrayal in the illustrations and his appearance in the text, and the same differentiation is valuable in Marietta's case. Appearing in the text as a "seduced innocent" and a figure of art, Marietta is a woman of the twenties, a flapper, in the illustrations. She displays her iconographical kinship to the Columbine type in the *Dramatis Personae* (Pl. 41) by turning away, and in effect rejecting, the kneeling Pierrot. Her dress no longer derives from literary tradition but from contemporary style. In fact, the daring short shirt evokes more the milieu of Reno DeVaux and Dot Wilcox, Faulkner's acquaintances in the *demi-monde* of Clarksdale and Memphis, than eighteenth-century French comedy.[15] Pierrot's dance partner on the left side of *Pierrot's Two Visions* (Pl. 39) is wearing a costume which, by virtue of the pointed fool's cap alone, returns to the tradition. On the right, however, as in *Marietta by the Pool* and *Marietta by the Fountain* (Pls. 94, 95), Marietta has bobbed hair and wears an evening gown in the style of the twenties. In *The Kiss* (Pl. 96) she is young, attractive, and a tease; with short hair and a shorter skirt, she becomes a forerunner of Cecily in *Soldiers' Pay*. Throughout the illustrations Marietta seems more realistic than her portrayal in the text, but despite this surface appearance, the drawings remain highly stylized. The type of stylization manifests itself above all in the adoption of specific poses. Standing statue-like in *Pierrot's Two Visions* and *Marietta by the Fountain* (Pls. 39, 95), Marietta is depicted in *Marietta by the Pool* (Pl. 94) in the manner of Rossetti, Beardsley, and William H. Bradley (Pls. 52, 86), gazing contemplatively and narcissistically into the mirroring water. In *Marietta's Apotheosis* (Pl. 97) the combination of realistic and stylized features creates an almost parodic effect, which Faulkner probably did not intend. As if in an apotheosis, a flapper in a bathing suit, with her vapid facial expression meant to radiate transfiguration, poses ceremoniously on a peacock throne resembling Beardsley's *Salome on Settle* (Pl. 98).

In attempting to trace Faulkner's literary development, there are a number of reasons for taking his drawings into account. The visual arts, no less than literature, pose fundamental questions concerning the problematic relationship between stylization and mimesis. The interaction between Faulkner's early texts and the accompanying illustrations provides various insights into his character representations in the following novels, for instance Margaret Powers and other characters in Faulkner's first novel, *Soldiers' Pay* as well as in *Light in August* and *Absalom, Absalom!*. The references to Beardsley in this novel function similarly to the visual allusions to him in the drawings of *The Marionettes*, enhancing the symbolic dimension of the realistic narrative.[16] Stylized as a "Beardsley woman," Mrs Powers is not only a war widow and a literary relative of Hemingway's Lady Brett Ashley, but also a symbolic figure suggestive of Proserpina. In the same vein, Marietta, a projection of Faulkner's vision of Estelle, appears at once a flapper of the Fitzgerald era and the subject of a Symbolist portrait.

In her sadness following her seduction and Pierrot's subsequent desertion, Marietta resembles Goethe's Gretchen or Housman's Prunella, who finally breaks down, "utterly worn out" and "weary of life."[17] On the whole, however, she differs considerably from Housman's Victorian schoolgirl. From the outset she displays a peculiar languorous sensuality instead of Prunella's artificial naiveté: "I cannot sleep, my narrow bed is not cool tonight. My bed is heavy and hot with something that fills me with strange desires" (*MAR*, 10). Faulkner's depiction of

94–5. Faulkner, from *The Marionettes*, 1920: *Marietta by the Pool* and
Marietta by the Fountain

96–7. Faulkner, from *The Marionettes: The Kiss* and *Marietta's
Apotheosis*

awakening sexuality and a closed interior – Marietta's bed is "narrow" and her garden "like a dark room when the candles are extinguished" (pp. 10–11) – recalls such Pre-Raphaelite paintings as Rossetti's *Ecce Ancilla Domini* and Millais's *Mariana* and suggests a claustrophobic atmosphere. Like his Victorian predecessors, Faulkner gives sensuality a somewhat obsessive quality, the social and psychological roots of which can be found in the sexual inhibitions and frustrations of his immediate surroundings, but the ritualistic pantomime in which Marietta enters the water, nears the wall of her *hortus conclusus*, and kisses Pierrot, foreshadows the vitalist love initiation of Emmy and Donald Mahon.

The Marionettes is not a unified work of art in the classic sense, because its themes and motifs do not grow organically out of one another. There is no narrative connection between the vitalistic breakthrough in the first part of the play, where Marietta escapes from her garden into life, and her embodiment in art at the end. In fact, this metamorphosis may appear a flaw if we do not relate it to a specific tradition extending from Baudelaire and Mallarmé into the twentieth century. Seen within this tradition, where sterility appears an unavoidable and fundamental characteristic of art, the second part of this Symbolist play becomes more credible. With regard to the abrupt transition from the first to the second part of *The Marionettes*, the Symbolist nature of the play should also be taken into consideration. Faulkner clearly does not aim at following the rules of Naturalist

98. Beardsley, *Salome on Settle*, from *Salome*, 1893

drama and fulfilling the expectations of a plausible, sequential plot. *The Marion-ettes* is perhaps best described as a series of Symbolist tableaux connected by a kind of ritualist movement: the pivotal events are either presented completely in pantomime or conveyed through movement, gesture, or pose before they are expressed in speech. Through the separation of action and speech, the dramatic action loses in immediacy and clarity, but acquires instead an aura of indetermi-nate suggestiveness characteristic of Symbolist imagery. This, however, endows *The Marionettes* with a certain thematic and metaphorical coherence. Following the climax of vitalism in the first part, the second part closes with a dialectic reversal: the cessation of movement in the stillness of art.

As a figure of art Marietta is not without literary precedent. Polk sees in her a particularly close resemblance to Mallarmé's Hérodiade (*MAR*, xxvii). A com-parison of "Hérodiade" with *The Marionettes* shows, however, that Faulkner was only partially aware of Mallarmé's subtle and complex use of such themes as beauty and death or such motifs as hair and mirrors. The essence of the Narcissus

99. William H. Bradley, title page of *The Inland Printer*

theme and the mirror imagery in "Hérodiade" is Mallarmé's aesthetic transform-ation of the void of being. But to the young Faulkner, for whom the motifs of mirrors, hair, and precious materials are purely decorative, the deeper Symbolist dimension of "J'attends une chose inconnue" remains hidden.[18] Still, together with Oscar Wilde's *Salome* and Amy Lowell's "Patterns," "Hérodiade" proves to be an important aid in understanding Faulkner's *Marionettes*. All three works have left their mark on this one-act play, with the Lowell and Wilde influences informing the style and Mallarmé providing a model for Marietta as an artistic figure.[19] In interpreting the heroine of *The Marionettes* it is also necessary to distinguish between two different symbolic types found in the *fin de siècle*. The *femme fatale* type has an entirely different set of thematic implications from the narcissistic, hermaphroditic, or lesbian representatives of the *femme fragile* type. There are only a few traces of the imagery commonly associated with the *femme fatale* in Faulkner's play (*MAR*, 43, 45), and in the second part the theme behind Marietta's depiction is the narcissism or longing for art familiar from "Hérodiade", and not fatal eroticism.

Since Faulkner dealt with the problem of narcissism in very different ways during the course of his long career as a writer, the various thematizations should also be taken into account.[20] Throughout his work narcissism has a psychosexual aspect that differs in application and extent. The mirror scenes in *Sanctuary* and *The Sound and the Fury* as well as the situations in *Light in August* in which Joe Christmas encounters his own image are an expression of the characters' psycho-logically and socially disturbed natures, their isolation, and in connection with the wraith motif, a foreshadowing of death. In contrast, the thematic implications of mirror imagery in *The Marionettes* do not fully emerge. The illustration *Marietta by the Pool* (Pl. 94), for example, is apparently meant to suggest Marietta's sexual frustration. Rossetti, Wilde, Beardsley (Pl. 52) and the Ameri-can *art nouveau* artist William Bradley (Pl. 99) all use the motif of reflection in water to convey a similar crisis of the self.[21] Faulkner's versions of this same scene in several of his early works, for example, in *The Marble Faun*, are indicative of his close relationship to late Romanticism and certain Pre-Raphaelite tendencies: "Pan sighs and broods upon the scene/Beside this hushèd pool where lean/His own face and the bending sky" (*MF & GB*, 17). Considered stylistically, *Marietta by the Pool* is much more closely related to these late Romantic predecessors than Faulkner's own realistic figure of Joe Christmas. More importantly, the cor-responding scene in the text calls for a different interpretation: Marietta, admiring the beauty of her reflection in the water, is surrounded by a pattern of esoteric reflections composed of peacocks, lilacs, and cypresses (pp. 42–3, 46–7, 50–1). Here mirroring expresses the "l'art pour l'art" ideal of art's self-suf-ficiency. As in Mallarmé, and in contrast to the usual psychological interpreta-tions, narcissistic sterility takes on positive connotations: Marietta transcends her suffering in life and love in the mirror of art.

It is significant that neither Mallarmé's nor Faulkner's heroines have need of human contact, but fulfill themselves instead with narcissistic beauty. Both authors emphasize this quality of self-sufficiency in their respective portrayals of Hérodiade and Marietta as part of an artistic world of mirrors and reflections: "Et tout, autour de moi, vit dans l'idolâtrie/D'un miroir qui reflète en són calme dormant/Hérodiade au clair regard de diamant . . . "[22] The green motion of Marietta's jade-colored dress finds its complement in the jade of her fingernails (MAR, 49). Her peacocks are mirrored in the pool, like herself, and thus become another component in a manneristic system of reflections, correspondences, and synesthesia:

> . . . and the purple on my feet will be thick with rubies to rival the red points of my peacocks' eyes like the eyes of wolves upon a wood's edge. My peacocks are white smeared with purple and cry to their reflections in the bottomless pool below the cypress trees. And the lilacs beside the pool stare unceasingly at the lilacs within the pool until the peacocks' cries shudder through them, then the lilacs beside the pool stir, and cry soundlessly to the lilacs within the pool. And the cypress trees struggle upward from the pool and brush the stars down into the garden.   (MAR, 50–1)

Here Faulkner makes his heroine a part of the decorative pattern of the "formal garden" by juxtaposing the purple of her ruby-bejeweled feet with the red of the peacocks' eyes. The correspondence between the peacocks' and the lilacs' reflections is then ingeniously elaborated, as Faulkner establishes a synesthetic crossover ("the peacocks' cries shudder through the lilacs" – "the lilacs cry soundlessly"). In addition, the downward movement from the peacocks and lilacs to their reflections in the pool is contrasted to the rising motion of the reflected cypresses, whose ascent leads in turn to the descent of the stars into the garden. The stars seem to represent an attempt to add a cosmic note to the decorative pattern emanating from the heroine, and the conceit of "brushing down the stars" conforms as well to the pattern of reflecting images: the fallen stars in the garden mirror the stars remaining in the sky. The motifs in this passage (peacocks, the colors white and purple, cypress tree, lake) closely resemble Herod's description of his park in Salome. This model is revealing not only for the motifs Faulkner derives from it, but more importantly, because Wilde, in line with his concept of masks and marionettes, formulates a principle of mirroring which Faulkner follows in his arrangement of these motifs: "Neither at things, nor at people should one look. Only in mirrors should one look, for mirrors do but show us masks."[23]

The striking parallels between this example of Faulkner's prose poetry and a poem by one of his contemporaries, Wallace Stevens's "Domination of Black," demonstrate that The Marionettes can hardly be dismissed as the idiosyncratic product of a fin de siècle mannerism which Faulkner soon outgrew:

> At night, by the fire,
> The colors of the bushes
> And of the fallen leaves,
> Repeating themselves,
> Turned in the room,
> Like the leaves themselves
> Turning in the wind.

Yes: but the color of the heavy hemlocks
Came striding.
And I remembered the cry of the peacocks.

The colors of their tails
Were like the leaves themselves
Turning in the wind,
In the twilight wind.
They swept over the room,
Just as they flew from the boughs of the hemlocks
Down to the ground.
I heard them cry – the peacocks.
Was it a cry against the twilight
Or against the leaves themselves
Turning in the wind,
Turning as the flames
Turned in the fire,
Turning as the tails of the peacocks
Turned in the loud fire,
Loud as the hemlocks
Full of the cry of the peacocks?
Or was it a cry against the hemlocks?

Out of the window,
I saw how the planets gathered
Like the leaves themselves
Turning in the wind.
I saw how the night came,
Came striding like the color of the heavy hemlocks.
I felt afraid.
And I remembered the cry of the peacocks.[24]

Not only is there a certain similarity in image content – the cries and colors of peacocks, stars, bushes, and unstationary trees which stride and struggle – but more importantly, there are affinities in image structuring. Both Faulkner and Stevens use techniques of synesthesia, correspondence, and repetition to achieve an ornamental effect in which the imagery has only a tenuous contact with its referential base, presenting itself as an endless chain of reversible relationships. Significantly, neither Faulkner's prose poetry nor Stevens's poem possess the transcendental dimension distinguishing Baudelaire's Symbolist sonnet "Correspondances."

In both *The Marionettes* and "Hérodiade" the reflection scenes convey a particular state of pure contemplation. Praz, in comparing the painters Gustave Moreau and Eugène Delacroix, contrasts the "sterile contemplation" of decadence with the "frenzied action" of Romanticism,[25] and, indeed, Pater, Wilde, and the early Yeats all differentiated between action and contemplation in a similar way, making contemplation their ideal: "the end of life is not action but contemplation."[26] As Wilde's comment shows, the choice of contemplation as the highest value is not a result of decadent whim, but of a social and spiritual dilemma: "While in the opinion of society, contemplation is the gravest sin of which any citizen can be guilty, in the opinion of the highest culture it is the proper occupation of man."[27] In contrast to this aesthetic contemplation or self-reflection Marietta's self-observation seems less purposeful. For Mallarmé, narcissism is a philosophical and aesthetic principle. Hérodiade, in an act of blasphemous provocation, decides against a normal human existence ("je ne veux rien d'humain et, sculptée, si tu me vois") in favor of the sterility of an ideal existence in art ("J'aime l'horreur d'être vierge et je veux/Vivre parmi l'effroi que me font cheveux").[28] Her equation of beauty with death ("Si la beauté n'était la mort") follows as a direct consequence of this choice.[29] Apparently Mallarmé's concept so impressed the young Faulkner that he accepted it in a simplified form: "Nothing save death is as beautiful as I am" (p. 49).

One of Faulkner's methods of expressing the theme of art is Marietta's contrast of her own beauty with the transient beauty of her garden. She juxtaposes her new beauty ("No, I have not changed. I am really beautiful now") against the decay of her garden ("how my garden is changed," pp. 43, 46). The joined images of "leaves" and "hands" show how Marietta's suffering in life and love in the first part of The Marionettes (summed up by the autumn motif) resolves into a state of aesthetic contemplation expressed by a system of self-reflecting images in the second part.[30] On her return to the garden, Marietta compares its fallen leaves to "wearied hands upon the pool" (p. 46). In a mannered elaboration, she indirectly links this extravagant image to her own suffering love: "The leaves are dead, like hands that have held love, they are like the hands of those who have seen happiness before them . . . " (pp. 46–7). When the limits of elaboration are reached, there is a clever reversal of the comparison, in which hands once again become leaves: "they are like the hands of those who . . . found that their hands were like dead leaves . . . " (p. 47). As if to counter this process of metamorphosis, Marietta contrasts her literal hands with metaphorical ones: "But my hands are not dead leaves, my hands are still beautiful" (p. 47). Just as in a musical composition, where one instrument picks up and varies the theme of another, the First Figure promptly reiterates the motif of "beautiful hands."

This passage, with the transformed Marietta in her never-fading garden, leaves no doubt as to Faulkner's close contact with both the French and English *fin de siècle* and the avant-garde movement growing out of *fin de siècle*. As in Amy Lowell's poem with the revealing title "Patterns" (1916), the heroine of Faulkner's *Marionettes* is woven into a decorative pattern by use of repetitions, reflections, and images composed of precious materials and colors. Once transformed into decoration, Marietta becomes part of an art landscape and takes her place as its ornamental centerpiece:

> I walk down the patterned garden-paths,
> In my stiff, brocaded gown.
> With my powdered hair and jewelled fan,
> I too am a rare
> Pattern. As I wander down
> The garden paths.

My dress is richly figured,
And the train
Makes a pink and silver stain
On the gravel . . .   (Lowell, p. 75)

I shall wear a jade gown, and walk on
the gravel paths in my garden. When I walk
the green motion of my gown will be repeated
upon the jade on my finger nails, and my hair
will be heavy with gold . . .   (Faulkner, p. 49)

The skillful handling of the image pattern in the Marietta passages is of vital importance for a deeper understanding of Faulkner the stylist, as we will see in the next chapter, where the impact of these image patterns on the poetic prose of Faulkner's novels is discussed in detail.

Faulkner's use of precious materials as a means of stylization in *The Marionettes* is not merely the result of a close study of "Hérodiade" and *Salome*, but derives from a wider artistic tradition in which Gautier, the inspiring force behind the "gold, marble, and purple" in the first of Faulkner's *New Orleans Sketches*, and the Baudelaire of "Rêve Parisien" are chief representatives. In the "terrible paysage" of Baudelaire's world of art the artist bans the organic ("le végétal irrégulier") and creates a world of reflecting metals, marble, and precious stones.[31] Along with other artists influenced by Symbolist tradition, Faulkner displays an affinity for older forms of stylized literary representation in *The Marionettes*. In this spirit he makes use of the Song of Solomon and relates particular parts of Marietta's body to precious metals and stones: "her hair is gold"; "Her breasts are like ivory crusted jewels"; "her hands are two links of silver chain . . . little pieces of smoothe silver" (pp 44, 45, 48). She is wearing a jade-colored dress, has jade-jewelry on her fingernails, gold on her forehead, and rubies, silver, and gold on her feet. Like Huysmans in his description of Moreau's Salome or Flaubert in his depiction of the Queen of Sheba, Faulkner takes the figure of Marietta as an opportunity to depict preciousness.[32] Like Wilde's Salome, Marietta has "gilded eyelids" (p. 54).[33] Her peacocks, also modeled after those in *Salome*, pick the gems from her feet and the jade jewelry from her fingers. The "sea of amethyst" and colored "lapis-lazuli" (p. 52) echo the "jardins d'améthyste" in Mallarmé's "Hérodiade".[34]

Faulkner's comparison of Marietta to an ivory tower is another example of the delight he and his predecessors took in the imagery of precious materials. The Second Figure initially compares Marietta, deep in contemplation of her own beauty, to an ivory tower in over-large dimensions; then, with an ingenious manneristic twist, to an ivory statue in miniature: "She is like an ivory tower builded by black slaves, and surrounded by flames, she is like a little statue of ivory and silver for which blood has been spilt . . . " (p. 43). As close comparison of a number of passages shows, Faulkner adapts and reworks imagery he found in Wilde's *Salome*:

He is like a thin ivory statue. He is like an image of silver. I am sure he is chaste as the moon is. He is like a moonbeam, like a shaft of silver. His flesh must be cool like ivory. Thy mouth is like a band of scarlet on a tower of ivory.

. . .

Thy body was a column of ivory set on a silver socket. It was a garden full of doves and of silver lilies. It was a tower of silver decked with shields of ivory.[35]

Salome uses imagery of sculpture and towers of ivory and silver to describe the chastity she finds so repelling in Jokanaan. In light of her narcissistic beauty, Faulkner's use of the same imagery to describe Marietta is quite appropriate and re-emphasizes that characteristic feature which she has in common with Mallarmé's Hérodiade: "rien d'humain et, sculptée." Such passages from *Salome* are composed of variations on imagery found in the Song of Solomon, a text that the young Faulkner had already attempted to utilize in his first attempts at poetry.[36] The rich and often bizarre imagery of the famous biblical poem exercised a fascination on many writers with Symbolist and aesthetic affinities. The tower image is not, however, limited to Old Testament love poetry; due to the ascription of the epithet "turris eburnea" to the Virgin Mary, it plays an important role in Christian iconography. It is this iconographic convention which Swinburne in "Dolores (Notre-Dame de Sept Douleurs)" and Wilde in "The New Helen" blasphemously reshape as a means of adding a mythical dimension to their Symbolist female portrayals: "O tower not of ivory" (Swinburne); "Tower of ivory! red rose of fire!" (Wilde).[37] In his depiction of Marietta, as in his poetry, Faulkner shares with the Symbolists a tendency to mythicize women, and these experiments with esoteric iconography will eventually help him to create the portrait of Eula.

Among the traditional means of stylized portrayal in *The Marionettes*, the hair motif is particularly striking. Because of the motif's sensual as well as ornamental possibilities, it was put to frequent use by Rossetti and Yeats, European *art nouveau*, and American artists like William Bradley. The painful weight of Marietta's hair ("my hair will be heavy with gold so that the weight of my hair will hurt my head," p. 49; "my heavy hair," p. 54) recalls Swinburne's association of hair with gold and gems ("Her hair most thick with many a carven gem . . .").[38] In turning Hérodiade's hair into something lifeless and precious, Mallarmé creates a symbol of art:

> Je veux que mes cheveux qui ne sont pas de fleurs
>
> . . .
>
> Mais de l'or, à jamais vierge des aromates,
> Dans leurs éclairs cruels et dans leurs pâleurs mates,
> Observent la froideur stérile du métal.[39]

In *The Marionettes* the hair motif is the occasion for a series of mannered and decorative alternations from one image and object to another. Marietta's golden hair initially suggests images of adventure, then danger, and finally, by way of contrast, images of the organic world:

Second Figure – Her hair is gold, it is as gold as a galleon captured by pirates, gold bleachened with blood and passion; her hair is like a panther's flank at night.

First Figure – No, her hair is not gold, her hair is like the sun upon a field of wheat, it is like sunlight combed through maple leafs . . .   (*MAR*, 44)

It is important to notice that this accumulation of decorative imagery around Marietta does not make her a more tangible figure. On the contrary, the heroine's personality is lost from view as the emphasis shifts from her hand to hair to foot by way of ornately analogous imagery. In addition, the images themselves become strangely insubstantial; they change quickly and are elaborated to such a degree that they lose their descriptive function. Identical images are often used in succession to describe different parts of the body: "Yes, her eyes are like *pools* in which one could drown oneself, her breast is a narrow white *pool*" (my italics, p. 45). Sometimes the opposite technique is employed and a single part of the body accumulates a number of totally different images in rapid succession: "her breast is a narrow white *pool*, and her breast points are the *twin reflections* of stars. Her breasts are like ivory crusted jewels" (my italics, p. 45). The effect of these various means of stylization is heightened by the fact that they all occur in close proximity. The aim is apparently a reduction of Marietta's reality as a character; overlaid with imagery she has herself become an icon.

The transformation of reality into pattern or ornament is a major characteristic of *art nouveau*. This process manifests itself not only in the text, but also in the illustrations to *The Marionettes*, and in the Beardsley *Salome* cycle which inspired them. In a painting typical of *art nouveau*, Gustav Klimt's *The Kiss* (Pl. 100), two lovers are so transformed into ornament that only their heads remain distinguishable. Although at first glance the European context of Klimt's painting seems to have little to do with the young Faulkner's own environment, we know from the study of several illustrations in the 1920–1 *Ole Miss* that *art nouveau* even had an impact on Faulkner's hometown Oxford. One drawing in particular depicting a "moon priestess" (Pl. 101) displays many representative tendencies of *art nouveau*. The figure of the priestess, or rather her clothing, dissolves into decorative bands which swing out to touch the border of the illustration. The wave motion captured by these bands neatly accords with the oval format and the roundness of the main motif, the moon. Following in the footsteps of Bradley and Beardsley, this student artist utilizes empty space as an important structural element in this illustration.

In light of the presence of such typical manifestations of *art nouveau* in *Ole Miss*, it is not surprising to find Faulkner using similar motifs and forms in works from the same period. Alongside the precious Parnassian imagery taken from Gautier and the exotic imagery from Flaubert, Faulkner uses nature imagery in which – from poems like "A Poplar" to the nymph-like Cecily in *Soldiers' Pay* – figures of young women take on the shapes of swaying trees: "she is like a slender birch tree . . . like a young poplar" (*MAR*, 43–4) or appear as dancers: "I shall swing my painted legs through intricate figures" (*MAR*, 52–3). It did not escape his attention that the dance motif plays a major role in Wilde's *Salome* and that the reconciliation of opposites – sensuality and spirituality, vitality and form, motion and stasis – embodied in the dance together with its fusion of movement, color, and light made it equally attractive to artists with diverse backgrounds. In contrast to the vertical shapes of stylized figures and poplar-shaped, "meretricious trees," the moon appears as a graphic motif in almost all the illustrations in *The Marionettes*. While Faulkner's inspiration was most probably Beardsley's *The Woman in the Moon* (Pl. 50), the use of the moon as an *art nouveau* ornament is not unusual even among illustrations in *Ole Miss* (Pl. 101). The moon as a graphic leitmotif, however, seems to be Faulkner's original idea. In *Pierrot Sleeping* (Pl. 48), the circular moon is set against the stylized linear trees and defines the center of the illustration. In *Marietta by the Fountain* (Pl. 95), it provides the background for the silhouettes of Pierrot and the peacock. In *Marietta's Apotheosis* (Pl. 97), the moon takes on the appearance of a halo over Marietta's head and thereby enhances the stylization of motifs and metaphors in the text. While the association of Pierrot with the moon (the moon is his "foster mother" and an ally in luring Marietta into "moon madness," p. 27) corresponds to a long-standing tradition evident in *Prunella*, the connection of Marietta with the moon has macabre connotations which can be traced to *Salome*. Faulkner's "the moon is like the bloated face of a scorned woman who has drowned herself" (p. 6) distinctly resembles Wilde's "The moon is like a woman rising from a tomb. She is like a dead woman."[40]

In various passages of the text, the moon motif appears in connection with the peacock motif: "and my peacocks will follow me in voluptuous precision, brushing the moonlight from the path with their heavy wings" (p. 53). Here it is interesting to note the intricacy with which Faulkner interweaves his imagery; the peacock motif reiterates the dance motif ("follow me . . . voluptuous precision" – "swing . . . intricate figures"), while "brushing the moonlight" is a variation on "brush the stars down into the garden" (p. 51). Such variations correspond to the pronounced tendency toward parallel and analogical patterning in the imagery used to depict the peacocks by the pool. Like the moon, the peacocks are brought into contact with the motif of precious materials: "they will approach and eat the jewels from my feet" (p. 54). The peacocks embody not only beauty and splendor, but also unfeeling inexorability and sterile, narcissistic greed: "their eyes will grow arid and thick and remorseless as the eyes of virgins growing old" (p. 53). There is little doubt that Faulkner's peacocks, derived from those in *Salome*, reflect the reversal of values evident in Wilde's "The Decay of Lying" and Baudelaire's "esthétique du laid." The paradox inherent in this concept of beauty – that it also comprises ugliness and destruction – characterizes the role of the peacocks, whose cries blight the ilex before the statue of Hermes at the conclusion of *The Marionettes*: *Marietta's Apotheosis* (Pl. 97). Her transformation in art complete, Marietta is flanked by two peacocks, whose curving necks and cloud-like, flattened bodies are typical of both European and American *art nouveau*.

But the motif found its way into literature as well. Besides Wallace Stevens, Amy Lowell combines the peacock with another motif appearing in *The Marionettes*, the statue of Hermes, in her poem "Sultry" (1925):

100. Gustav Klimt, *The Kiss*, 1907–8

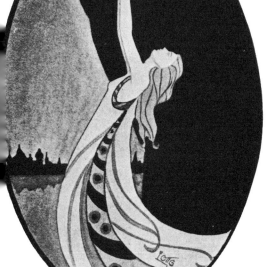

101. Drawing of a "moon priestess," *Ole Miss*, 25, 1920–1

> A peacock spreads his tail on the balustrade
> And every eye is a mood of green malice,
> A challenge and a fear.
>
> . . .
>
> And Hermes,
> Hermes the implacable,
> Points at me with a fractured arm. (pp. 469–70)

The coincidence of the combination of the peacock and Hermes motifs reveals two important features: the way avant-garde poetry assimilated *art nouveau* motifs and the close relationship of *The Marionettes* to the literature and art of its time. A sketch in the 1921–2 *Ole Miss* also shows full consciousness of the implications of the motif and combines the peacock with a *femme fatale* and a ferocious-looking cat (Pl. 102). Faulkner was obviously well aware of the popularity of the peacock motif and capitalized on it in *The Marionettes*. How he used his immediate model, the white peacocks in Wilde's *Salome*, can be seen in the following quote in which the phrases he borrowed are italicized:

Salome, you know my *white peacocks*, my beautiful white peacocks, that walk in the garden between the myrtles and the tall *cypress trees*. Their beaks are *gilded with gold*, and the grains that they eat are gilded with gold also, and their feet are stained with *purple*. When they *cry out* the rain comes, and the *moon* shows herself in the *heavens* when they spread their tails. *Two by two* they walk between the cypress trees and the black myrtles, and each has a slave to tend it. Sometimes they fly across the trees and anon they crouch in the grass, and round the lake . . . *and in the midst of them* you will be like the moon in the midst of a great white cloud . . . [41]

102. M. B. Howorth, drawing of a *femme fatale*, *Ole Miss*, 26, 1921–2

Besides Wilde's text, Beardsley's *Salome* illustrations, especially *The Peacock Skirt* (Pl. 103), had a strong influence on Faulkner's use of the peacock motif: *Marietta by the Fountain* (Pl. 95) and *Marietta's Apotheosis* (Pl. 97).

Considering Faulkner's familiarity with the graphic and literary possibilities of the peacock motif, it seems only natural that he would also use other *art nouveau* motifs such as roses and candles in *The Marionettes*. He probably derived his rose motif from Beardsley's *The Mysterious Rose Garden* (Pl. 104), the frontispiece for Dowson's *Pierrot of the Minute* (Pl. 44), or *Salome*, from the design for the title page and the border design for the *Contents* (Pl. 40). The rose garlands in *The Marionettes* resemble those in the *Salome* illustrations, and the rosebushes, often with a trellis (Pls. 39, 41, 93, 95, 96), are strongly reminiscent of the frontispiece for *Pierrot of the Minute* (Pl. 44). Roses also appear in the text as part of the scenery. There they are linked to the heroine's erotic experience, either directly ("Marietta . . . goes over to the rose bush . . . and draws a great armful of them about her face," p. 9) or metaphorically ("the pool . . . is like a naked girl lying on her back among the roses," p. 13).[42]

The candle motif in the play first appears in the midst of imagery that is decorative rather than descriptive, out of which the First and Second Figures ingeniously build an imaginary landscape in their dialogue: "the air is like a candle flaming in a dusty colonnade . . . The sky is like a blue candle flame" (p. 4). The candle found its way naturally into the world of neo-rococo feasts. As a self-consuming source of light, it was perfectly suited to decadent taste. Moreover, it implied ritual and mystery to the *fin de siècle* imagination. Besides the attraction of such connotations, the candle motifs offered a new set of graphic possibilities to the artist. While the candle flame suggests the form of the arabesque, the candle stem provides linear strength and symmetry helping to offset the rounded and curved forms of roses and peacock necks. Both linear form and arabesque are evident in the treatment of the candle motif in Beardsley's *The Eyes of Herod* (Pl. 51) and Faulkner's "Nocturne" (Pl. 32). In "Nocturne" the arabesque effect is further enhanced by the way the figures Pierrot and Columbine emerge from the candle flames. The positioning of the figures between the moon in the center and the rectangular space reserved for text on the right- and left-hand pages corresponds to the emphasis on symmetry. In combining linear elements with the arabesque, stasis with motion, the candle is closely related to the fountain, another favorite *art nouveau* motif. Fountains and trees have, of course, in both *The Marionettes* and the *art nouveau* tradition, erotic implications which will provide the dominant counterpoint to the war trauma in *Soldiers' Pay*.

SUMMARY OF PART III

As our comparative treatment has shown, the poetic play *The Marionettes* belongs within the context of anti-realist tendencies that mark the transition from Ibsen's Realistic drama to Gordon Craig's Symbolist productions, Yeats's study of Noh plays, and O'Neill's concern with masks. Like Millay's *Aria Da Capo*, Faulkner's

103. Beardsley, *The Peacock Skirt*, from
Salome, 1893

104. Beardsley, *The Mysterious Rose
Garden*, from *The Yellow Book*, 4, January
1895

105–6. Beardsley, from *Salome*, 1893: *The Toilette of Salome I* and *Enter Herodias*

"contribution to the Little Theater Movement" uses marionettes in the sense of figures of art and the type of rococo setting which authors as diverse as Wallace Stevens and F. Scott Fitzgerald find fascinating in Verlaine, Beardsley, and George Moore's *Confessions of a Young Man*. Both Faulkner's Pierrot and Marietta reflect – besides the inconsistencies of the fledgling writer – the paradoxical nature of the twenties. While the melancholy Pierrot of the illustrations corresponds to the traditional Pierrot image, the hero of the play has become a bold Lothario with a Faustian touch. Marietta, in the first part of the play, is a variant of the Gretchen figure; in the second, an embodiment of art modeled on Mallarmé's *Hérodiade* and Wilde's *Salome*.

This play of stylized characters or marionettes unfolds not as a conventional drama but in a series of Symbolist tableaux featuring a highly contrived syntax and elaborate imagery reminiscent of the Song of Solomon, of Wallace Stevens's "Domination of Black," and Amy Lowell's "Patterns." Close comparisons show the "simple country boy from the deep South" to be amazingly familiar with *fin de siècle* motifs (hair, mirror effects, precious metals, jewels, peacocks, and candles). Through his experiments with these motifs the young Faulkner apparently develops into a very conscious craftsman, yet the enduring influence of these exercises with unnatural, un-American materials on the later portrayals of his native Mississippi has yet to be determined. Since critics have been unable to discover a continuity on the level of motifs, they have generally tended to represent Faulkner's artistic development as a total rejection of the early, non-American influences. Once we have also become more knowledgeable about the New Orleans years, the assimilation of Swinburne and Joyce, of late Romantic and Modernist inspirations will emerge even more clearly.

Following the study of Faulkner's initial endeavors in art, poetry, and poetic drama (Parts I, II, III), in Part IV I shall consider related aspects of his major prose works that suggest the broader relevance of detailed research on the juvenilia. An example from *Absalom, Absalom!* serves to demonstrate how Faulkner's youthful *fin de siècle études* modified his sensibility and enabled him to give his regional references universal importance. The adaptation of a particular metaphoric pattern from the Song of Solomon and Wilde's *Salome*, in *The Marionettes*, and its later transference to the realistic context of *Soldiers' Pay*, *Flags in the Dust*, and *Light in August*, together with the impact of the early color studies on that symphony in gray in *The Sound and the Fury*, illustrate the gradual and indirect ways in which the shaping power of Faulkner's imagination evolved.

PART IV

The Creation of a New Prose

7

From *The Marionettes* to *A Fable*: The Impact of the Early Work on Faulkner's Novels

WHILE *fin de siècle* iconography and early Modernist forms are most readily found in Faulkner's earlier works, where they are often direct and unassimilated, it is in major works like *Absalom, Absalom!* that they take on the greatest significance. Faulkner draws on material from the Wilde-Beardsley era to express his own themes from the twenties and thirties. As in Thomas Mann's *The Magic Mountain* and *Doctor Faustus*, the decadent character of *fin de siècle* motifs is taken up and transformed, redeemed, as it were, by their Modernist usage. With *Absalom, Absalom!* in particular, Faulkner uses Beardsley and Wilde allusions to evoke the exotic culture of New Orleans, which is contrasted with the rural and puritanical world of Jefferson and the barbarous founding of the new feudal estate, Sutpen's Hundred. In this context the *fin de siècle* iconography is functionalized thematically and lends a specific quality to the related tensions in the text. New Orleans had undoubtedly impressed the young Faulkner no less than Henry Sutpen; it is the sophisticated world from which Charles Bon's Creole mistress and her child descend into the untamed wilderness of northeastern Mississippi. Mr Compson's comparison of this scene to settings from Wilde and Beardsley focuses attention on himself as narrator, on his own son Quentin as listener, and on the style of the description itself. Through his references to these Decadent artists, Faulkner endows the scene with a note of stylization and almost sinister exoticism:

It must have resembled a garden scene by the Irish poet, Wilde: the late afternoon, the dark cedars with the level sun in them, even the light exactly right and the graves, the three pieces of marble . . . looking as though they had been cleaned and polished and arranged by scene shifters who with the passing of twilight would return and strike them and carry them, hollow fragile and without weight, back to the warehouse until they should be needed again; the pageant, the scene, the act, entering upon the stage – the magnolia-faced woman a little plumper now, a woman created of by and for darkness whom the artist Beardsley might have dressed, in a soft flowing gown designed not to infer bereavement or widowhood but to dress some interlude of slumbrous and fatal insatiation, of passionate and inexorable hunger of the flesh, walking beneath a lace parasol and followed by a bright gigantic negress carrying a silk cushion and leading by the hand the little boy whom Beardsley might not only have dressed but drawn – a thin delicate child with a smooth ivory sexless face who, after his mother handed the negress the parasol and took the cushion and knelt beside the grave and arranged her skirts and wept, never released the negress' apron but stood blinking quietly who, having been born and lived all his life in a kind of silken prison lighted by perpetual shaded candles, breathing for air the milklike and absolutely physical lambence which his mother's days and hours emanated, had seen little enough of sunlight before, let alone out-of-doors, trees and grass and earth . . .   (*AA*, 193)

Even a brief glance at this passage shows the subtlety with which Faulkner interweaves Wilde, Beardsley, and *fin de siècle* elements associated with them, like the motifs of the theater and the formal garden. Wilde, for example, used stylized gardens in *The Importance of Being Earnest* and in the descriptions of Herod's park in *Salome*. Beardsley often went so far as to combine formal gardens and theatrical scenes in a single illustration, a technique recognized and imitated by Faulkner in his drawings for *The Marionettes*. The characters appear as if drawn by Beardsley, and Faulkner does not hesitate to link their design to him: "whom the artist Beardsley might have dressed . . . whom Beardsley might not only have dressed but drawn." Charles Bon's mistress, "created of by and for darkness," is apparently of the same stuff as the Beardsley woman and late Romantic *femmes fatales* like Pater's Mona Lisa.[1] Her description is reminiscent of Beardsley's tendency to dissolve outward appearance, especially dresses, into suggestive arabesques. She embodies a kind of peculiar sensuality alien to Jefferson, but similar to the Swinburnean qualities of "slumbrous and fatal insatiation, of passionate and inexorable hunger of the flesh" which were captured by Beardsley in the *Salome* illustrations so familiar to Faulkner (for instance, in *The Toilette of Salome I*, Pl. 105). She also brings with her the atmosphere of foreign and perverse pageantry that marks such Beardsley illustrations as *Enter Herodias* (Pl. 106).

With his "smooth ivory sexless face," the small boy has just as much of the Beardsley manner as his mother and suggests the hermaphrodite. It would be presumptuous to read into this "sexless face" the complexity of meaning given the hermaphrodite by *fin de siècle* artists.[2] But there is an important correspondence: the hermaphrodite type in late Romantic texts often appears as the symbolic projection of a sterile and esoteric existence, characteristic of *fin de siècle* idealism and its anti-idealist aesthetics. Faulkner's description of the boy in *Absalom, Absalom!* recalls the artificial existence described by Max Beerbohm in "A Defense of Cosmetics" as well as by Joris-Karl Huysmans in *A Rebours*, a novel much admired by both the French Symbolists and the English Decadents.[3] Like Des Esseintes, the hero of *À Rebours* who lives by candlelight, Charles Bon's son has "lived all his life in a kind of silken prison lighted by perpetual shaded candles." His artificial life (he "had seen little enough of sunlight before, let alone out-of-doors, trees and grass and earth") embodies the Aesthetic principle which Wilde, in "The Decay of Lying," set in opposition to the "nature cult" of the Romantic period.

But here in *Absalom, Absalom!* Faulkner no longer makes use of *fin de siècle* motifs for their own sake. Rather, it is the implications and lingering connotations of these motifs, personified in Faulkner's memory by the *fin de siècle* artists Wilde and Beardsley that inspire him to create his own stylization of events and their setting in the American South. The cloying, alliterative effects of Faulkner's *paradis artificiels* "lived all . . . life . . . kind of silken prison lighted . . . milklike . . . physical lambence . . . little . . . sunlight . . .") echo in prose the music of Swinburne's poetry. Together with allusions to Wilde and Beardsley, this Swinburnean prose creates the exotic atmosphere surrounding the arrival of the figures from New Orleans on the barren, provincial scene of northern Mississippi. Through this pattern of references to the European *fin de siècle*, Faulkner adds a universal dimension to the fate of the Sutpen-Coldfield-Bon families and to the particular social and cultural struggles of the South. These strategies of stylization in *Absalom, Absalom!* give the constellation of figures from the American twenties and thirties the generality of a mythical pattern, fitting in a novel which explores the contrasts between different degrees of consciousness and different stages of civilization.

The influence of the early experiments with modes of stylization is most important in the sphere of metaphor, the profoundest impact being on the structure of the imagery. A comparison of passages from *The Marionettes* and *Vision in Spring* with others from *Soldiers' Pay*, *Flags in the Dust*, and *Light in August* will show how Faulkner came by a particular image structure, experimented with it, and finally incorporated it into his own style. Like Oscar Wilde and many of the Symbolists, Faulkner was fascinated by the poetic quality of biblical prose and the imaginative beauty and unrealistic nature of its images. Characteristically, he assimilated the biblical style in *The Marionettes* through Wilde's *Salome*:[4]

His legs are as pillars of marble, set upon sockets of fine gold (Song of Solomon 5:13)

Thy body was a column of ivory set on a silver socket   (*Salome*, 574)

She is like an ivory tower builded by black slaves, and surrounded by flames, she is like a little statue of ivory and silver for which blood has been spilt   (*MAR*, 43)

Because of its esoteric qualities and rich symbolic associations, the garden from the Song of Solomon as a metaphor for a love relationship is a favorite with both Faulkner and his *fin de siècle* master: "I am a garden sprung beneath your footsteps . . . Your hands that have fallen like plum petals within my garden" (*MAR*, 19).[5] Here the use of garden imagery is obviously rather contrived and reveals Faulkner's conscious effort to vary and develop the traditional image. In Wilde's *Salome*, the young Syrian addresses the heroine with the same imagery: "Princess, thou who art like a garden of myrrh" (p. 560), combining two images from the Song of Solomon, myrrh and the garden: "A bundle of myrrh is my wellbeloved" (1:13) and "A garden inclosed is my sister, my spouse" (4:12).

Since biblical imagery plays a major role in the development of Faulkner's prose, the recurrence of the same type of garden imagery approximately six years later in "Hong Li," the final story in *Royal Street: New Orleans*, also deserves some attention. There, in line with the allegorical mode of the prose poem, it is used to organize an entire paragraph:

The husbandman winnows his grain ere he sow it; the wise husbandman destroys the seed of tares. So do I, in the nurtured garden of my soul, winnow carefully the grain given me; so do I root out and destroy the tares which her dead and delicate foot sowed across my heart, that my soul may be as a garden beyond the rumors of the world for the contemplation of the evening of my life. For it is written that sorrow is as the fire in which the sword is tempered, but that despair is an attribute of beasts.   (*HO*, 29)

The repetition and variation of the image and the carefully composed rhetoric of its setting point forward to Faulkner's later efforts to metaphorically structure his prose at the high points of his novels.

Wilde's variations in *Salome* had particularly alerted Faulkner to the conspicuous arrangement of imagery in the Song of Solomon. As the following passages demonstrate, Wilde and Faulkner are both intrigued by the parallel construction of the comparison with its ritual solemnity and ingenious poetic expansion:

Thy lips are like a thread of scarlet, and thy speech is comely: thy temples are like a piece of a pomegranate within thy locks.   (Song of Solomon 4:3)

Thy body is white like the snows that lie on the mountains, like the snows that lie on the mountains of Judea, and come down into the valleys.   (*Salome*, 558–9)

She is like a slender birch tree stripped by a storm, she is a birch tree shivering at dawn upon a dim wood.   (*MAR*, 43–4)

In approaching his biblical model Wilde uses two parallel similes. Faulkner twice illustrates the same subject, moving from simile to metaphor in the process. By this simplification he reinforces the basic impression of rhythmic symmetry and introduces in his language an effect similar to the parallel structure of *art nouveau* drawings.

The unorthodox tendency of the Song of Solomon to use parts of the body as points of departure for metaphoric expansion is just as pronounced in Faulkner's *Marionettes* as in Wilde's *Salome*: "Her eyes are like pools . . . her breast is a narrow white pool . . . her breast points are the twin reflections of stars . . . Her breasts are like ivory crusted jewels . . . " (*MAR*, 45). Although Wilde attempts to preserve the identity of each object referred to in his metaphors,[6] Faulkner seems to lose control in his fascination with combining images, and the concreteness of his subjects as well as his metaphors threatens to disappear in the fluctuation of comparison. Apparently the aims behind these exercises are quite different from those of Oscar Wilde. As we will see from his modified use of the biblical image structure in the novels, in *The Marionettes* Faulkner was striving less to give shape to individual images than to larger prose passages. Significant in this regard are his attempts to interweave the poetic sound patterns imitated in his Swinburne paraphrases with biblical image patterns:

First Figure – Her breasts are white roses asleep upon a pool, and her breathing stirs her breast like the wind within a bed of roses; her breasts are like two white birds after a long flight. How beautiful she is!
Second Figure – How beautiful she is?   (*MAR*, 46)

Along with the metaphoric emphasis on breasts, the repetition of words and sound effects contributes to the overdone quality of the prose. Marietta's breasts, the reference point of this description, are related not only by means of comparison, but also by alliteration to "*b*reathing," "*b*ed of roses," "*b*irds," and "*b*eautiful." The images of roses and birds are linked by the color white. The words "like," "white," and "flight," as a result of their assonance, give the image cluster a melodic cohesion. Several smaller acoustical units, which are brought together by alliteration and assonance, contribute to the musical effect: "as*l*eep upon the *pool*," "*h*er *b*reathing s*t*irs *h*er *b*reast," and "*w*ind *w*ithin."

Despite the artificiality of the metaphors and the obtrusiveness of the sound effects, there is little doubt that we are observing here the emergence of an essential feature of the poetic prose of the novels. Of equal importance for the genesis of Faulkner's unique novelistic style are the experiments with the biblical image structure in *Vision in Spring*. The continuity and relevance of stylization in Faulkner's art is confirmed by the fact that the poetic prose of the play and the poems share the metaphoric structures informing the prose of his first novels. "The World and Pierrot: A Nocturne," the third poem of the *Vision in Spring* cycle, compares the stars to pilgrims and follows the same abstract, musical principles of composition found in *The Marionettes*. At the beginning of the poem, the two variations of this comparison taking shape in Pierrot's consciousness are patterned on the style of the Song of Solomon and Wilde's *Salome*: "These stars, thinks Pierrot, freezing there/Are like so many pilgrims in a forest,/They are like blind people, they are so calm and white" (*VS*, 15). This twofold comparison is followed by a similar modulation of the twofold metaphor from the perspective of the dead: "But you are young, Pierrot; you do not know/That we are souls prisoned between a night and a night;/That we are voiceless pilgrims here alone" (p. 16). The attribution of several comparisons to a single subject in immediate succession is another striking feature that links the structures of the imagery in the prose of Faulkner's one-act play and the poetry of *Vision in Spring*. In the same poem, after the stars have been scattered like confetti, a comparison melodramatically intensified by alliteration ("confetti" – "coffin"), they take the form of an *art nouveau* image, the blossoms in the hair of dancing girls: "the stars like confetti blown on a wind/Across an open coffin,/Blown like petals in the hair of dancing girls" (p. 22).

The continued relevance of these biblical image patterns is clearly demonstrated by the parodistic prose of *Mayday* (1926). It is perfectly understandable why Faulkner would imitate Cabell's parody of the Pre-Raphaelite vision of the Middle Ages with such enthusiasm; parody enabled him to continue his experiments with stylized art forms and, at the same time, allowed him to distance himself from the idealism of chivalrous love and esoteric speech patterns. In this sense *Mayday* can be seen as a continuation of *The Marionettes*. As a medium of parody, the language in *Mayday* is ironic as in Cabell's *Jurgen* and not poetic as in *The Marionettes*. But whenever imagery is employed it is of the elaborate kind familiar from *The Marionettes* with the biblical double comparison very prominent:

So he rose up and put on his polished armour and the golden spurs like twin lightnings, and his bright hair was like a sun hidden by the cloudy silver of his plumed helm, and he took up his bright unscarred shield and his stainless long sword and young Sir Galwyn went out therefrom.

(*MAY*, 51)

What is evident here is not only that the brightness depicted in the interest of parody is too bright to be true. No less apparent is that the parodist Faulkner employs the double comparison as an axis to connect the individual parts of this image cluster and give it coherence. Since we have found Faulkner still working with highly artificial metaphors in *Mayday*, it is hardly surprising to see him continuing these experiments in the early novels. Again, the stylized content and the structure of biblical imagery are closely linked, as can be seen from numerous passages in *Soldiers' Pay* and *Flags in the Dust* where Faulkner uses the double comparison in connection with Pre-Raphaelite imagery:

Her body prone and naked *as a narrow pool, flowing* away *like two silver streams from a single source.*

(my italics; *SP*, 212)

Outward, above and beyond buildings peaceful and gray and old, within and beyond trees in an untarnished and gracious resurgence of green, *afternoon was like a* blonde woman going slowly in a windless garden; *afternoon and June were like* blonde sisters in a windless garden – close, approaching without regret the fall of day.   (my emphases; *FD*, 164)

In these excerpts the two image clusters appear less conspicuous because the young writer makes serious efforts to relate the esoteric imagery to the particular realistic situation in each novel. The example from *Flags in the Dust* constitutes a creditable attempt to express Horace Benbow's Oxford experience and his weak, pseudo-aesthetic quietism metaphorically. In any case, the biblical image pattern enhances the esoteric quality of the images, the Pre-Raphaelite garden motif, and the personifications. The overall impression gained from Faulkner's early fiction reveals that the frequency of the biblical image structure is directly related to the extent of esoteric image material and accordingly more frequent in *Soldiers' Pay* than in *Flags in the Dust*.

Does it then vanish with the disappearance of the late Romantic motifs in the later novels? Not without having strongly affected Faulkner's image-making faculties. The serious test of the relevance of the biblical image structure are those passages where the author attempts to put it to use in handling realistic material. A good example occurs in the description of Mrs Marders at Belle Mitchell's tennis party, proof that Faulkner was also one of the great satirists of the twenties:

"Horace is a poet," the other woman said . . . *Her flesh* draped loosely from her cheekbones *like rich, slightly soiled velvet; her eyes* were *like the eyes of an old turkey*, mucous and predatory and unwinking. "Poets must be excused for what they do. You should remember that, Belle."

(My italics; *FD*, 170)

The markedly parallel structure of the similes, one of the many variants of the biblical prototype that Faulkner devises, causes the evil content of the imagery to stand out all the more. The artificial quality of the double comparison, contrasting with the realism of the ironic conversation, caricatures Mrs Marders quite vividly. The following passage from *Soldiers' Pay* contains two variants of parallel images and seeks to catch the afternoon atmosphere in which Negroes and their mule-drawn wagons figure prominently:

Niggers and mules. Afternoon lay in a coma in the street, like a woman recently loved. Quiet and warm: nothing now that the lover has gone away. Leaves were *like a green liquid arrested in mid-flow*, flattened and spread; leaves were *as though cut with scissors* from green paper and *pasted flat* on the afternoon: someone dreamed them and then forgot his dream. Niggers and mules.
  Monotonous wagons drawn by long-eared beasts crawled past. Negroes humped with sleep, portentous upon each wagon and in the wagon bed itself sat other negroes upon chairs: *a pagan catafalque* under the afternoon. Rigid, *as though carved in Egypt* ten thousand years ago.   (my italics; *SP*, 148–9)

In addition to the first image cluster "years ago" devoted to the leaves and the second to the mythic qualities of the wagon, the use of the leitmotif "niggers and mules" at the beginning and end of the first paragraph and the variation on the famous introductory image from "Prufrock" ("Afternoon lay in a coma in the street") show how consciously the young novelist was striving for a poetic quality in his prose. Interestingly, the essentially Modernist Prufrock metaphor is followed by the simile "like a woman," acquiring something of the flavor of the biblical image pattern. In the first part of the leaves image cluster, the combination of synesthesia with the motion–stasis theme is dominant; in the second part, the silhouette effect, which Faulkner will later use so effectively, is cleverly introduced to illustrate the afternoon. In the second image cluster, Faulkner, anticipating later stylizing strategies, connects the bareness of his Southern realities with the rich associations of ancient ritual and Egyptian art which receive additional dignity from their parallel arrangement. There are echoes of both content and structure of this imagery in *Light in August* (1932) when Faulkner attempts to elevate the wagons to a mythic level:

she advanced in identical and anonymous and deliberate wagons *as though* through a *succession* of creakwheeled and limpeared *avatars*, *like* something *moving forever* and without progress across an urn.   (my italics; *LA*, 5)

These trivial mule-drawn wagons somewhere in the deep South become timeless icons by their metamorphosis into vehicle and mule combining avatars and by their appearance on an ancient urn,[7] Faulkner carefully avoids any direct reference to Keats's "Grecian Urn" as it would produce an inappropriate, arty flavor. What distinguishes his handling of stylizing images and image structures in *Light in August* from those in *Soldiers' Pay*, *Flags in the Dust*, and above all *The Marionettes* is its unobtrusiveness. When Lena experiences Brown's "harried and desperate eyes *like two terrified beasts . . . like two beasts* about to break" (p. 406), we no longer feel the ostentatious literariness that had originally made the young artist imitate the biblical image patterns in *Salome*, because Faulkner has broken up the double comparison and inserted a speech fragment between the two similes that realistically catches Brown's sheepishness and embarrassment: "Well, well," he said. "Well, well, well. It's Lena." The result is a paragraph in which

Naturalism and stylizing forces are so ideally balanced that the mannerist allegorization ("*eyes. She watched him* herd *them by will, like two terrified* beasts . . .*") can display its full force:

> . . . while ceaselessly here and there about the empty room went his harried and desperate eyes. She watched him herd them by will, like two terrified beasts, and drive them up to meet her own. "Well, well," he said. "Well, well, well. It's Lena." She watched him, holding his eyes up to hers like two beasts about to break . . .   (*LA*, 406)

What this and other passages from Faulkner's mature prose share with *The Marionettes* is the role of imagery as the decisive structuring force. Faulkner's subtle use of sound, his rich sensitive memory, his verbal intelligence developed in the Swinburne, Aiken, and Eliot *études* are all subordinate to the structuring element of his metaphoric power. The carefully contrived chains of images in *The Marionettes* are an indication of what he was striving for. For this reason the double beat of the pseudobiblical comparisons of *Salome* still echo in *Light in August* contributing to the mythic dignity of Joe Christmas's miserable death:

> about his hips and loins the pent black blood *seemed to rush like a released breath. It seemed to rush* out of his pale body *like the rush of sparks from a rising* rocket; upon that black blast the man *seemed to rise soaring* into their memories forever and ever.   (*LA*, 440)

In light of Faulkner's development as a narrative artist, his peculiar use of the biblical image patterns in dialogue form in *The Marionettes* deserves mention. The First and Second Figures, seemingly contradicting but really supplementing each other, often present an image cluster together:

> Second Figure – Her hair is gold, it is as gold as a galleon . . .
> First Figure – No, her hair is not gold, her hair is like the sun . . .   (*MAR*, 44)

The repetition of the metaphoric key words combined with the simple sentence structure (is, is not) produces a strange, ritualistic tone. These word repetitions in Faulkner's *Marionettes* are also modeled after syntactical variations in Wilde's *Salome*. The following comparison between the dialogue of the young Syrian and Herodias's page in *Salome* and that of the two figures in *The Marionettes* demonstrates Wilde's method of creating and varying patterns out of single words and coupled images and Faulkner's Wildean imitations:

> The Young Syrian: How beautiful is the Princess Salome tonight!
> The Page of Herodias: . . . How strange the moon seems! She is like . . .
> . . .
> The Young Syrian: How pale she [the Princess] is! Never have I seen her so
>   pale. She is like . . .   (*Salome*, 554–5)
>
> First Figure: How still it is! The air does not stir, the air is like a candle
> . . .
> Second Figure: The sky is like a blue candle flame, the sky is a curtain of
>   thin blue silk . . .   (*MAR*, 4)

The repetition of images and their syntactical tags in *Salome* and *The Marionettes* serves Symbolist purposes; it suggests that there is more to the description than meets the eye. We do not experience these two plays rationally like dramas of ideas by Racine or Schiller; instead, the word repetitions and recurring image patterns affect us poetically or magically. The fascination of repetition and its effect on the reader are concomitant with the discovery of the human sub-conscious by many authors of the late nineteenth and early twentieth centuries. This discovery of repetition as a central literary device took many forms; Joyce's use of repetition as a means of non-discursively structuring the stream of consciousness is one example, Hemingway's experiments with Gertrude Stein's repetition patterns is another.[8] Seen in this historic context, Faulkner's odd imitations of Wilde's decadent style become understandable. His exacting work with repetition patterns in *The Marionettes* marks an important preparatory stage for the repetitions in the stream of consciousness sections of *The Sound and the Fury* as well as the repetitions of dialogue in "That Evening Sun."

It becomes even more apparent that *The Marionettes* is not an unaccountable youthful venture from Faulkner's deliberate use of color patterns. Their stylistic effect is similar to that of the repetitive element in the biblical image patterns in so far as these "color symphonies" too belong to the category of metaphoric devices and are a means of structuring verbal contexts by sensuous modes rather than discursive logic. In the following example, this is confirmed by color patterns used closely together with word repetitions, synesthesia, and the biblical double comparison:

> The wind combs the pines from grey to black, while the cacophonous cries of my peacocks shiver the ilex before the statue of Hermes.
> The ilex is grey, from a white island in a sea of amethyst, then a wind stiff with the voices of subterranean things streaked the sea with lapis-lazuli and faded the ilex gray; the ilex is grey as a grey wall and the white statue of Hermes is an island in a sea of ink, and the wind combs the sky from grey to black.   (*MAR*, 51–2)

Faulkner here makes use of a common version of the color poem, characterized by a modulation of colors within a particular color scheme (here grey, black, white, violet, blue). At the heart of the passage is the statue of Hermes, embodying the theme of art. The statue collects a set of contrasting and differentiated colors around itself, highlighted by the jewels amethyst and lapis-lazuli. The pains Faulkner takes in completing this prose exercise become all too evident by the end of the passage, where he returns to the initial color transition, grey to black, and slightly varies the wind's object: "The wind combs the sky [instead of the pines] from grey to black."

There is little doubt that Faulkner is basically working in the same literary tradition recognizable in Amy Lowell's *Can Grande's Castle* ("Sea-Blue and Blood-Red"), Dos Passos's *Manhattan Transfer*, and many other contemporary prose poems and lyrical novels:

> Blue as the tip of a salvia blossom, the inverted cup of the sky arches over the sea. Up to meet it, in a flat band of glaring colour, rises the water. The sky is unspecked by clouds, but the sea is flecked with pink and white light shadows, and silver scintillations snip-snap over the tops of the waves.

Something moves along the horizon. A puff of wind blowing up the edges of the silver-blue sky? . . . Beautiful ballooning thunderheads dipping one after another below the blue band of the sea.   (Lowell)[9]

The river was smooth, sleek as a bluesteel gunbarrel. Don't matter where I go; can't go nowhere now. The shadows between the wharves and the buildings were powdery like washingblue. Masts fringed the river; smoke, purple chocolatecolor fleshpink climbed into light. Can't go nowhere now.   (Dos Passos)[10]

What separates the three prose poems by Faulkner, Lowell, and Dos Passos are differences in nuance and quality and not in literary strategy. While Dos Passos employs the color scheme to beautify and symbolically charge a real cityscape, Faulkner's scenery is wholly imaginary. In contrast to the liveliness of sensual perception in Lowell, Faulkner's prose appears remote from experience and too consciously formulated. In *Elmer* he will attempt to rid himself of this literariness, although the color patterns there also have the exaggerated quality of apprentice work:

. . . Burnt sienna. Ultramarine. That's blue, that one. Brown and blue. The colors of war, to Elmer. Not red: red was heat and there had been no heat about his part of the war. Brown, khaki, the color of his ill-fitting uniform with its accursed brass to be shined everyday; and blue, the starched grayish blue of nurses' uniforms. And dark blue enveloping cloaks with brass insignia on the shoulders . . . The day was brisk and blue. In New Orleans it was August and hot but here on this ship surging its slow bulk across the everchanging monotony of seas, riding with a heavy reluctance the long swells off the Portuguese coast – long swells wind-tortured to a clear white-crested blue . . . The wind whipped steadily around the corner of the Captain's cabin and Elmer buttoned his new thick soft blue flannel coat.   (*ELM*, 356–7)

The obvious reason for the inclusion of color patterns in *Elmer* is that the hero, like the young Faulkner, hopes to be an artist.[11] A more profound explanation seems to be that in these color experiments of the novel fragment the author was searching for more essential and lasting features of his style. Following mainstream developments in the history of the novel, Faulkner did not continue his work with color schemes in his major prose, but it left a deep impact on his verbal sensitivity. Like other prose writers in the period between William Morris's late Romantic "Golden Wings," J. A. Symonds's Impressionist "In the Key of Blue" and the early Modernism of John Gould Fletcher's "White Symphony" and Amy Lowell's "Town in Color," it helped him to open up the new poetic dimension of twentieth-century prose still absent in the Victorian novel. The early Modernist color symphony in *Elmer* is valuable in tracing Faulkner's genesis from the decorative color scheme in *The Marionettes* through the functional form in *Flags in the Dust* to its exaltation in the "Symphony in Gray" of *The Sound and the Fury*. In the episode depicting Bayard's stallion ride in *Flags in the Dust*, bronze is the leitmotif signaling the "kingly" animal's superior power in contrast to Bayard's destructive violence ("like a motionless bronze flame," p. 116; "like a bronze explosion," p. 119; "The beast burst like unfolding bronze wings," p. 119). Against the background of this leitmotif, a kind of counterpoint is developed by the "bright small spots of color . . . children in bright colors . . . white shirt and diminutive pale blue pants . . . then rushing green" of Bayard's rushing vision terminating in "a red shock, then blackness" (p. 120). The pivotal role these color experiments must have played in the development of Faulkner's style becomes apparent from the use of gray in one of the decisive Quentin-Caddy episodes in *The Sound and the Fury*. Unrelieved gray not only sets the tone impressionistically but through careful combinations with the other leitmotifs structures the scene:

I was running in the gray darkness   (p. 149)

her face tilted back in the gray light   (p. 150)

to get any air at all out of that thick gray honeysuckle   (p. 151)

the gray it was gray with dew slanting up into the gray sky   (p. 153)

the ditch was a black scar on the gray grass   (p. 153)

the gray light drizzling like rain   (p. 154)

the gray light like moss in the trees drizzling   (p. 155)

the gray grass among the crickets the honeysuckle getting stronger and stronger and the smell of water then I could see the water the color of gray honeysuckle   (p. 156)

she went on in the gray light the smell of rain   (p. 157)

outside the gray light the shadows of things like dead things in stagnant water (p. 157)

The montage of quotes lets us not only recognize the contours of one of the great scenes in Faulkner but also understand why the young man would work so hard mechanically arranging unrealistic images in *The Marionettes*. By allocating the same vehicle to several tenors or by reversing and doubling these metaphoric patterns, Faulkner was not, of course, consciously planning the verbal strategies that affect the reader so subtly and imperceptibly in *The Sound and the Fury*. Yet it seems safe to say that without the strange insistent experiments in the early work, one of the greatest novels in American literature could not have been written. The deceptively simple and natural way Faulkner handles language in the quoted passage from *The Sound and the Fury* makes it more difficult to see the stylistic continuity than the elaborate prose of *A Fable* with its more striking forms of synesthesia and other rhetorical devices:

Then for a time the sound of the hooves seemed to have dissolved into, been smothered by, the yelling, until suddenly the cavalry had ridden as though into the yelling as into a weightless mass of dead leaves, exploding them, flinging and hurling them, to reappear the next second like centaurs in furious soundless motion intact in an intact visible cloud of swirling frantic screams which continued to swirl and burst in that faint frenetic tossing even after the horses must indubitably have been gone, still swirling and tossing in scattered diminuendo when the other sound began. It came up beneath them, beginning not as sound at all but rather as light, diffused yet steady from across the plain beyond the city: the voices of men alone, choral almost, growing not in volume but in density as dawn itself increases, filling the low horizon beyond the city's black and soaring bulk with a band not of sound but light . . .   (*FAB*, 243)

While synesthesia in *The Sound and the Fury* seems to come effortlessly, appears wholly sensuous and not intellectually controlled, the elaborate patterning of the passage from *A Fable* shows considerable sophistication. What makes its synesthetic imagery difficult over and above the involved syntax is a certain daring in the metaphoric combination of the sense perception ("ridden . . . into yelling . . . leaves") as well as the Impressionistic exuberance conveyed by the choice, repetition, and grouping of the words enhanced by Swinburnean alliterations and rhythms. Also responsible is the arrangement of the imagery in dramatic contrasts ("sound of hooves – smothered, ridden into dead, sound of hooves . . . soundless motion"). Most important, however, are the ingenious expansions and carefully calculated symmetries of the synesthetic imagery. It is here that the unlikely affinity between *The Marionettes*, where the peacock cries "shudder" among the lilacs (p. 51) and they, in turn, cry soundlessly to their reflections in the pool, and *A Fable* becomes clear. The study of the role of the prose poems in the development of the poetic prose of Faulkner's novels may help us to more fully assess respective characteristics of Faulkner's image-making.

8

From "The Hill" to *The Hamlet*: The Role of the Prose Poem in Faulkner's Development

THE MANY DIFFERENT MANIFESTATIONS of lyricism in Faulkner's early works and his novels are characteristic of the transition between late Romanticism and Modernism and the disintegration of the traditional boundaries between genres. On the one hand, the novel, under the impact of James Joyce and Virginia Woolf, tends toward a specific lyricism; on the other hand, the poem renounces its strict form and opens itself to the prose poem. Both the lyricism of the new novel and the prose of the poem make it possible to transcend – in epiphanies – the established conceptions of reality. In this desire for Symbolist expression, a desire which Faulkner shares with many contemporaries, lies the deeper motivation for his fascination with the more strongly stylizing language of the lyric. What connects the stylization in prose poems like "The Hill" or "Nympholepsy" with poems like "L'Après-midi d'un faune" or the nymph episode in "The Lilacs" is that it serves to transmit experiences with cannot be expressed in realistic, narrative prose.

Faulkner may have come into contact with the different techniques used in the prose poem, a fashionable genre at the turn of the century, in the works of Oscar Wilde and Ernest Dowson or in those of his compatriots, John Gould Fletcher and Amy Lowell. The musical concept of counterpoint, utilized by Fletcher in his discussion of polyphonic prose, became one of the structural principles of this new medium:

The new form was neither, strictly speaking, prose nor verse . . . its basis was the elaborately rhymed prose of Sir Thomas Browne, de Quincey, of Melville with this addition: that all the wealth of English rhyme, assonance, verbal onomatopoeia, was deliberately woven into it exactly as the masters of polyphony, such as Bach, had woven over their simple chorales the most elaborate contrapuntal forms.[1]

Fletcher envisioned polyphonic prose as a prose free of discursive and logical order, structured along the lines of a fugue or an abstract painting. The analogy drawn between literature and music by so many authors of the time reflects the same poetic ideal informing the color poem, and we could say that in *The Marionettes* Faulkner strives for form not only in the sense of the color poem discussed earlier but also in the sense of Fletcher's, Lowell's or Aiken's polyphonic prose. The fugal composition of Faulkner's metaphors – their symmetries, reflections, and reversals – and his melodic repetition patterns are attempts to transpose extraliterary musical or graphic structures into literary devices that are consistent with his praise of "Mr Aiken's abstract three dimensional verse patterned on polyphonic music form" (*EPP*, 76). The analogies to painting and music, sometimes combined as in the term "color symphony," play a key role in the poetics of the prose poem.[2]

Prose poems by the French Symbolists were of fundamental importance for *fin de siècle* or early Modernist attempts in English; George Moore left no doubt about this in his *Confessions of a Young Man*.[3] Faulkner may have been familiar with Mallarmé's prose poems from this book, which had the force of a revelation for young English and American writers. Moore specifically mentions the prose poem in connection with the formation of a new prose and treats Gautier's novel *Mademoiselle de Maupin*, which Faulkner returns to in "Wealthy Jew" and *Mosquitoes*, as a point of reference alongside Pater's novel *Marius the Epicurean*:

> . . . this book [Marius] was the first in English prose I had come across that procured for me any genuine pleasure in language itself, in the combination of words for silver or gold chime, and unconventional cadence, and for all those lurking half-meanings, and that evanescent suggestion, like the odour of dead roses, that words retain to the last of other times and elder usage.[4]

Moore's discussion of these books provides a context for the young Faulkner's own rarefied style as well as for his critical awareness of major stylistic trends of the time: of "Hergesheimer [as] a decayed Pater" and of that "infatuation with words" evoked in *Mosquitoes*.[5] Later Faulkner refers to his own experience of language in terms reminiscent of Moore's literary sensitivity:

> I wrote this book [*The Sound and the Fury*] and learned to read. I had learned a little about writing from *Soldiers' Pay* – how to approach language, words: not with seriousness so much, as an essayist does, but with a kind of alert respect, as you approach dynamite; even with joy, as you approach women: perhaps with the same secretly unscrupulous intentions. But when I finished *The Sound and the Fury* I discovered that there is actually something to which the shabby term Art not only can, but must, be applied.[6]

Stephen Dedalus's experience of language in Joyce's *A Portrait of the Artist as a Young Man* (1916) suggests the wider historical framework for Faulkner's unique verbal imagination and the genesis of his poetic prose:

> His own consciousness of language was ebbing from his brain and trickling into the very words themselves which set to band and disband themselves in wayward rhythms:
>
> > The ivy whines upon the wall
> > And whines and twines upon the wall,
> > The ivy whines upon the wall
> > The yellow ivy on the wall
> > Ivy, ivy up the wall.
>
> Did anyone ever hear such drivel? Lord Almighty! Who ever heard of ivy whining on a wall? Yellow ivy; that was all right. Yellow ivory also. And what about ivory ivy?
>
> The word now shone in his brain, clearer and brighter than any ivory sawn from the mottled tusks of elephants.[7]

What links the two greatest English-speaking novelists of the first half of the twentieth century with Moore's "gospel of Decadence" is the new sense of prose as an artistic medium, a feature unknown to the Victorian novelists and central to Hugh Kenner's assessment of the literary goals of the twenties: "A prose . . . as absolute as paint, that was a dream of the twenties. It was a decade of writing, a craft with a mystique."[8]

For the development of this new sense of prose, the prose poem constitutes a center of artistic energy around which the creative impulses of these two writers gravitate. It is interesting to note that here as well Faulkner continues along lines visible in Moore's *Confessions of a Young Man*:

The poem in prose is the form, above all others, they prefer; handled by an alchemist of genius, it should contain in a state of meat the entire strength of the novel, the long analysis and the superfluous description of which it suppresses . . . the adjective placed in such an ingenious and definite way, that it could not be legally dispossessed of its place, would open up such perspectives, that the reader would dream for whole weeks together on its meaning at once precise and multiple, affirm the present, reconstruct the past, divine the future of the souls of the unique epithet.[9]

Writing characteristically from Paris where an up-and-coming American author had to go, the young man from Mencken's "Sahara of the Bozart" shows a full awareness of the new ideals and their implications for the writer as craftsman and *poeta faber*:

I have just written such a beautiful thing that I am about to bust – 2000 words about the Luxembourg gardens and death. It has a thin thread of plot, about a young woman, and it is poetry though written in prose form. I have worked on it for two whole days and every word is perfect. I havent slept hardly for two nights, thinking about it, comparing words, accepting and rejecting them, then changing again. But now it is perfect – a jewel. (*SL*, 17)

The new ideals appeal to Faulkner because they allow him to explore fully his rich lyrical talent in strict but congenial form – without the constraints of traditional poetry and without renouncing his narrative gift.

Probably the most important outcome of Faulkner's Parisian "poetry in prose form" is the magnificent conclusion to *Sanctuary*. Its striking synesthesia ("she seemed to follow with her eyes the waves of music,"*SANC*, 291) and the Symbolist tableau recall the young writer's fondness for the Luxembourg Gardens and the allegorical paintings of Puvis de Chavannes: "dead tranquil queens in stained marble mused, and . . . the sky . . . in the embrace of the season of rain and death" (*SANC*, 291). But there are also more clearly recognizable contributions to the genre of the prose poem among the *New Orleans Sketches* (1925) and in pieces like "The Hill" (1922) and "Nympholepsy" (1925). Among them those texts that seem to lead most directly to Faulkner's great Realist fiction have received the most critical attention. But before turning to "The Hill" we should not overlook that in "Hong Li," the last selection in *Royal Street: New Orleans* (1926), Faulkner returns once more to the style of *The Marionettes*. This is in line with the handlettered, handbound, and illuminated quality of this version of the *New Orleans Sketches* which Faulkner gave to

Estelle.[10] In the first paragraph, the disappointment and sadness over Estelle are transformed into ornate, Symbolist prose, the unhappy lover telling himself that "The Honey's sweetness is but comparative." In the next paragraph, he reflects on the moral advantage of sorrows over happiness, in a style pointing to "The Doer of Good" and other prose poems by Oscar Wilde. And in the third paragraph, he decides to remove the memory of the beloved as "the husbandman destroys the seeds of tares" (*HO*, 29). Fortunately, he has retained enough of a sense of self-irony to add the poetic afterthought: "But Ehee, Ehee, her little, little feet," placing the effectiveness of his resolution in doubt. "Hong Li," stylistically so close to the one-act play, has a circular structure with the biblical phrase "it is written" as an opening and concluding formula. The text also displays the same symmetrical sentence patterns, stylized image structures, and esoteric metaphors familiar from *The Marionettes*: "Misfortune is . . . happiness is as the orchid that . . .," ". . . that my soul be as a garden" (*HO*, 29). Since this somewhat contrived style appears in countless forms and modifications in Faulkner's later prose, it is time that we finally differentiate between realistic and stylized modes of expression in interplay and accept the artificial prose of *The Marionettes* along with the so-called natural prose of "The Hill."[11] The more so, since, as the analyses of "The Hill" by Gresset, Momberger, and Kreiswirth have shown, its prose is anything but realistic or natural.[12]

Just as the style of "The Hill" resembles the new prose of Gertrude Stein, Ernest Hemingway, and Sherwood Anderson in its artificial simplicity and seems to prefigure many descriptive passages in *Light in August*, the complicated metaphorical structures in *The Marionettes* prepare the way for the mannerism of *Absalom, Absalom!*, the synesthetic image structures in *A Fable*, and the Ike Snopes episode in *The Hamlet*. Particularly notable in "The Hill" is the persona Faulkner creates to embody his new Cubist manner of seeing and expression. The protagonist is clearly different from Pierrot in *The Marionettes*, who was born in "Paris town" and remained a descendant of the late European Romantic era. A Sherwood Anderson hero conceived before Faulkner's acquaintance with the writer, his simplicity and earthiness prefigure the protagonist of "Out of Nazareth." Behind this new hero stands the inherited Naturalism of Hamlin Garland (*Main-Travelled Roads*, 1891; *Prairie Folks*, 1893) and the overt simplicity and primitivism of the generation of Sherwood Anderson and Willa Cather. Phil Stone's preface to *The Marble Faun* and Faulkner's self-stylization "a simple heart . . . a man steeped in the soil of his native land" (*MF & GB*, 6–7) – in replacement of his earlier dandy mask – are located in this tradition. As the focus of a simplifying type of vision, the new hero is an important factor in the development of Faulkner's specific poetic prose.

Faulkner conveys his vision by giving it an "un-literary" painterly quality in the Cubist mode of Gertrude Stein and Hemingway.[13] In contrast to the merely decorative color arrangements in *The Marionettes* and some of the color poems, in "The Hill" he places the individual color segments of the trees and buildings against a specially prepared background, showing the structural awareness admired by the Cubists in Cézanne:

The opposite valley rim came first into sight, azure and aloof, in the level afternoon sun. Against it, like figures rising in a dream, a white church spire rose, then housetops, red and faded green and olive half hidden in budded oaks and elms. Three poplars twinkled their leaves against a gray sunned wall over which leaned peach and apple trees in an extravagance of fragile pink and white . . .   (*EPP*, 90)

The city is viewed by the protagonist from his elevated position, not from the perspective of an omniscient narrator in a Naturalistic novel ("no piles of winter ashes and rusting tin cans," p. 91). In the process, three-dimensional space is reduced to a flat surface: "from the hilltop the valley was a motionless mosaic of tree and house" (p. 91). The climax reveals the thematic purpose behind the careful arrangement of landscape and shadow, a technique expected more from a Symbolist poem than a regionalist story: "His monstrous shadow lay like a portent upon the church, and for a moment he had almost grasped something alien to him, but it eluded him" (p. 91). An ecstatic experience, or more precisely, the frustrating sense of a vision which vanishes at the last moment, "an epiphany manquée" as Gresset so aptly puts it, is the theme of "The Hill."[14]

"The Hill" has a hero, a setting, and a plot, but, as a comparison with the related poem "Twilight" (*A Green Bough*, X) confirms, it resembles a prose poem more closely than a short story. Its division into five sections clearly serves a thematic function: section one – ascent, suggestion of a visionary mood with the strange description of the shadow; section two – view of a Cubist landscape; section three – backward glance from the hilltop, relation of the visionary to the world; section four – approaching vision, social and philosophical situation of the hero; and section five – reverberation of the ecstatic moment with the descent from the mountain, the traditional setting of visions. But the beginning and the ending of the text and its individual sections show the strong emphasis on form characteristic of the lyric genre. As Martin Kreiswirth writes, they have "something of the linguistic density of poetry."[15] Only a superficial reader could miss the fact that the pronounced simplicity of the prose in "The Hill" is just as artistically ordered as the decorative symmetries in *The Marionettes*.

Faulkner's "Nympholepsy" may not be as cryptic as some of Mallarmé's prose poems, but ever since its publication in 1973 by James B. Meriwether the text has generated considerable controversy among scholars.[16] For those who previously assumed that Faulkner, with "The Hill," finally became the creator of an indigenous Yoknapatawpha, "Nympholepsy" is especially puzzling. This text, generally considered an expanded and more important version of the material in "The Hill," curiously includes prominent features of late Romantic stylization in addition to its realistic elements. Nymphs and their lovers have attracted poets and painters since Daphne escaped Apollo by her metamorphosis into a laurel tree. For obvious reasons, the theme of "nympholepsy" exercised a particular fascination on the Romantic imagination. Cleanth Brooks, discussing the possible

sources of Faulkner's "Nympholepsy," observes that the "experience of nympholepsy – catching a glimpse of the nymph or goddess – is traditional in romantic
poetry."[17] But a comparison of Faulkner's prose poems with texts central to this
tradition such as Swinburne's "A Nympholept" or Browning's "Nympholeptos"
reveals more differences than affinities. With this in mind, it seems less desirable
to search for the ultimate source of a theme like "nympholepsy" and more
productive to examine the causes that led to its frequent use around 1900.

In his introduction to the *Helen* poems, Carvel Collins makes a valuable point
concerning this question by connecting Faulkner's prose poem to George
Moore's comment on "nympholepsy."[18] Moore's comment may indeed constitute a direct source for Faulkner's piece. But it is more significant that Moore,
one of the "Janus" figures between decadence and Modernism, identifies the
spirit which inspired so many authors of the era including Swinburne and Pound,
Browning and H.D., Donald Davidson and William Faulkner, to reactivate the
traditional motif of the nymph–faun–"nympholepsy":[19]

You ask me why I like the landscape? Because it carries me back into the past times when
men believed in nymphs and satyrs. I have always thought it must be a wonderful thing to
believe in the dryad. Do you know that men wandering in the woods sometimes used to
catch sight of a white breast between the leaves, and henceforth they could love no mortal
woman. The beautiful name of their malady was nympholepsy. A disease that every one
would like to catch.[20]

Moore's formulation discloses both the longing for a golden age of nymphs and
satyrs and the awareness that such beliefs are no longer tenable in the modern
period. Typical in the use of the "nymph–satyr" motif in Faulkner's novel
Soldiers' Pay and his short story "Black Music," as in Donald Davidson's poems
"Dryad" and "Twilight Excursion," is the ironic contrast between mythological
figure and "modern setting":

> She saw the faun's ears in his hair
> Beneath a Leghorn – latest cut –
> And goat-legs underneath his suit
> Crooked with a strangely familiar strut.[21]

Faulkner, too, was obviously fascinated by the nymph motif in his early poems,
but, as we have seen, in "L'Après-midi d'un faune" and "Naiads' Song" he
remains indebted to the late Romantic or Pre-Raphaelite manner of presentation.
In "Nympholepsy" and "The Lilacs," however, he combines stylized and
realistic elements into a Modernistic montage. The nymphs in these examples are
poetic sisters of the "mermaids" in T. S. Eliot's "Prufrock."

The contemporary preference for nymphs, oreads, dryads, fauns, and satyrs
was doubtlessly a manifestation of the era's specific vitalistic desires: "Hurl your
green over us/Cover us with your pools of fir" (H.D., "Oread").[22] But the
heightened desire for closeness to nature ("The tree has entered my hands,"
Pound, "A Girl") was destined to remain unsatisfied in the given stage of

civilization. Pound's nymph-poem "A Girl" ends with the realization: "And all this is folly to the world."[23] The era which can with equal right be categorized as the "Jazz Age" or the "lost generation" found precisely this dual aspect of the nymph motif – its sense of a vitalistic but unrequited longing – especially fascinating. Faulkner also invokes this double aspect in quite different treatments of the nymph-faun motif: in "Nympholepsy," the prose poem closely associated with Sherwood Anderson, and in the sonnet "The Faun" with Pre-Raphaelite mannerisms ("leafed close and passionate"; "musical leaves"; "cup unlipped"; "sweet-sunned"). The double aspect of frustrated vitality also governs the structure of the nymph–faun motif in *Soldiers' Pay*. The faun Donald Mahon is wounded, like the "fisher king" in the *Waste Land* mythology, while Emmy, his former lover and a predecessor of Faulkner's "earthwomen," is left behind. Cecily, a modish, banal flapper of the twenties who acquires nymph-like features through the tree metaphor, tempts and then dupes the lecherous satyr Januarius Jones. Similarly, in the "war" poem, "The Lilacs," the protagonist wonders whether the union with the nymph really took place, and the youthful hero of "Nympholepsy" tries to convince himself afterward that the brief meeting with the nymph brought him fulfillment: "But I touched her!" (*US*, 336).

Faulkner conveys this ambiguity in a convincing manner: the "nympholept" senses only the nymph's limbs in the churning water ("a startled thigh," "a swift leg," "the point of a breast"); everything is threatening ("thigh slid like a snake," "among dark bubbles," p. 335) and erotically fascinating. It is not the nymph the hero sees, but "death like a woman shining and drowned and waiting" (p. 335). Her appearance simultaneously implies attraction ("shining," "waiting") and menace ("drowned," "body tortured"). The ambiguity of the nymph's appearance and the unrequitable nature of the longing for her cannot be satisfactorily explained in Freudian terms alone; the numinous dimension of the nymph experience is just as important. The unorthodox, religious character of the nymph experience also plays an important role in the structure of the prose poem. Through this mysterious, sensual–spiritual condition, the bounds of reality are overstepped. In a visionary moment, an unusual transcendence occurs: "For an arrested fragment of time he felt, through vision without intellect, the waiting dark water . . . and the branches like an invocation to a dark and unseen god" (p. 334). Here Faulkner articulates one of the central themes of Symbolism, whether we think of Baudelaire, Verlaine, and Mallarmé, or of Rossetti, Swinburne, and Yeats.

Like "The Hill," "Nympholepsy" presents itself at first glance as a realistic sketch of contemporary Mississippi: "his overalls gray with dust" (p. 331); "horses . . . barn . . . ammonia . . . smell of sweaty harness," "blue shirt wet with sweat" (p. 333). But alongside the realistic details, a complex of decorative metaphors is built into the text which has a stylizing effect: a country girl appears "moist with heat, in blue gingham" (p. 331) or "in this calico against the heat" (p. 336), and yet her realistic appearance is modified in both cases by the extravagant simile "perhaps a girl like defunctive music."[24] Similarly, the unshaven beard of the Sherwood Anderson hero is gilded, maple and beech trees appear as abstract color fields, and the pines are converted into Symbolist metal sculptures:

> . . . the west alchemized the leaden dust upon him, gilding the tips of his unshaven beard. Hardwood, – maple and beech trunks, – were twin strips of red gold and lavender upright in the earth . . . Pines were half iron and half bronze, sculptured into a symbol of eternal quiet . . .   (p. 332)

Another distorted impression results when elements from the Catholic ritual are incorporated into the landscape sketches of Mississippi, a combination which has an odd effect in the Baptist South: "from the blacksmith's . . . ring of hammer and anvil like a call to *vespers*" (p. 332); "this green *cathedral* of trees" (p. 332); "repeating slow *orisons* in a green nave"; "a priest . . . reading his soul" (p. 333). The same effect ensues from such rarefied similes as "the rising harvest moon, like a ship on a silver sea" (p. 335), especially when they are repeated at brief intervals in slightly varied form: "the moon sailed up like a fat laden ship before an azure trade wind" (p. 336).

Unquestionably, one of the decisive impulses governing the imagery in "Nympholepsy" is the transformation of nature or everyday surroundings into works of art. The "court-house columns" at the center of town in "The Hill" are stripped of triviality and simplified in a Cubist manner, the modest town in the deep South becoming "a dream dreamed by Thucydides" (p. 331). In the conclusion even a country silo receives a certain dignity through its placement in the Classical world: "and a silo became a dream dreamed in Greece" (p. 336–7). The idealization of profane buildings finds an interesting parallel in William Carlos Williams's poem "Classic Scene" and in paintings by his friends Charles Demuth (*My Egypt*, 1927) and Charles Sheeler (*Classic Landscape*, 1931). "Nympholepsy" is of special interest for assessing the impact of the *Marionettes* style on the mature work, because Faulkner also uses variants of the pseudo-biblical image patterns assimilated from *Salome* to structure and stylize material from the world of everyday life and labor:

> His heavy shapeless shoes *were gray* in the dusty road, his overalls *were gray* with dust: dust was like a benediction *upon* him and *upon* the day of labor behind him.
> (my emphases; p. 331)

In the following sentence the statement "he did not recall" is repeated three times in the varied form "he had forgotten":

> He *did not recall* the falling of slain wheat and his muscles *had forgotten* the heave and thrust of fork and grain, his hands *had forgotten* the feel of a wooden handle worn smooth and sweet as silk to the touch; he *had forgotten* a yawning loft and spinning chaff in the sunlight like an immortal dance.   (my italics; p. 331)

The image clusters in another passage closely resemble the style of *The Marionettes* in the curious quality of the similes following the repetitions:

> The *sun was* a red descending furnace mouth . . .
> The *sun was* in the trees . . . , the *sun was* like a little little silver flame . . .

maple and beech trunks, *were* twin strips of red gold and lavender . . . *they were like* the hands of misers reluctantly dripping golden coins of sunset.   (my italics; p. 332)

The use of this image pattern in countless variations heightens the stylizing effect. Word repetitions which keep these image structures closely linked to the larger context also contribute to the text's lyricism. In the last quotation, for example, a sentence is added which echoes the image of "dripping gold." Sometimes the patterns of the biblical double comparison constitute intricate sound systems as well:

though the *t*ips of *t*rees were still as gold-dipped *b*rushes and the *t*runks of *t*rees upon the summi*t* were like *b*arred grate *b*eyond which the evening *b*urned slowly away.
(my italics; p. 333)

By and large the acoustic and metaphoric patterning in "Nympholepsy" is not more than apprentice work, although the combination of the verbal strategies first developed in *The Marionettes* with the Sherwood Anderson material signifies a giant step forward. Occasionally the young artist even comes close to the fusion of the stylized and the realistic he will achieve in *The Hamlet*:

There she was, in a wheat field under the rising harvest moon, like a ship on a silver sea.
   He plunged after her. His furrow broke silver in the wheat beneath the impervious moon, rippling away from him, dying again into the dull and unravished gold of standing grain.   (p. 335)

Two prose poems among the *New Orleans Sketches* (1925), "Wealthy Jew" and "The Priest," represent interim stages in the genesis of Faulkner's great narrative prose. What obviously fascinates Faulkner in the protagonist of "Wealthy Jew" is a certain breadth of historical and geographical perspectives:

The waves of Destiny, foaming out of the East where was cradled the infancy of the race of man . . . Upon the tides of history has my race ever put forth . . . my ancient Phoenician ancestors breasted the uncharted fabulous seas with trading barques . . . No soil is foreign to my people . . .   (*NOS*, 3–4)

This widening of horizons probably corresponds to the young Faulkner's general frame of mind after leaving the provincial confines of his hometown for the urbane and international culture of New Orleans in 1925. The cosmopolitan "Judaism" in "Wealthy Jew" and the "Catholicism" in "The Priest" lead far beyond the small Baptist and Presbyterian town in Mississippi. In order to transform Oxford into Yoknapatawpha, Faulkner clearly needed to take a "detour through the world." In "Wealthy Jew" the wider perspectives become visible in the inclusion of the emperor figures ("Ahenobarbus . . . Alexanders and Caesars and Napoleons") whose pomp and absolute power ("rise in blood and gold") had intoxicated the *fin de siècle* and in the mention of the First World War (Passchendaele). Daringly, Passchendaele and Ahenobarbus's gardens are forced together on the same level in the spirit of Modernistic montage.

   Blotner has correctly established the biographical situation behind "Wealthy Jew," and through friends like Julius Weis Friend and his sister, Faulkner undoubtedly became aware of the long historical Jewish tradition.[25] The narrative voice of his dramatic monologue does not express a personal destiny; instead, the "wealthy Jew" is a representative of the Jewish culture, or, to be more precise, a projection of the late Romantic image of this culture. As in the Salome paintings by Moreau, the *Salome* of Wilde and Beardsley, or the opera of Richard Strauss, Faulkner's depiction of Judaism in this prose poem is characterized by a longing for exoticism. Above all, the protagonist is a "wealthy Jew" in the sense that he represents an age-old, world-wide culture rich in tradition in contrast to the "roaring twenties." Faulkner conveys this richness with his favorite line from Gautier's *Mademoiselle de Maupin*: "I love three things: gold; marble and purple; splendor, solidity, color," and by repeating it at the beginning and end of the sketch he establishes, as in "The Hill" and "Nympholepsy," that firmness of outline essential to the prose poem.

What links "The Priest," the second of the *New Orleans Sketches*, with the first, "Wealthy Jew," is the technique of montage or transfer. As in "Wealthy Jew," where the protagonist is allotted the Gautier quotation, the protagonist in "The Priest" employs a line from Swinburne's "In the Orchard." The transfer in "The Priest" is considerably more sensational, since the Swinburne quotation and Faulkner's variation ("Ah, God, ah God, that night should come so soon"; "hold my hair fast, and kiss me through it – so: Ah, God, ah God, that day should be so soon!") refer to the woman's words in an *aubade*, a secular love poem in the medieval style of the Pre-Raphaelites. The priest emerges with even vaguer contours than the "wealthy Jew" and can with right be deemed a mouthpiece for the Swinburne quotation. Like the First and Second Figures in *The Marionettes*, he is not an individual so much as a means of organizing the decorative prose.[26] Because of his association with the Virgin Mary tradition ("Ave, Maria") and the passionate eroticism of Swinburne's "Provençal burden," the "priest" stands at the center of the blasphemous tension in Faulkner's text.

Many details in this prose poem and in the novel *Mosquitoes* stem from the very real world of Catholicism which Faulkner experienced with such captivation in New Orleans. But the way the religious imagery is used in "The Priest" suggests that literary tradition, not personal experiences, had the greatest impact. The most striking elements are the delicate and sentimental qualities the prose poem shares with the Pre-Raphaelite sonnet XXXIV in *A Green Bough*. In both texts similar colors (gold, silver) and metaphors (ship of night, boat) introduce the image of the madonna:

> The ship of night, with *twilightcolored* sails,
> Dreamed down the *golden* river of the west,
> And Jesus' mother mused the sighing gales
> While Jesus' mouth shot drinking on her breast. (my italics, *MF & GB*, 57)

> The moon is a *silver* sickle . . . the moon is a little
> *silver* boat . . . on shoreless seas . . . How like birds with
> *golden* wings the measured bell notes fly outward and
> upward . . . Ave Maria! a little *silver* virgin, hurt and
> sad and pitiful, remembering Jesus' mouth upon her breast.
>
> (my italics, *NOS*, 5)

Among the numerous Pre-Raphaelite paintings and lyrics infused with this artificial simplicity, Rossetti's poem "The Blessed Damozel" reprinted in *The Oxford Book of English Verse* is probably the best-known. But Faulkner's complete command of the Pre-Raphaelite tone ("sighing," "soft," "little," "hurt," "sad"), diction (compound forms: "twilightcolored," "doveslippered"), and imagery ("Evening like a nun shod with silence," *NOS*, 4) suggests he knew much more than the Rossetti poem alone. The "St Dorothy" legend in Swinburne's *Poems and Ballads* exemplifies this type of poetry, where the main concern is not really religious sentiment, but the adoption of stylized postures. Other works reflecting these pseudoreligious, Aestheticist tendencies include Rossetti's poems "Ave" and "Mary's Girlhood," Wilde's volume of poetry *Rosa Mystica* with the poems "Ave Maria Gratia Plena" and "San Miniato," and Beardsley's *Christmas Card* (Madonna and Child).[27]

From the fusion of religious attitudes with erotic intentions it soon becomes clear that Faulkner is no more interested in presenting an orthodox religious subject than Rossetti in "The Blessed Damozel." As in Rossetti's poem, the erotic implications of the imagery in "The Priest" stand in vivid contrast to the devotional tone. That pattern so familiar from *The Marionettes* – the reiteration of the subject of an image cluster with two different similes ("Evening like a nun," "evening like a girl") – enables Faulkner to express the inherent moral tensions from the very beginning: "Evening like a nun shod with silence, evening like a girl slipping along the wall to meet her lover . . . " (*NOS*, 4). The first comparison ("like a nun") connects with the Virgin Mary imagery and with the concept of mortification, while the second ("like a girl") points ahead to the "flesh" and Swinburnean eroticism. The second bar of the first movement of this "polyphonic prose" supplements the description of the evening not only by referring to the New Orleans atmosphere ("whispering . . . palms"), but also, as in "Sapphics" and *Soldiers' Pay*, by introducing Lesbos, a literary setting suggestive of frustrated sexual relationships. The mythical "hyacinth bells" prefigure the Angelus bell in the main body of the text. This preluding sound is reinforced by the three syntactically sustaining participles "stirring," "ringing," and "whispering." The bell motif receives additional emphasis from a group of 'b' and 'l' alliterations, which are synesthetically connected ("spikes of bloom bells") to the preceding group of 'ai' assonances and to the 'l' and 'k' alliterations:

The twilight is like the breath of contented kine, stirring among the lilacs and shaking spikes of bloom, ringing the soundless bells of hyacinth dreaming briefly of Lesbos. (*NOS*, 4)

The central passage of the sketch opens with the Swinburne quote "Ah, God, ah, God," which subsequently becomes, in leitmotif-like variations, the dominant structuring force. Interestingly, the young montage artist combines these Swinburne variations with an image apparently borrowed from the "Gloomy Orion" in Eliot's "Sweeney Among the Nightingales," but varied from "Orion and the Dog" to "Orion and the Wain" and appropriately modified to suit his idealized context: "Orion through the starry meadows strays . . ." (p. 5). The final lines "Ave, Maria; deam gratiam . . . tower of ivory, rose of Lebanon . . ." – despite the faulty church Latin – are an astonishing feat of religious dandyism for someone whose roots were firmly planted in Protestant soil. But the guiding inspiration behind Faulkner's literary Catholicism is not the Church of Rome but the gospel according to Swinburne and Wilde, who had often inverted the Catholic iconography ("O tower not of ivory . . . O mystical rose of the mire"; "Tower of ivory! red rose of fire!") for their unorthodox Symbolist purposes.[28]

In the *New Orleans Sketches*, "Wealthy Jew" and "The Priest" are followed by the sketch entitled "Frankie and Johnny." The vaguely Symbolist overture of the volume gives way to Realistic experiments ("I knowed it was all up with me," p. 6) that have received considerably more attention from critics.[29] From our point of view, however, the most interesting texts of the mid-twenties are not those dominated by an almost Andersonian Realism like "Out of Nazareth," but those like "Nympholepsy" where the idealized forms from *The Marionettes* are used to structure "Realistic" material. In this respect, the comparison of the image structures in *The Marionettes* and several of the novels was relevant because it showed us how the tensions between stylization and mimesis develop into the chief organizing force of Faulkner's mature prose. The love story of Ike Snopes where Faulkner achieves a reconciliation of these tensions illustrates particularly well how close attention to the formation of stylizing forces in his early work enables us to appreciate his major novels more fully.

> . . . how can a creature who is so nearly animal in his lack of intellect have the depth of emotion and sheer intensity of poetry with which Faulkner endows him? It is the poetry itself which provides the solution, for insofar as the reader participates in the poetry, he gains an imaginative vision of the world in which the idiot lives, moves, and has his being. (Cleanth Brooks, *William Faulkner: The Yoknapatawpha Country*, 190)

For many Faulkner critics *The Hamlet* would have been his most convincing novel if it were not for the "regrettable" episode with Ike Snopes and the cow. On its publication in 1940 it was received with widely varying reviews, ranging from Don Stanford's denunciation of it as "Faulkner's latest explosion in a cesspool" to its positive appraisal by his colleague Robert Penn Warren in the *Kenyon Review*.[30] Not surprisingly, many critics since then have stressed the necessity of providing a plausible interpretation for this "bizarre" or "offensive" passage. Valiant attempts have been made to shed light on the episode, either by viewing it within the context of the numerous and varied love relationships in the novel or by interpreting it as a parody of the traditional theme of courtly love.[31] Monique Pruvot, in her perceptive article "Le Sacre de la vache," has explored the mythic and archetypal aspects of "Ike and the Cow." Her thorough investigation also leads her to remark on its lyrical language, which will be the focus of our discussion of Ike's love story (*HAM*, 180–6) as a prose poem.[32]

The day begins in the darkened barn with the groping movements of the feebleminded Ike Snopes. From the start, the imagery places the ensuing scene in a dimension beyond the ordinary: "the door, he can see it now, gray, lighter in tone yet paradoxically no more luminous, *as if a* rectangle of opaque glass had been set into nothing's self . . . " (*HAM*, 180). Similarly, in an effort to convey the prehuman power of sexual attraction, Faulkner presents Ike in grotesque distortion:

. . . breathing in the reek, the odor of cows and mares as the successful lover does that of a room full of women, his the victor's drowsing rapport with all anonymous, *faceless female flesh* capable of walking the *female earth*.   (my italics; p. 181)

Realistic impressions are interwoven with Symbolist implications in the description of the early morning light: ". . . light, is not decanted onto earth from the sky, but instead is from the earth itself suspired" (p. 181). Both the choice of words and their arrangement, the lofty imagery and its Swinburnean sound repetitions elevate this scenery to a realm above the Mississippi countryside: "Roofed by the woven canopy of *blind* annealing grass-*roots* and the *roots* of trees, *dark* in the *blind dark* of time's silt and *rich* refuse . . . " (p. 181).

This sets the stage for the montage from Synge's *Playboy of the Western World* and allows Faulkner to give his native region mythical overtones of timelessness. The careful structuring of images here and in the conclusion of the passage reflects the impact of the experiments in *The Marionettes* and in prose poems like "Nympholepsy":

. . . in the blind dark of time's *silt* and rich *refuse* – the constant and unslumbering anonymous *worm-glut* and the inextricable known bones – *Troy's Helen* and the *nymphs* and the *snoring mitred bishops*, the *saviors* and the *victims* and the *kings* . . . (my italics; p. 181)

The same images of Helen and the bishops are now arranged into two different groups, giving a decisive ring to the passage. Following the erotic ecstasy and the world-embracing conception, the hero steps lightly across the earthly canopy where, rounding off the prose poem, Helen and the bishops continue their eternal sleep. The Synge montage has an even stronger impact through its association with other repeated motifs: the dwindling light growing fainter and fainter at the end of the passage is captured just as originally by Faulkner ("in that gathered last of light, she owns no dimension against the lambent and undimensional grass," p. 186) as the first appearance of the morning light:

. . . it wakes, upseeping, attritive in uncountable creeping channels: first, root; then frond by frond, from whose escaping tips like gas it rises and disseminates and stains the sleepfast earth with drowsy insect-murmur; then, still upward-seeking, creeps the knitted bark of trunk and limb where, suddenly louder leaf by leaf and dispersive in diffusive sudden speed, melodious with the winged and jeweled throats, it upward bursts and fills night's globed negation with jonquil thunder.   (p. 181)

This prose is characterized by rich metaphoric inventiveness and a deliberate intention to impose form. The organization of its overall structure ("upseeping . . . first . . . then . . . then, still *upward-seeking* . . . it *upward* bursts . . ."), like the ingenious imagery ("fills night's globed negation with jonquil thunder"), testifies to a highly accomplished artist. Expressions such as "melodious with the winged and jeweled throats" (p. 181) or "flamboyant summer's spendthrift beginning" (p. 184) call to mind his studies in Romantic poetry, but the conventional material is now put to conspicuously different use. In *The Hamlet*, as in the Wilde–Beardsley allusions in *Absalom, Absalom!*, Faulkner employs stylizing elements with the consciousness of a montage writer to transcend the surface of everyday reality. "Realistic" treatment of the love story of Ike Snopes would have led to the form the episode takes for those who focus only on the content and ignore the manner of representation: an unpleasant and uninteresting case of a feebleminded sodomite in Northern Mississippi.

Closer examination of the "Ike" episode shows that even the most striking mannerisms contribute to the realization of the novel's theme. The mythological association of the cow with Juno, for example, is accompanied by an idealizing description of the beast, while, at the same time, her animal features are retained: "The shifting shimmer of incessant leaves gives to her a quality of illusion as insubstantial . . . a hand's breadth of contact shapes her solid and whole out of the infinity of hope" (p. 182). Juno–Hera, to whom cows were sacrificed in antiquity, bore the epithet βοῶπιζ, "cow-eyed," because of her "beautiful" protruding eyes. Evidently this allusion to Juno inspired the image group "eyes-sees-look-mirror" in the description of Ike's relationship with the cow. The stylizing effects of the Juno archetype and the optical imagery are in turn enhanced by one of the subtle sound patterns the young Faulkner had imitated from Swinburne:

Within the *mild* enormous *moist* and *pupilless globes* he *sees* himself in twin *miniature mirrored* by the *inscrutable* abstraction; one with that which *Juno* might have *looked* out with, he *watches* himself *contemplating* what those who looked at Juno saw. (my italics; p. 182)

The mirror imagery is elaborated in the description of the spring where Ike and the cow drink, assonance and imagery combining to emphasize the growing closeness between man and animal:

. . . [the spring] which now at each return of light stood full and clear and leaf by leaf repeating until they lean and interrupt the green reflections and with their own drinking faces break each other's mirroring, each face to its own shattered image wedded and annealed.
(p. 183)

What distinguishes the use of mirror images here and in *The Marionettes* is not the poetic intensity and ingenuity which constitute an essential dimension of Faulkner's language from the beginning, but the moral scope of its content. Here it takes the form of a satirical contrast between the seemingly abnormal relationship of Ike and the cow and the cow and the really unnatural conventional human behaviour: "They eat from the basket together . . . things which the weary long record of shibboleth and superstition had taught his upright kind to call filth . . ." (p. 182). This tongue-in-cheek remark, along with other ironic references to higher evolutionary stages equally critical of civilization ("who has learned success and then precaution and secrecy and how to steal and even providence; who has only lust and greed and bloodthirst and a moral conscience to keep him awake at night, yet to acquire," p. 183), demonstrate that Ike Snopes and Benjy Compson are not clinical cases but human beings that extend the scope of our vision. Ike's movements parallel those of the sun, the earth is represented as a heavenly body, and rain appears as a cosmic sexual metaphor. The exuberance of the imagery and sounds in the prose suggests the overcoming of the gap between man and animal and a new, vitalistic vision of innocence. Ike's "love," like Eula's mythicized sexuality, stands in obvious contrast to the several frustrated human love affairs portrayed in the novel.

The implied Symbolist transcendence of ordinary reality here could not have been expressed in the language of mimetic realism. Following Rossetti and Swinburne, Faulkner had experimented in "Une Ballade des femmes perdues" and "Sapphics" with the accumulation of assonance and alliteration required for the indirect conveyance of themes like cosmic eroticism in the "Ike Snopes" episode. The frequent use of complex systems of sound, exemplified in the vitalist rain theme with its 'r' alliteration and different acoustic counterthemes ("*l*ike gauzy um*b*i*l*ica*l l*oops from the *b*e*ll*ied cumu*l*ae, the sun-*b*e*ll*ed ewes of *s*ummer . . . *f*inding them *f*inally in a bright intransigent *f*ury," p. 184), gives this prose a distinctly lyrical flavor. Similarly, in *The Hamlet* the delight in carefully contrived image patterns central to *The Marionettes* is convincingly put to use:

> The air is still loud with birds, but the cries are no longer the mystery's choral strophe and antistrophe rising vertical among the leafed altars, but are earth-parallel, streaking the lateral air in prosaic busy accompaniment to the prosaic business of feeding. (p. 183)

The religious imagery ("mystery's choral strophe . . . altars") is effectively related to the vertical movement, which is then replaced by the "earth-parallel" in the horizontal movement of the birds' feeding. This change in the Symbolist imagery of correspondences quite naturally coincides with the day's progression. The description of the birds' cries as "strophe and antistrophe . . . among the leafed altars" is of the rarefied kind found in Faulkner's Symbolist one-act play and his early poetry. To the dismay of some readers Faulkner insists on linking the sublime leitmotif – "Helen and the bishops, the kings and graceless seraphim" – with zoological description: "first the forequarters, then the hinder ones" (p. 186). But this juxtaposition of Symbolist stylization and Realistic depiction characterizes much of Faulkner's great prose. It obviously represents the great challenge in his writing, which he has already struggled with in the prose poem "Nympholepsy." The description of Ike's shadow, which serves as a prelude to the ecstatic experience, and the descent from the hill which draws the episode to a close are several details in the "Ike Snopes love story" that recall the early prose poems "The Hill" and "Nympholepsy."

But the most telling similarity between *The Hamlet* and these two earlier works is the shared theme of an erotic encounter elevated to a visionary experience. And it is equally important that in "Nympholepsy" as in *The Hamlet* Faulkner insists on uniting features of a banal and often repugnant reality with the presentation of ecstasy:

It is the well of days, the still and insatiable aperture of earth. It holds in tranquil paradox of suspended precipitation dawn, noon, and sunset; yesterday, today, and tomorrow – star-spawn and hieroglyph, the fierce white dying rose, then gradual and invincible speeding up to and into slack-flood's coronal of nympholept noon. Then ebb's afternoon, until at last the morning, noon, and afternoon flow back . . . in one last expiring inhalation. (p. 186)

In light of this kind of prose, it is hardly surprising that Faulkner considers *Moby Dick* the greatest American novel.[33] His style clearly shares with Melville's that unorthodox blend of metaphoric ingenuity and richness reminiscent of Metaphysical poetry and mannerist art. A further peculiarity that Faulkner has in common with Melville is that "prose poems" such as the love story of Ike Snopes are not isolated "purple" passages but intimately related parts of the larger narrative cosmos. This poetic dimension is a distinctive and essential feature of the Faulkner narrative at its best. To explore this art of stylization will perhaps eventually reveal to us how his unique fusion of the poetic and the narrative affect the reader.[34] It will certainly help us to discover a new dimension of *Absalom, Absalom!*; and this novel, which has been the subject of so many brilliant appraisals of its narrative strategies, may also turn out to be Faulkner's most original attempt to regain for the epic genre the poetry it had lost in the Naturalist novel.

The Background of Faulkner's *Fin de Siècle* Interests: *The Chap-Book* and the American Reception of Beardsley

SINCE the purely literary products of American Aestheticism are admittedly insignificant, the reception of the Aesthetic movement has not yet received the full attention it deserves. This is particularly true if we view it as a comprehensive movement encompassing artwork and literature and affecting the artistic climate from which such Modernist writers as diverse as Sandburg and Fitzgerald, Pound, Stevens, and Faulkner eventually drew their inspiration. In this context, periodicals like *The Chap-Book* played a major role as intermediaries. This small fortnightly magazine, published by the Arts and Crafts printers Stone and Kimball (first in Cambridge, Massachusetts, then in Chicago, from 1894 to 1898), is worthy of mention for both its graphic and literary contributions. Here such Europeans as Verlaine and Mallarmé appeared beside Americans such as Henry James and Hamlin Garland. The first issue contained a translation of Verlaine's "Clair de Lune," a poem which Faulkner would also attempt to translate. During the magazine's second year, readers had the opportunity to read Mallarmé's "Hérodiade" in Richard Hovey's translation. Although closely connected to *The Yellow Book* (both magazines numbered Max Beerbohm among their contributors, for instance), *The Chap-Book* was not merely a contemporary imitation, but proved itself an equal in artistic quality. Even more important, *The Chap-Book* gave the American public its first taste of motifs and styles which had already spread throughout Europe. Figures like Pierrot and the Blessed Damozel, motifs like the dance, mirrors, the seasons, and floral decoration fill the editions.

The many decorative ensembles in *The Chap-Book* seem to have been particularly important in establishing the fashion of *art nouveau* and winning acceptance for it. A characteristic example, "The Love of a Summerday" by John Bennet, begins with an epigram from Omar Khayyám and is accompanied by a Frank Hazenplug illustration influenced by Beardsley. To the left of the poem, a narrow ornamental band with waterlilies appears; to the right, a madonna-like "beloved" in a forest. The international perspective of *The Chap-Book* was just as significant as the emphasis on the interaction between the arts. French (Eugène Grasset), English (Ricketts), and American *art nouveau* artists of the time (Hazenplug, Bragdon, John Sloan) are found in close proximity within its pages. William Bradley has a prominent place as well, and his famous drawing *The Serpentine*

Dance appeared in the magazine in 1895. Aubrey Beardsley's dominant influence is evident in the works of a number of the American graphic artists represented in *The Chap-Book*. The journal published his *Mask of Red Death* and a self-portrait in 1894 and characterized him as a "clever, more than clever draftsman," who had made his name with "his pictures to Mr Wilde's *Salome*." That same year a limerick, "The Yellow Book-Maker," managed to combine parody and advertisement in a manner perfectly typical of the time:

> There once was a certain A.B.
> And a yellow bookmaker was he.
> His dead black and white
> Was such a delight
> All Vigo street came out to see.
> . . .
> P.S. If you're anxious to see
> This most up to date Salome,
> Send over the way
> To Copeland and Day,
> Cornhill, in the Hub, dollars three –.

As the references to *Salome* and Beardsley in *The Chap-Book* indicate, Beardsley was the subject of discussion and parody in America as early as 1894 and this reception in America shows that it was not at all unusual for Faulkner to own a copy of the book and use it in writing *The Marionettes*. From the advent of magazines like *The Chap-Book* (1894) to the publication of *Soldiers' Pay* (1926) and beyond, Beardsley's influence was a major force on the American cultural scene. By 1916, not only artists in Chicago and critics in New York, but even artistically inclined students in major American colleges were familiar with the *fin de siècle* tradition. Princeton's *Nassau Literary Magazine* opened its May 1916 issue with a charming drawing of a neo-rococo "lady" in the style of Beardsley and a perceptive article on Beardsley by C. Lawton Campbell. Here Beardsley is linked to Swinburne, Mallarmé, and more revealingly, to the "new movement in scenery design Léon Bakst and the pantomime-ballet." Campbell's differentiation between Beardsley's decadent image and his lasting importance as a graphic artist is of particular significance in connection with a reappraisal of Beardsley's reputation in America and Faulkner's own perception of him: "The 'Beardsley Craze' is dead. And now after two decades his work may be viewed not as a *succès de scandale* of fashionable London but as a real contribution to art and an entirely new departure in the development of black and white." Campbell praises Beardsley not only for his superb style, but above all for his penetrating analysis of the "sin-sick soul faces" of his time.

That Campbell, like Arthur Symons before him, perceives Beardsley to be the artist of the modern Pierrot, sheds considerable light on Faulkner's own use of Pierrot and the mask and marionette motifs. A number of illustrations in both *The Nassau Literary Magazine* and *The Princeton Tiger* in 1915 and 1916 demonstrate the popularity of Pierrot and the configuration of scenes in which he traditionally appears. The stylistic impact of *art nouveau* on these illustrations and on the Princeton student publications in general between the years 1916 and 1920 is unmistakable. The situation was similar at Harvard. In *Exile's Return*, Cowley notes that the "Harvard Aesthetes of 1916" "discussed the harmonies of Pater, the rhythms of Aubrey Beardsley," and an article on *The Yellow Book* in *The Dial* in 1915 indirectly attests to the accuracy of his memory. Its author praises Beardsley and Dowson and makes a point of being open-minded about their apparent Decadence: "The notion that the years from 1881 to 1898 were a period of decadence in English letters is already a legend." In a 1918 issue, *The Dial* gave Arthur Symons's *The Art of Aubrey Beardsley* a favorable review and emphasized how poorly imitators measured up to "Beardsley's imperious art." The Beardsleyesque illustrations of Djuna Barnes, republished together with her early short stories dating from 1916 onward (*Smoke*, edited with an introduction by Douglas Messerli, 1982), exemplify well how Modernist and *fin de siècle* elements fuse.

By 1920, the time when Beardsley had an active influence on *The Marionettes* and on Faulkner's graphic work in *Ole Miss*, the Englishman's fame was at its zenith, and even magazines of a more general appeal like *The Smart Set* were giving him attention. Just as characteristic is a reference in 1922 in *The Double Dealer*, in which Beardsley takes his place along with Wilde, Moore, Huysmans, Dowson, and Marinetti as one of the "Catchwords of the Sophisticated." This magazine, which Faulkner himself was associated with during his New Orleans period, clearly reveals the close proximity of the Aesthetic movement to new literary currents. In a single 1922 issue, for example, an essay from Symons's *Trees in Paris: 1890* is directly followed by reviews of Dos Passos's *Three Soldiers*, H.D.'s *Hymns*, and Beerbohm's essays. It is not to be denied, however, that tone and emphasis were on the verge of change. Later in 1922, the year in which *The Double Dealer* published Faulkner's poem "Portrait," another contributor considered Beardsley, together with Wilde, Dowson, and Symons, as representatives of a movement that had exhausted itself and discarded them in favor of the modern "isms" of a new generation: Joyce, Wyndham Lewis, Pound, and Eliot. Edmund Wilson also shared this opinion, which was soon to become fact. In his 1923 review of Carl Van Vechten's *The Blind Bow-Boy*, Wilson subtly assesses the *fin de siècle* concept of evil and considers Van Vechten and English writers like Ronald Firbank to be the last representatives of a generation "brought up on Beardsley and Wilde."

APPENDIX 2

The Old and the New Sound: On the Verse in *Vision in Spring*

IN THE VERSES AND STANZAS of *Vision in Spring*, regularity and irregularity occur side by side and often in a productive state of tension that reminds us of T. S. Eliot, William Carlos Williams, and many other contemporaries. Thus in "Vision in Spring" (I), only the second and fourth lines rhyme in each stanza, and long and short lines are alternated. The loose iambic rhythm and long, run-on lines create the impression of a flowing rhythm, in accordance with the visionary state, and are only occasionally restrained by a few simple lines:

> And then another bell slid star-like down the silence
> Stagnant about him, and awoke
> A sudden vagueness of pain. That – he said, and trembled –
> Was my heart, my ancient heart that broke.   (*VS*, 1)

In the poem "Portrait" (V), this four-line stanza form is cleverly varied, so that the rhyme in the final stanza mirrors the rhyme in the first. The content of the two stanzas demonstrates the function of the portrait's fixed frame.

Like Eliot in "Prufrock" and "Portrait," Faulkner often replaces orthodox stanza forms with unrhymed or only occasionally rhymed verse groups of varying lengths. Within these verse groups, points of intensity receive a surprising emphasis through the combined use of rhyme and the parallel structure of the imagery:

> The <u>moon</u> *is a* luminous bird against a window flown
> And Pierrot *is a* <u>moth</u> on the dark, alone . . .   (my emphases, *VS*, 10)

This clever contrivance is perfectly suited to the stylized world of Pierrot and Columbine and would be out of place in the shabby modern world of "Love Song" (XIV), where there are units of different lengths, in which a free iambic meter is countered by the rhythm of colloquial speech with irregular rhymes – mostly couplets – providing acoustic emphasis. Although Faulkner imitates simple and trivial rhymes ("cup . . . pick a napkin up," p. 57), we do not have the feeling that he fully appreciates Eliot's superb, parodic use of rhyme as in the lines "In the room the women come and go/Talking of Michelangelo."

Many of the experiments in *Vision in Spring* are unsatisfying, but few are uninteresting, as, for example, those passages which relax the metrical pattern either too little or too much, leaving the medium hovering awkwardly between prose and poetry. There is little doubt that these kinds of experiments would later help the young writer to develop a masterful handling of rhythmic prose in the Rosa Coldfield passages of *Absalom, Absalom!* In the poems without traditional rhyme schemes, Faulkner conspicuously uses rhymelessness and the massing of rhyme to create structure; his effort to emphasize the ending of poems by the accumulation of rhymes is particularly noticeable.

The juxtaposition of regularity and irregularity is striking not only within the poems themselves, but also as regards the overall structure of Faulkner's late Romantic–Modernist cycle. After the basically regular stanza forms and rhyme schemes in the opening poems, "Vision in Spring" (I) and "Interlude" (II), a freer pattern of form and structure appears in "The World and Pierrot: A Nocturne" (III) and the first set of the Eliot *études*, poems IV, V, and VI. "A Symphony" (VII) goes further, beginning to resemble Aiken's "This Dance of Life" with its motifs of dance and music and similar consonance of rhymes. Although the stanzas are of different lengths, the relatively short and metrically regular rhyming couplets create a prevailing effect of harmony and regularity. Moving in the opposite direction, poem VIII ("Rain, rain") and "Love Song" (IX) return to freer forms. It is hardly an accident that "The Dancer" (X), a formal *art nouveau* portrait ("I am Youth," stanzas I and V, 65–6) in five regular four-line stanzas, is set as a contrast between the Modernistic Eliot *études* IX and XI and strongly affects the rest of the cycle.

As with many of the individual poems, the elements of consonance and harmony increase towards the end of the cycle. In the singer poem "Orpheus" (XII), the rhymes bear the same close relationship to the music motif as in "A Symphony" (VII). But Faulkner proves himself a restless experimenter once again. In contrast to the couplets in "A Symphony," "Orpheus" is marked by unorthodox combinations of different rhyme schemes. The repetition of rhymed words from other stanzas, the use of rhyme to link stanzas, the identical rhyme, and the frequent repetition of individual words and rhetorical formulas combine to intensify the musicality of this poem. Yet the dominant impression is Modernistic and thus in contrast to "Philosophy" (XIII) and particularly the final poem "April" (XIV). Here Faulkner employs a difficult, ten-line stanza form which even Swinburne, his late Romantic model, seldom used. The ingenious rhyme scheme, a-b-a-b-c-d-e-d-c, is exactly suited to the artificiality of the Pre-Raphaelite "nature" and "love" scenery and gives the cycle an emphatic final accent. "April" demonstrates that, within the late Romantic formal tradition, there was little more for Faulkner to learn at this point.

Notes

Introduction

1. Edmund Wilson, "William Faulkner's Reply to the Civil Rights Program," in Robert Penn Warren, ed., *Faulkner: A Collection of Critical Essays* (Englewood Cliffs: Prentice Hall, 1966), pp. 219–25; p. 221.
2. On Faulkner's idealism see Michel Gresset and Patrick Samway, SJ, eds., *Faulkner and Idealism: Perspectives from Paris* (Jackson: University Press of Mississippi, 1983).
3. For an overview of research up to 1983 see my article "Faulkner's Poetry," *Yearbook of Research in English and American Literature*, 2 (1984), 355–69.
4. Richard P. Adams, "The Apprenticeship of William Faulkner," *Tulane Studies in English*, 12 (1962), 113–56; Joseph Blotner, *Faulkner: A Biography*, 2 vols. (London: Chatto and Windus, 1974), and the updated edition *Faulkner: A Biography* (New York: Random House, 1984); Cleanth Brooks, *William Faulkner: Toward Yoknapatawpha and Beyond* (New Haven and London: Yale University Press, 1978).
5. Athens: University of Georgia Press, 1983.
6. Austin: University of Texas Press, 1984.
7. Thomas L. McHaney, "Brooks on Faulkner: The End of the Long View," *Review* (Charlottesville), 1 (1979), 29–45; 40.
8. On the concept "Pre-Raphaelite" see especially William E. Fredeman, *Pre-Raphaelitism: A Bibliocritical Study* (Cambridge, Mass.: Harvard University Press, 1965), pp. 1–5.
9. On the concept *art nouveau* see Robert Schmutzler, *Art Nouveau-Jugendstil* (Stuttgart: Hatje Verlag, 1977).
10. On the term *fin de siècle*, see the definitive essays of Fritz Schalk ("Fin de Siècle") and Wolfdietrich Rasch ("Fin de Siècle als Ende und Neubeginn") in Roger Bauer *et al.*, eds., *Fin de Siècle: Zur Literatur und Kunst der Jahrhundertwende* (Frankfurt am Main: Klostermann, 1977). On the term "Modernism" in the sense I use here, see Hugh Kenner, *A Homemade World: The American Modernist Writers* (New York: William Morrow, 1975) and Monroe K. Spears, *Dionysus and the City: Modernism in Twentieth Century Poetry* (New York: Oxford University Press, 1970).
11. For an understanding of the concept "Symbolism," especially relevant for the early Faulkner, see Arthur Symons, *The Symbolist Movement in Literature* (London: Constable, 1899).
12. On the term "Modernism" as applied to Faulkner, see Thomas L. McHaney's articles "The Modernism of *Soldiers' Pay*," *William Faulkner; Materials, Studies, and Criticism*, 3, No. 1 (1980), 16–30, and "Literary Modernism: The South Goes Modern and Keeps on Going," in Philip Castille and William Osborne, eds., *Southern Literature in Transition: Heritage and Promise* (Memphis: Memphis State University Press, 1983), pp. 43–53.

13. For various biographical explanations and theories see Judith L. Sensibar, *The Origins of Faulkner's Art* (Austin: University of Texas Press, 1984), pp. 42, 50–1, 233–4; Joseph Blotner, *Faulkner: A Biography*, 2 vols. (London: Chatto and Windus, 1974) and *idem*, *Faulkner: A Biography* (New York: Random House, 1984); David Minter, *William Faulkner: His Life and Work* (Baltimore: Johns Hopkins University Press, 1980); and Judith B. Wittenberg, *Faulkner: The Transfiguration of Biography* (Lincoln: University of Nebraska Press, 1979).

Faulkner, *Fin de siècle*, and Early Modernism

1. *Literary Essays of Ezra Pound*, ed. T. S. Eliot (London: Faber and Faber, 1954), pp. 290–4.
2. Lincoln Kirstein, "The Eyes of Ez," *The New York Review of Books*, 28, No. 7 (30 April, 1981), p. 3.
3. See Robert Buttel, *Wallace Stevens: The Making of "Harmonium"* (Princeton: Princeton University Press, 1967).
4. *i: six nonlectures* (Cambridge, Mass.: Harvard University Press, 1953), p. 29.
5. See Frances J. Bowen, "The New Orleans *Double Dealer*, 1921–1926," *Louisiana Historical Quarterly*, 39 (1965), 443–56.
6. On the influence of *Jurgen* and other works by Cabell on *Mayday*, see Carvel Collins's introduction to Faulkner's *Mayday* (Notre Dame: University of Notre Dame Press, 1976), pp. 15–23. For its influence on *Soldiers' Pay*, see Michael Millgate, *The Achievement of William Faulkner* (London: Constable, 1966; Lincoln: University of Nebraska Press, 1978) and Margaret Yonce, "*Soldiers' Pay*: A Critical Study of William Faulkner's First Novel" (Unpublished Ph.D.thesis, University of South Carolina, 1971).
7. See Frederick L. Gwynn and Joseph Blotner, eds., *Faulkner in the University: Class Conferences at the University of Virginia, 1957–1958* (Charlottesville: University Press of Virginia, 1959), pp. 20, 33.
8. *Exile's Return: A Literary Odyssey of the 1920s* (New York: Knopf, 1956), p. 35.
9. See Rebecca Meriwether, "The Copyright of Faulkner's First Book," *Mississippi Quarterly*, 36, No. 3 (1983), 263–87.
10. Mr Louis Daniel Brodsky, the well-known Faulkner collector, kindly responded to my questions with the following description of *The Lilacs*: "F definitely *did* bind the little Lilacs booklet himself . . . it is of red velvet cloth; the pages were handstitched together with delicate thread . . . strands of the thread remain as does about half of the red-velvet cover . . . it was *not* printed on a printing press, rather lettered by hand by F on tiny sheets that he personally gathered and stitched with needle and thread and possibly even trimmed with a scissors."
11. Sherwood Anderson, *The Modern Writer* (San Francisco: The Lantern Press, 1925; rpr. Darby, Pa: The Arden Library, 1979), p. 31.
12. Elinor Wylie, *Collected Prose* (New York: Knopf, 1946), pp. 872, 873–4. My emphasis.
13. *The Mississippian* (26 Nov. 1919), p. 3.
14. *The Mississippian* (29 Oct. 1919), pp. 4, 7.
15. *The Mississippian* (19 Jan. 1921), p. 8; *The Mississippian*, 27 April 1921.
16. *Ole Miss*, 25 (1920–1), pp. 170 and 129.
17. *Ole Miss*, 25 (1920–1), p. 153.
18. *Ole Miss*, 26 (1921–2), p. 29.
19. *Ole Miss*, 24 (1919–20), p. 257.
20. *Ole Miss*, 26 (1921–2).
21. *Ole Miss*, 24 (1919–20), p. 125.

22. *Ole Miss*, 25 (1920–1), p. 111.
23. *Ole Miss*, 25 (1920–1), p. 31. The Japanese girl is obviously modeled after one in an advertisement for the New York dressmaking firm Homer in *Vanity Fair*, 13 (1919), p. 127, which shows how international fashions in art reached more provincial areas by way of advertising.
24. See Roger B. Stein, *John Ruskin and Aesthetic Thought in America: 1840–1900* (Cambridge, Mass.: Harvard University Press, 1967).
25. *Chapters in the History of the Arts and Crafts Movement* (1902; rpr. New York: Ayer, 1973).
26. See H. Allen Brooks, *The Prairie School: Frank Lloyd Wright and His Midwest Contemporaries* (New York and London: Norton, 1976), p. 17.
27. Brooks, p. 19.
28. On Bradley and the influence of Beardsley, see Robert Koch, "Artistic Books, Periodicals, and Posters of the Gay Nineties," *The Art Quarterly*, 25 (1962), pp. 370–83, esp. p. 374. See also Roberta Wong, "Will Bradley and the Poster," *The Metropolitan Museum of Art Bulletin*, 30 (1972), pp. 294–9.
29. C. P. Rollins, as quoted in Susan Otis Thompson, "The Arts and Crafts Book," in Robert Judson Clark, ed., *The Arts and Crafts Movement in America: 1876–1916* (Princeton: Princeton University Press, 1972), p. 94.
30. James M. Wells, "Buchgestaltung in den Vereinigten Staaten," in *Internationale Buchkunst im 19. und 20. Jahrhundert*, ed. Georg K. Schauer (Ravensburg: Otto Maier, 1969), pp. 45–95, esp. p. 67. See also Albert Kapr, *Schriftkunst: Geschichte, Anatomie und Schönheit der lateinischen Buchstaben* (Dresden: Verlag der Kunst, 1971).
31. Susan Otis Thompson in Clark, ed. *Arts and Crafts*, p. 94.
32. *Carl Sandburg, Philip Green Wright, and the Asgard Press, 1900–1910: A Descriptive Catalogue of Early Books, Manuscripts, and Letters in the Clifton Waller Barnett Library*, comp. Joan St C. Crane (Charlottesville: University Press of Virginia, 1975), p. 17.
33. For a discussion of the problem of script in *art nouveau*, see Roswitha Baurmann, "Schrift," in Helmut Seling, ed., *Jugendstil: Der Weg ins Zwanzigste Jahrhundert* (Munich: Keysersche Verlagsbuchhandlung, 1979), pp. 169–214. On American designers of typeface during the period, see Kapr, *Schriftkunst*, pp. 204, 207, and Wells, in Schauer, ed., *Internationale Buchkunst*, p. 62.
34. See my book, *Grundprobleme der englischen Literaturtheorie des neunzehnten Jahrhunderts* (Darmstadt: Wissenschaftliche Buchgesellschaft, 1977), pp. 151–2. See also Sherwood Anderson, *The Modern Writer*, pp. 13, 26 on the baneful effects of standardization and factory work.
35. The poem "A Dead Dancer" was first published in *Man Collecting. Manuscripts and Printed Works of William Faulkner in the University of Virginia Library*, comps. Joan St C. Crane and Anne E. H. Freudenberg (Charlottesville: University Press of Virginia, 1975), pp. 131–3. See also Louis Daniel Brodsky, "Additional Manuscripts of Faulkner's 'A Dead Dancer,'" *Studies in Bibliography*, 34 (1981), pp. 267–70.
36. Roswitha Baurmann's analysis of van de Velde's scripts (see n. 33) could also be applied to Faulkner's handwriting: "The lines of the letters seem . . . as if drawn with a trembling pencil, so that straight lines make little S-curves . . . The entire script has a soft, uncertain touch" (p. 183, my translation).
37. See Robert Schmutzler, *Art Nouveau – Jugendstil*, pp. 110–12.
38. Joseph Blotner, *Faulkner: A Biography* (1974), vol. 1, p. 307. Although *VS* is in typescript, it was, as Blotner emphasizes, typed decoratively with some thought to its appearance: "This time he (or perhaps Stone's secretary) had typed the poems neatly, using a purple ribbon and making few overstrikes or erasures."
39. For a discussion of *art nouveau* book illustration in America, see the examples suggested by Thompson's essay.

40. The interaction of text and space was the subject of much debate among *art nouveau* artists in Europe; see Baurmann in Seling, ed., *Jugendstil*, p. 193.
41. Hugo von Hofmannsthal, "Englischer Stil," in *Gesammelte Werke: Prosa I* (Frankfurt: Fischer, 1956), p. 257; my translation.

2 Faulkner as Cartoonist and Parodist of the Twenties

1. Faulkner drew three illustrations for the Red and Blue Club, which I identify according to the publication dates in *Ole Miss: Red and Blue I*, in *Ole Miss*, 22 (1917–18), p. 119 (Pl. 65); *Red and Blue II*, in *Ole Miss*, 24 (1919–20), p. 157 (Pl. 82); and *Red and Blue III*, in *Ole Miss*, 25 (1920–1), p. 137 (Pl. 66). *Red and Blue III* ("Jazz Musicians") appears in *EPP*, p. 81. Faulkner also drew two illustrations for the Social Activities section of *Ole Miss*, which I also identify according to the publication dates: *Social Activities I*, in *Ole Miss*, 22 (1917–18), p. 111 (Pl. 70) and *Social Activities II*, in *Ole Miss*, 24 (1919–20), p. 155 (Pl. 46).
2. "The Lesser Arts" was the title of a lecture delivered by William Morris in 1873 and a term he often used for the decorative arts.
3. On poster art, see Jean Louis Sponsel, *Das moderne Plakat* (Dresden: G. Kühtmann, 1897), esp. pp. 177–228 and Annemarie Hagner, "Plakat," in Helmut Seling, ed., *Jugendstil*, pp. 249–77.
4. Ilse Dusoir Lind, "The Effect of Painting on Faulkner's Poetic Form," in *Faulkner, Modernism, and Film: Faulkner and Yoknapatawpha, 1978*, eds. Evans Harrington and Ann J. Abadie (Jackson: University Press of Mississippi, 1979), pp. 127–48; 130.
5. M. Thomas Inge, "Faulkner Reads the Funny Papers," in *Faulkner and Humour: Faulkner and Yoknapatawpha, 1984*, eds. Fowler and Abadie, (Jackson: University Press of Mississippi, 1986), pp. 153–90.
6. Many of the stylistic characteristics and motifs (humorous auto and ship scenes, formal wear with striking striped and checkerboard patterns) appear not only in drawings by Held (*Judge*, 21 August 1920), but also in illustrations by other artists including Fish (*Vanity Fair*, April 1918 and May 1918), Ralph Barton (*Judge*, 24 July 1920 and 11 Sept. 1920), Herman Palmer (*Judge*, 3, 10, and 24 July 1920), and L. Fellows (*Judge*, 18 Sept. 1920).
7. Thomas L. McHaney of Georgia State University in Atlanta kindly brought these similarities to my attention.
8. Even before Faulkner mentions the "Vorticist schools" in the *NOS* (1925), he uses swirling imagery ("stars/vortex together again," p. 69) in the lyric cycle *VS*. A later reference appears in the novel *SAR* (1929): "the red vortex" (p. 136).
9. On Faulkner's familiarity with contemporary jazz, see Joseph Blotner, *Faulkner: A Biography* (1974), vol. 1, pp. 155, 175. W. C. Handy or Bynum's band played at the Red and Blue Club dances which Faulkner attended.
10. Barbara Rose, *American Art since 1900* (New York and Washington: Praeger, 1975), p. 66.
11. "Miniver Cheevy," in *Collected Poems of Edwin Arlington Robinson* (New York: Macmillan, 1952), pp. 347–8; 348.
12. See Blotner, *Faulkner: A Biography* (1974), pp. 183–8.
13. See Blotner, *Faulkner: A Biography* (1984), pp. 172–5.
14. Noel Polk writes, "*Royal Street: New Orleans* is a small handsome pamphlet hand-lettered and bound apparently in late October 1926 . . . Faulkner carefully decorated and painted, in a variety of shades, the initial letter of each sketch, giving *Royal Street* something of the appearance of an illuminated medieval manuscript." ("William Faulkner's 'Hong Li' on *Royal Street*," *The Library Chronicle of the University of Texas at Austin*, 13 (1980), 27–30). See also Blotner, *Biography* (1984), p. 190 and Collins, *MAY*, p. 5.

15. For purposes of identification, I have given the three watercolors in *Mayday* the following titles: *I. The Vision in the Chapel* (Pl. 77); *II. The Return to Earth* (Pl. 78); *III. The Final Vista* (Pl. 79).
16. See also *FAB*, p. 261: "as when in the old days the cadet would spend that last night of his maiden squiredom on his knees on the lonely chapel's stone floor before the cushion bearing the virgin spurs of his tomorrow's knighthood."
17. For the "ideal beloved" type, see my book *Präraphaeliten und Fin de Siècle: Symbolistische Tendenzen in der englischen Spätromantik* (Munich: Fink, 1971), pp. 263–315; esp. p. 306.
18. In the upper right-hand corner there are also traces of a figure remaining from an earlier version.
19. "The falcons planed plummetting beside the chariot and the wind screamed through the feathers of their wings" (*MAY*, p. 78).
20. James G. Watson sees the gate-like setting as symbolizing Galwyn's hovering between life and death: "For Galwyn the scene in the painting represents the ideal life he has envisioned and an alternative to suicide; for Faulkner the hoped for outcome of his courtship to Helen." ("Faulkner in Fiction on Fiction," *Southern Quarterly*, 20 (Fall 1981), 46–62, esp. 53–7).
21. On the relationship of *MAY* to *SF*, see Collins's introduction, *MAY*, pp. 27–40 and Gail Moore Morrison, "Time, Tide and Twilight: *Mayday* and Faulkner's Quest Toward *The Sound and the Fury*," *Mississippi Quarterly*, 31 (1978), 337–52, esp. 345–51.
22. On the drawing as a "multiple self-portrait," see Watson, p. 56. On the various faun and Pierrot masks of the author, see André Bleikasten, "Pan et Pierrot, ou les premiers masques de Faulkner," *Revue de Littérature Comparée*, 5 (1979), 299–310, and Judith L. Sensibar, *The Origins of Faulkner's Art* (Austin: University of Texas Press, 1984), esp. pp. 129–32.
23. *MAY*, p. 34.
24. *MAY*, p. 11.
25. See Meta Carpenter Wilde and Orin Borsten, *A Loving Gentleman: The Love Story of William Faulkner and Meta Carpenter* (New York: Simon and Schuster, 1976), p. 75.
26. Guy Davenport, "Narrative Tone and Form," in *The Geography of the Imagination* (San Francisco: North Point Press, 1981), p. 312; Ilse Dusoir Lind, "Effect"; and Jürgen Peper, *Bewußtseinslagen des Erzählens und erzählte Wirklichkeiten* (Leiden: E. J. Brill, 1966).

3 Points of Departure: Faulkner's Pre-Raphaelite Poems

1. See my article, "The Novel as Poem: The Place of Faulkner's *Absalom, Absalom!* in the History of Reading," *Amerikastudien/American Studies*, 31, 1986, pp. 127–40.
2. See Cleanth Brooks, *Toward Yoknapatawpha*, pp. 1–31, Martin Kreiswirth, *The Making of a Novelist* (Athens: University of Georgia Press, 1983), and especially Judith Sensibar, *The Origins of Faulkner's Art* pp. 105–25, 153, and Notes, pp. 147–55.
3. Blotner, *Faulkner: A Biography*, 2 vols. (1974), vol. 1, p. 299.
4. Ibid., p. 543.
5. The following survey is based on volumes of this anthology from the period 1913–26.
6. For Faulkner's review of Percy's *In April Once*, see *EPP*, pp. 71–3. For Faulkner's familiarity with ironic references to Sara Teasdale, see *WP*, 100, and Thomas L. McHaney's account in *William Faulkner's 'The Wild Palms': A Study* (Jackson: University Press of Mississippi, 1975), pp. 84–5.
7. William Stanley Braithwaite, ed., *Anthology of Magazine Verse for 1921 and Yearbook of American Poetry* (Boston, 1922), p. 37.

8. Braithwaite, *Anthology* (1919), p. 70; (1921), p. 115.

9. Braithwaite, *Anthology* (1921), p. 180.

10. Title of a poem by Winifred Wellers in Braithwaite, *Anthology* (1921), p. 193.

11. Edna St Vincent Millay, "Elaine," in Braithwaite, *Anthology* (1919), p. 70.

12. Louis Ginsberg, "April," in Braithwaite, *Anthology* (1920), p. 22. See also Hazel Hall's "Spring from a Window": 1. "Blossomtime," 2. "In April," and 3. "When There is April" in Braithwaite, *Anthology* (1921), pp. 66–7 as well as W. A. Percy's collection of poetry reviewed by Faulkner, *In April Once* (New Haven: Yale University Press, 1919/20).

13. John Dos Passos, *Three Soldiers* (New York: Random House, 1932), p. 240.

14. Braithwaite, *Anthology* (1920), pp. 44–5. See also the stanzas from Swinburne's poem "Masque of Queen Bersabe," "I am the Queen Semiramis . . . All these were cast beneath my feet." (Algernon Charles Swinburne, *Poems and Ballads*, 1st edn London: John Camden Hotten, Piccadilly, 1866, p. 264).

15. Herbert S. Gorman, in Braithwaite, *Anthology* (1920), p. 45.

16. Antoinette De Coursey Patterson, "In a Moonlit Garden," in Braithwaite, *Anthology* (1921), p. 122: "The spell upon my fountain, no naiad . . . "; Edgar Lee Masters, "A Lady," in Braithwaite, *Anthology* (1919), p. 70: "she sleeps beneath a canopy of carnation silk/Embroidered with Venetian lace . . . Her eyelids . . . "

17. Maxwell Bodenheim, "Sonnet," in Braithwaite, *Anthology* (1920), p. 35; Alfred Kreymborg, "Dorothy," in Braithwaite, *Anthology* (1920), p. 48; Hildegarde Flanner, "Allegiance," in Braithwaite, *Anthology* (1921), p. 47.

18. Hildegarde Flanner, "Communion," in Braithwaite, *Anthology* (1921), p. 46.

19. Braithwaite, *Anthology* (1921), p. 157.

20. Braithwaite, *Anthology* (1920), p. 113.

21. See also poems by Agnes Kendrick Gray, in Braithwaite, *Anthology* (1921), p. 62; Amy Lowell, in Braithwaite, *Anthology* (1920), p. 27; Marjorie Allen Seiffert, in Braithwaite, *Anthology* (1921), p. 157, and Nelson Autrun Crawford, in Braithwaite, *Anthology* (1919), p. 57. Crawford's "In the Key of Blue" bears the same title as the famous Decadent collection of poetry by John Addington Symonds (1893).

22. See Blotner, *Biography* (1974), vol. 1, pp. 194–5. See also Sensibar, *Origins*, pp. 25–7, on Marietta in *The Marionettes* and Estelle Oldham Franklin.

23. Accessible in printed form in the catalogue of the Massey exhibition, *Man Collecting*, comps. Crane and Freudenberg, pp. 125–6.

24. William Faulkner Collections, Acc. No. 9817-i, University of Virginia Library.

25. *The Great Gatsby*, Vol. 1 of *The Bodley Head Scott Fitzgerald* (London: Bodley Head, 1963), pp. 101–2.

26. "Faulkner as Translator: His Versions of Verlaine," *Mississippi Quarterly*, 30 (1977), 429–32.

27. For a discussion of the evolution of the text of "L'Après-midi d'un faune," see Robert W. Hamblin and Louis Daniel Brodsky, "Faulkner's 'L'Après-midi d'un faune,'" *Studies in Bibliography*, 33, (1980), 254–63.

28. See Michael Millgate, "Starting out in the Twenties: Reflections on *Soldiers' Pay*," *Mosaic*, 7 (1973), 5 and Martin Kreiswirth, "Faulkner's *The Marble Faun*: Dependence and Independence," *English Studies in Canada*, 6, iii (1980), 333–44. See also Kreiswirth's *The Making of a Novelist*, pp. 14–15. For different readings, see Brooks, *Toward Yoknapatawpha*, p. 3, and Sensibar, *Origins*, pp. 70–71.

29. See my article "Faulkner's First Published Poem: 'L'Après-midi d'un faune,'" *William Faulkner: Materials, Studies, and Criticism*, 6, No. 1 (1984), 1–19.

30. Quotations from the manuscript and typescript versions of "L'Après-midi d'un faune" are taken from *Man Collecting* (comps, Crane and Freudenberg); quotations

from the final version and the *New Republic* version are from *EPP*, pp. 39–40 and pp. 124–5. Where not otherwise indicated, quotations are from the final version.

31. For a discussion of the complex development of the prose from *Mayday* to *The Sound and the Fury*, see Gail Moore Morrison, "Time, Tide, and Twilight," 337–52.

32. Swinburne, "In the Orchard," in *Poems and Ballads*, p. 116.

33. "Look in my face; my name is Might-have-been;/I am also called No-more, Too-late, Farewell" ("A Superscription," in Dante Gabriel Rossetti, *Poems*, ed. Oswald Doughty (London: J. M. Dent, 1957), p. 126).

34. For examples of the traditional use of these motifs, see the "lute-strings" in Swinburne's poem "A Ballad of Life," (*Poems and Ballads*, pp. 1–4) or the motif of the "windflowers" present in the title of Oscar Wilde's collection of poetry *Wind Flowers*. The originality of Faulkner's formulations, which my italics highlight, results from both his choice of language and his use of alliteration.

35. On the unifying element, see Sensibar, *Origins*, pp. 105–205. On the relationship of *VS* to Faulkner's other poetry, see Patrick Samway, "Faulkner's Poetic Vision," in *Faulkner and the Southern Renaissance*, eds. Doreen Fowler and Ann J. Abadie (Jackson: University of Mississippi Press, 1982), pp. 204–44.

36. All citations are taken from Judith Sensibar's recent edition of *Vision in Spring* (Austin: University of Texas Press, 1984). The poems in this cycle are numbered I–XIV; poem III ("Nocturne") has eight sections and will be referred to as III, i, etc.

37. Conrad Aiken, *Nocturne of Remembered Spring and Other Poems* (Boston: Four Seas Company, 1917), p. 11. The same company published Faulkner's volume of poetry *The Marble Faun* in 1924.

38. Faulkner still enjoyed the paintings of Puvis de Chavannes in 1925 and refers to him twice in his letters from Paris (*SL*, 13, 18).

4 From Swinburne to Eliot

1. For a more extensive treatment of the following, see my article "The Role of Swinburne and Eliot in Faulkner's Literary Development," *Amerikastudien, American Studies*, 28 (1983), 467–83. For a description of the booklet *The Lilacs*, which also contains a version of the poem "The Lilacs," see *Selections from the William Faulkner Collection of Louis Daniel Brodsky: A Descriptive Catalogue*, comps. Robert W. Hamblin and Louis Daniel Brodsky (Charlottesville: University Press of Virginia, 1979), pp. 31–4.

2. But see also Pound's Imagistic couplet "Alba": "As cool as the pale wet leaves of lily-of-the-valley/She lay beside me in the dawn" (Ezra Pound, *Selected Poems*, ed. T. S. Eliot (London: Faber and Faber, 1928), p. 113).

3. The following quotations from "Before Dawn" are from Swinburne, *Poems and Ballads*, pp. 174–7. All quotations from "Aubade" are from the catalogue of the exhibition honoring Linton Reynolds Massey: *Man Collecting*, comps. Crane and Freudenberg (Charlottesville: University Press of Virginia, 1975), p. 126.

4. See Swinburne, *Poems and Ballads*, p. 79.

5. Cleanth Brooks lists the Kipling quotation in the notes to *Toward Yoknapatawpha*, p. 349.

6. All quotations from Faulkner's "Sapphics" are from *EPP*, pp. 51–2. For different readings of the poem, see Cleanth Brooks, *Toward Yoknapatawpha*, pp. 2–3, Judith Sensibar, *Origins* (Austin: University of Texas Press, 1984), pp. 78–82, and Martin Kreiswirth, *The Making of a Novelist*, pp. 7, 21–2.

7. Swinburne, *Poems and Ballads*, p. 238. All quotations from "Sapphics" are from this edition, pp. 235–8.

8. See the introduction to *MAR*, ed. Noel Polk (Charlottesville: University Press of Virginia, 1977), pp. xxvi-xxvii.

9. See Hans H. Skei, *William Faulkner: The Short Story Career. An Outline of Faulkner's Short Story Writing from 1919 to 1962* (Oslo, Bergen, and Tromsø: Universitetsforlaget, 1982), p. 50.

10. *The Poetical Works of John Keats*, ed. H. W. Garrod (London: Oxford University Press, 1956), p. 210. For a perceptive discussion of this theme, see Joan S. Korenman, "Faulkner's Grecian Urn," *Southern Literary Journal*, 7 (1974), 3–23.

11. See also Faulkner's reference to poetic vase-making in "Introduction for *The Sound and the Fury*," ed. James B. Meriwether, *Southern Review*, 8 (1972), 710.

12. See Edwin T. Arnold, "Freedom and Stasis in Faulkner's *Mosquitoes*," *Mississippi Quarterly*, 28 (1975), 281–97, esp. 289–92.

13. *The Works of Walter Pater* (London: Macmillan and Company, 1901), 8, pp. 246–54; 253. On the hermaphrodite as the expression of a way of perceiving the world, see A. J. L. Busst, "The Image of the Androgyne in the Nineteenth Century," in Ian Fletcher, ed., *Romantic Mythologies* (London: Routledge and Kegan Paul, 1967), pp. 1–95. On the image of the hermaphrodite in Faulkner's works, see Kreiswirth, *William Faulkner*, pp. 7–10 and André Bleikasten, "Pan et Pierrot, ou les premiers masques de Faulkner," *Revue de Littérature Comparée*, 53 (1979), 299–310.

14. Swinburne, "Hermaphroditus," in *Poems and Ballads*, p. 91.

15. Swinburne, *Poems and Ballads*, p. 92.

16. See, for example, T. S. Eliot, "Swinburne as Poet," in *Selected Essays* (London: Faber and Faber, 1951), pp. 323–7.

17. *Literary Essays of Ezra Pound*, ed. T. S. Eliot (London: Faber and Faber, 1954), pp. 290–4; 292.

18. Ezra Pound, *Selected Poems*, ed, T. S. Eliot (London: Faber and Faber, 1928), p. 117.

19. *The Complete Poems and Plays of T. S. Eliot* (London: Faber and Faber, 1969), p. 19. All quotations from poems by Eliot are taken from this edition. Sensibar, differing from other critics (Blotner, Brooks, Yonce), sees Aiken, not Eliot, as the dominant influence in "The Lilacs" (*Origins*, pp. 67–8). On fragmentation and multiple personalities in the poem, see Margaret Yonce's valuable article " 'Shot Down Last Spring.' The Wounded Aviators of Faulkner's Wasteland," *Mississippi Quarterly*, 31 (1978), 359–68.

20. Swinburne, "Dolores," in *Poems and Ballads*, pp. 178–95, 188.

21. On Faulkner and Eliot, see Brooks, *Toward Yoknapatawpha*, pp. 11–16, 30, 65, 347–9; Joseph Blotner, *Faulkner: A Biography* (1974), vol. 1, pp. 241, 307, 309–10 and *Faulkner: A Biography* (1984), pp. 70, 79, 95–7; Sensibar, *Origins*, pp. 105–7, 164–78, as well as in her introduction to *Vision in Spring* (Austin: University of Texas Press, 1984), xiv-xvi; and Patrick Samway, SJ, "Faulkner's Poetic Vision," in *Southern Renaissance*, eds. Fowler and Abadie, esp. pp. 212–44.

22. This poem ("Laxly reclining, he watches the firelight going") is quoted from *MF & GB*. For slight variations see poem II in *VS*.

23. Sensibar sees a four movement musical structure in the cycle *VS*. See *Origins*, pp. 105, 116–25 and her introduction to *VS*, pp. xxi-xxiii.

24. Conrad Aiken, *Collected Poems* (New York: Oxford University Press, 1970), p. 1027.

25. The image of the whirling dance as vortex also occurs in Aiken's poems "Episode in Grey" ("the gigantic vortex of our hearts") and "The House of Dust" ("A vortex of soundless hours"). (*Collected Poems*, pp. 21, 125). Ezra Pound coined the word "vorticist" in 1913, but Wyndham Lewis's "Composition" (1913) is usually considered the first example of the term.

26. Tms/Tccms-two burned fragments, one with an emendation; ACLT (Academic Center Library, University of Texas, Austin).

27. James Joyce, *A Portrait of the Artist as a Young Man* (New York: Viking, 1964), pp. 217–18.
28. See Faulkner's "Introduction for *The Sound and the Fury*," 710.
29. I am indebted to Dr Nonn from the History Department of the University of Bonn for information relating to this question. There are several figures named "Aelia" or "Aelius" in Roman history, but none of them can be convincingly linked to Faulkner's sonnet. It is, however, worth mentioning Aelia Paetina, wife of the Emperor Claudius, who is included in the book on the emperors' lives which according to Blotner was in Faulkner's library (Suetonius, The Lives of the Twelve Caesars (New York: Modern Library, 1931)). See Joseph Blotner, *William Faulkner's Library-A Catalogue* (Charlottesville: University Press of Virginia, 1964), p. 80.
30. *The Rivet in Grandfather's Neck*, Vol. 14 of *The Works of James Branch Cabell* (New York: Robert McBride and Co., 1929), p. 53.
31. Tms/Tccms, MS file Faulkner, ACLT.

5 A Theater of Masks and Marionettes

1. For Hergesheimer's influence on Faulkner's work, see Phyllis Franklin, "The Influence of Joseph Hergesheimer upon *Mosquitoes*," *Mississippi Quarterly*, 22 (1969), 207–13.
2. On Faulkner's knowledge of Moore, see Michael Millgate, *The Achievement*, p. 300, note 95.
3. *Vanity Fair*, 14 (July 1920), p. 29.
4. *Wallace Stevens: The Making of "Harmonium"* (Princeton: Princeton University Press, 1967), p. 58; see also p. 43.
5. Richard Ellmann, ed., *The Artist as Critic: Critical Writings of Oscar Wilde* (London: W. H. Allen, 1970), pp. 290–320; 291.
6. *The Yellow Book*, 1 (April 1894), p. 71.
7. *The Yellow Book*, 1 (April 1894), p. 66.
8. For a psychoanalytic approach to this problem, see John T. Irwin, *Doubling and Incest/ Repetition and Revenge: A Speculative Reading of Faulkner* (Baltimore: Johns Hopkins University Press, 1975).
9. T. S. Eliot, *Selected Essays* (London: Faber and Faber, 1951), p. 21–2.
10. Edward Gordon Craig, *On the Art of the Theatre* (London: Heinemann, 1911), pp. 84, 85, 87, 85, 89–90, respectively.
11. See W. B. Yeats, "Certain Noble Plays of Japan," in *Essays and Introductions* (London: Macmillan and Co., 1961), pp. 221–37, esp. p. 236: "I know that some among them [the Japanese of the time of the Noh plays] would have understood the prose of Walter Pater, the painting of Puvis de Chavannes, the poetry of Mallarmé and Verlaine."
12. Karl E. Zink discusses this concept in his article "Flux and the Frozen Moment: The Imagery of Stasis in Faulkner's Prose," *PMLA*, 71(1956), pp. 285–301.
13. See, for example, Christine Edwards, *The Stanislavsky Heritage* (London: Peter Owen, 1966), pp. 186–207, Petra Fröhlich, *Das nicht-kommerzielle amerikanische Drama* (Rheinfelden: Schäuble, 1974), pp. 31–62, and Glenn Hughes, *A History of the American Theatre: 1700–1950* (London and Toronto: Samuel French, 1951), pp. 355–79.
14. "Faulkner's Uses of Poetic Drama," in *Faulkner, Modernism, and Film: Faulkner and Yoknapatawpha, 1978*, eds. Evans Harrington and Ann J. Abadie (Jackson: University Press of Mississippi, 1979), pp. 66, 81; 68.
15. Ever since the censorship of *Salome* in England and its premiere in Paris, an air of scandal had surrounded it and heightened its attraction for young readers like Phil

Stone and Faulkner. "Richard Strauss's *Salome* (based on Oscar Wilde's notorious play) created a scandal on its presentation at the Metropolitan Opera House" in 1907 and "Mary Garden continued to shock the city with Salome" in 1910 (Hughes, pp. 345, 353). Phil Stone may have seen a performance of Wilde's *An Ideal Husband* at Yale during the 1915–16 academic year, but *Salomé* was never performed during the same period in New Haven.

16. On Faulkner and avant-garde theater, see James E. Kibler, Jr, "William Faulkner and Provincetown Drama, 1920–2," *Mississippi Quarterly*, 22 (1969), pp. 226–36.
17. Quoted in Blotner, *Faulkner: A Biography* (1974), vol. 1, p. 283. According to Blotner, Faulkner had even made an attempt at a one-act play before *The Marionettes*. In it "an emancipated young woman rejected a worldly suitor in favor of another whom she considered dominating though he was actually subservient. Faulkner talked about plots of plays he knew, about characterization, about actors and the theater. He especially like George Bernard Shaw's *Candida*." See also p. 284.
18. Lind, in Harrington and Abadie eds., *Faulkner*, pp. 68–9.
19. Lind, in Harrington and Abadie eds., *Faulkner*, p. 68.
20. Elizabeth Atkins, *Edna St. Vincent Millay and Her Times* (New York: Russell and Russell, 1964), pp. 70, 71.
21. Kibler, "Provincetown Drama," pp. 233, 235. The play was first printed in *Reedy's Mirror* (March 1920) and reprinted in *The Chap-Book* (August 1920).
22. Fröhlich, *Das nicht-kommerzielle amerikanische Drama*, p. 52.
23. B.F.W., Jr., "Potpourri," in *The Mississippian* (27 April 1921), p. 8.
24. Edna St Vincent Millay, *Aria Da Capo*, in *Fifteen American One-Act Plays*, ed. Paul Kozelka (New York: Washington Square Press, 1961), p. 81. All quotes from *Aria Da Capo* are taken from this collection.
25. See, for example, Joseph Blotner, *Faulkner: A Biography* (1984), pp. 53–6, 58–9, 94; David Minter, *William Faulkner: His Life and Work* (Baltimore: Johns Hopkins University Press, 1980), pp. 27–9, 34; and Judith Sensibar, *Origins* (Austin: University of Texas Press, 1984), pp. 24–7, 38–9, 250–1.

6 The Iconography of Faulkner's *Marionettes*

1. George Moore, *Confessions of a Young Man*, ed. Susan Dick (Montreal and London: McGill-Queen's University Press, 1972), p. 176.
2. Moore, *Confessions*, p. 176.
3. On the Pierrot figure and his tradition, see Robert F. Storey, *Pierrot: A Critical History of a Mask* (Princeton: Princeton University Press, 1978). See also A. G. Lehmann, "Pierrot and Fin de Siècle," in Ian Fletcher, ed., *Romantic Mythologies* (London: Routledge and Kegan Paul, 1967), pp. 209–24.
4. Quoted in Storey, *Pierrot*, p. 122.
5. Quoted in Hans Hellmut Hofstätter, *Geschichte der europäischen Jugendstilmalerei: Ein Entwurf* (Cologne: DuMont, 1963), p. 185. My translation.
6. Arthur Symons, *Studies in Seven Arts* (London: Martin Secker, 1924), pp. 96–7.
7. *Geschichte der Kunst* (Munich: Droemer, 1954), vol. 2, p. 678. My translation.
8. On the biographical implications of the Pierrot persona, see Sensibar (Austin: University of Texas Press, 1984), pp. 115–16.
9. Faulkner's poem "Nocturne" (*EPP*, 82–3) appears in slightly modified form as section ii of the third poem ("The World and Pierrot: A Nocturne") in the cycle *VS*, pp. 12–14.
10. *The Complete Poetical Works of Amy Lowell* (Boston: Houghton Mifflin, 1955), p. 148. This poem was first published in *The Little Review* in March 1916. All quotations from Lowell's poems are taken from this edition.

11. Silhouette effects, still favored by Faulkner in important later works like "Barn Burning" and *Sanctuary*, are conspicuously repeated in the text and illustrations of *The Marionettes*. Faulkner's use of silhouettes is especially interesting in the context of modern art, since the *art nouveau* silhouette became an important technique in the reduction of cubic forms to flat planes and ultimately to lines. In *Marietta by the Fountain* (Pl. 95), as in an illustration from Beardsley's cycle, Pierrot is projected against the moon as a miniature next to a peacock while he plays the mandolin. In accordance with the emphasis of the second half of the play, Marietta dominates the foreground in the drawing.

12. See Storey, *Pierrot*, pp. 136–7.

13. Cf. Polk, "Faulkner's 'Hong Li' ": "Faulkner seems to have intended, in Pierrot, to synthesize both types: the Don Juan-Jurgen-like Pierrot" (*MAR*, xxix).

14. Goethe's Gretchen is the most well-known example of this type, which is the subject of Hellmuth Petriconi's *Die verführte Unschuld: Bemerkungen über ein literarisches Thema* (Hamburg: Cram, de Gruyter, and Co., 1953).

15. See Joseph Blotner, *Faulkner: A Biography*, (1974), vol. 1, pp. 235–8, 352–4.

16. On Beardsley's influence in *Soldiers' Pay*, see Addison Bross, "*Soldiers' Pay* and the Art of Aubrey Beardsley," *American Quarterly*, 19, No. 4 (1967), 3–23.

17. Laurence Housman and Harley Granville-Barker, *Prunella or Love in a Dutch Garden* (Boston: Little, Brown, and Co., 1919), pp. 72, 76.

18. Stéphane Mallarmé, "Hérodiade," in *Oeuvres complètes* (Paris: Librairie Gallimard, 1945), p. 48.

19. For the influence of Amy Lowell's poem "Patterns" on *The Marionettes*, see Carvel Collins's introduction to *EPP*, p. 18.

20. On Faulkner's treatment of narcissism, see André Bleikasten, "Pan et Pierrot," 299–310.

21. Compare, for example, Rossetti's "Willowwood" Sonnets, "Love's Nocturn," and "How They Met Themselves" and Wilde's "The Disciple" with these graphic works by Beardsley and Bradley.

22. Mallarmé (see n. 18), p. 48.

23. Oscar Wilde, *Salome*, in *Complete Works of Oscar Wilde* (London and Glasgow: Collins, 1966), p. 571.

24. Wallace Stevens, *Harmonium* (New York: Knopf, 1950), pp. 13–15. The poem originally appeared in *Others*, vol. 2, no. 3 (March 1916).

25. Mario Praz, *The Romantic Agony*, trans. Angus Davidson, 2nd ed. (London, New York, Toronto: Oxford University Press, 1951), p. 289.

26. *The Works of Walter Pater* (London: Macmillan and Company, 1901), 5, p. 62.

27. Oscar Wilde, "The Critic as Artist," in Richard Ellmann, ed., *The Artist as Critic: Critical Writings of Oscar Wilde* (London: W. H. Allen, 1970), p. 381.

28. Mallarmé (see n. 18), p. 47.

29. Mallarmé (see n. 18), p. 44.

30. The autumn motif is, of course, also embodied in the Spirit of Autumn. In the text, he is described as playing the violin; with Pierrot and Marietta's festival of love at an end, the music accompanies a dance of death evidenced in the falling leaves: "while he is speaking, an occasional leaf falls slowly" (*MAR*, 31). His melancholy, downcast pose corresponds to the downcast head and indistinct features of the figure in the illustration *Marietta by the Pool* (Pl. 95). A precedent for Faulkner's Spirit of Autumn can be found in the Pre-Raphaelite interest in brooding figures with heads turned downward (for example, Rossetti's *Dante's Dream at the Time of the Death of Beatrice*). The personification of the seasons and the times of day enjoyed wide popularity among the English Pre-Raphaelites (Burne-Jones), the French *art nouveau* artists (Puvis de Chavannes), and their American disciples (*The Chap-Book*, for example).

31. Charles Baudelaire, *Les Fleurs du Mal* (Paris: Garnier Frères, 1961), pp. 113–14.
32. Cf. Praz, *Romantic Agony*, pp. 291–3.
33. Wilde, *Salome*, in *Complete Works*, p. 558, 565. For Wildean and other echoes in *The Marionettes*, see Cleanth Brooks, *Toward Yoknapatawpha* pp. 348–9.
34. Mallarmé (see n. 18) p. 47. There are countless instances of this fondness for jewels in American poetry of the period, for instance, Lowell's "Paradox."
35. Wilde, *Salome* in *Complete Works*, p. 558, 559 and 574.
36. Cf. Blotner, *Biography* (1974), vol. I, pp. 142, 186.
37. Swinburne, *Poems and Ballads*, p. 179; Wilde, *Complete Works*, p. 735.
38. Swinburne, "Laus Veneris," in *Poems and Ballads*, p. 21.
39. Mallarmé (see n. 18), p. 45.
40. Wilde, *Salome* in *Complete Works*, p. 552.
41. Wilde, *Salome* in *Complete Works*, p. 571. The words I have italicized are in *MAR*, pp. 50–6.
42. See also *MAR*, pp. 12, 27, 28 and 31.

7 From *The Marionettes* to *A Fable*

1. On the *femme fatale* type and its many variants, see Mario Praz, *Romantic Agony*, pp. 187–411. See also my book *Präraphaeliten*, esp. pp. 264–71.
2. On the hermaphrodite type, see A. J. L. Busst, "The Image of the Androgyne in the Nineteenth Century," in Ian Fletcher, ed., *Romantic Mythologies* (London: Routledge and Kegan Paul, 1967), pp. 1–95 and Praz, *Romantic Agony*, pp. 287–412.
3. For the impact of *A Rebours* on English literature, see, for example, Oscar Wilde's *The Picture of Dorian Gray* in *Complete Works* pp. 96–115, esp. p. 101: "His eye fell on the yellow book that Lord Henry had sent him . . . It was a poisonous book."
4. Cf. Cleanth Brooks, *Toward Yoknapatawpha*, pp. 36–7. The passages from The Song of Solomon are cited according to the King James Version of the Bible published by Cambridge University Press. The quotations from Oscar Wilde's *Salome* are taken from *The Complete Works of Oscar Wilde*.
5. For many of these insights I am indebted to Claus Daufenbach, one of my doctoral candidates, who undertook a systematic comparison of the three texts.
6. See, for instance, the parallel structure in the eulogy and diatribe of Salome's three-part confession of love (Wilde, *Salome*, in *Complete Works*, pp. 558–9).
7. For a more recent account of this image in Faulkner's poetry and prose, see François L. Pitavy, "Faulkner Poète," *Etudes Anglaises*, 29 (1976), 456–67.
8. See Frank Baldanza, "Faulkner and Stein: A Study in Stylistic Intransigence," *Georgia Review*, 13 (1959), 274–86.
9. *The Complete Poetical Works of Amy Lowell*, p. 153.
10. *Manhattan Transfer* (Boston: Houghton Mifflin, 1953), p. 125.
11. On the art theme in *Elmer*, see Thomas L. McHaney, "The Elmer Papers: Faulkner's Comic Portraits of the Artist," *Mississippi Quarterly*, 26 (1973), 281–311.

8 From "The Hill" to *The Hamlet*

1. *Life is My Song: The Autobiography of John Gould Fletcher* as quoted in Wilhelm Füger, *Das englische Prosagedicht* (Heidelberg: Carl Winter, 1973), p. 375.
2. See Füger, *Das englische Prosagedicht*, pp. 366–401; Volker Bischoff, *Amerikanische Lyrik zwischen 1912 und 1922. Untersuchungen zur Theorie, Praxis und Wirkungsgeschichte der 'New Poetry'* (Heidelberg: Carl Winter, 1983). On Aiken and the structural aspect of the musical analogy, see Judith L. Sensibar, *Origins*, pp. 116–20.
3. See George Moore, *Confessions*, esp. pp. 167–72.

4. Moore, *Confessions*, p. 166.
5. See James B. Meriwether, ed., "Faulkner's Review of *Ducdame*," *Mississippi Quarterly*, 28 (1975), 343.
6. Faulkner, "Introduction for *The Sound and the Fury*," ed. Meriwether, 708.
7. James Joyce, *A Portrait of the Artist as a Young Man* (New York: Viking, 1964), p. 178.
8. Hugh Kenner, *A Homemade World: The American Modernist Writers* (New York: William Morrow, 1975), p. 123.
9. Moore, *Confessions*, p. 169. According to Susan Dick, the editor, this passage is "a literal and accurate translation from pages 265 and 264" of Huysmans' *À Rebours* (Paris: Charpentier, 1899).
10. See Noel J. Polk, "Faulkner's 'Hong Li,' " 27–30.
11. Cf. Cleanth Brooks, *Toward Yoknapatawpha*, pp. 40–1.
12. See the following complementary interpretations: Michel Gresset, "Faulkner's 'The Hill,' " *The Southern Literary Journal*, 6 (1974), pp. 3–18; Philip Momberger, "A Reading of Faulkner's 'The Hill,' " *The Southern Literary Journal*, 9 (1977), pp. 16–29; and Martin Kreiswirth, *The Making*, pp. 19–23.
13. See Ilse Dusoir Lind, "The Effect of Painting on Faulkner's Poetic Form," in Harrington and Abadie eds., *Faulkner, Modernism, and Film*, pp. 127–48; Momberger (see n. 12), p. 24; and Jürgen Peper, *Bewußtseinslagen*, esp. p. 209.
14. On "The Hill" as a prose poem, see Gresset, pp. 4 and 16.
15. Kreiswirth, *William Faulkner*, p. 23.
16. First published by James B. Meriwether in the *Mississippi Quarterly*, 26 (1973), 403–9, the story has since appeared in *US*.
17. Brooks, *Toward Yoknapatawpha*, p. 45. On "Nympholepsy" see also Momberger (see n. 12), pp. 26–7.
18. See William Faulkner, *Helen: A Courtship*, introductions by Carvel Collins and Joseph Blotner (New Orleans: Yoknapatawpha Press, 1981), pp. 51–2.
19. I am indebted to Thomas L. McHaney and Cleanth Brooks for the reference to Donald Davidson's nymph poems.
20. George Moore, *Memoirs of my Dead Life* as quoted in the introduction to *Helen: A Courtship* (see n. 18), pp. 51–2.
21. Donald Davidson, "Dryad," *The Double Dealer*, 4 (Oct. 1922), p. 188.
22. Quoted from Peter Jones, ed., *Imagist Poetry* (Harmondsworth: Penguin, 1972), p. 62.
23. Ezra Pound, *Selected Poems*, p. 75.
24. For an interesting discussion of this image, see Masaji Onoe, "Some T. S. Eliot Echoes in Faulkner," in *Faulkner Studies in Japan*, comps. Kenzaburo Ohashi and Kiyoyuki Ono, ed. Thomas L. McHaney (Athens: University of Georgia Press, 1985), pp. 49–51.
25. See Joseph Blotner, *Faulkner: A Biography* (1974), vol. 1, esp. p. 517 as well as the new edition *Faulkner: A Biography* (1984), pp. 120–1, 131, 183 and 191. On the *NOS*, see James K. Feibleman, "Literary New Orleans between World Wars," *Southern Review*, 1 (1965), 102–19.
26. The "sketch" of "The Priest," published by James B. Meriwether in the *Mississippi Quarterly* 29 (1976), 445–50 and appearing later in *US*, pp. 348–51, portrays a much more realistic and clearly defined figure of a priest than the "prose poem."
27. See my book *Präraphaeliten* pp. 293, 315.
28. Algernon Charles Swinburne, "Dolores," in *Poems and Ballads*, p. 179; Oscar Wilde, "The New Helen," in *Complete Works*, p. 735.
29. See Brooks, *Toward Yoknapatawpha*, pp. 101–14 and Kreiswirth, *William Faulkner*, pp. 26–36.
30. See Don Stanford, "*The Beloved Returns* and Other Recent Fiction," *Southern Review*,

6 (1941), 610–28, esp. 619; Robert Penn Warren, "The Snopes World," *Kenyon Review*, 3 (1941), 253–7.

31. On Ike as a "courtly lover," see, for example, Richard P. Adams, "Faulkner: The European Roots," in *Faulkner Fifty Years After 'The Marble Faun'*, ed. George H. Wolfe (University: University of Alabama Press, 1976), pp. 33–6; Cleanth Brooks, *William Faulkner: The Yoknapatawpha Country* (New Haven and London: Yale University Press, 1963), p. 180; and Olga W. Vickery, *The Novels of William Faulkner* (Baton Rouge: Louisiana State University Press, 1964), p. 176.

32. Monique Pruvot, "Le Sacre de la vache," *Delta*, 3 (1976), 105–23. As early as the famous collection *William Faulkner: Three Decades of Criticism* (eds. Frederick J. Hoffman and Olga W. Vickery (East Lansing: Michigan State University Press, 1960)), several critics connected the unique style of the "Ike" episode with its unusual content: Warren Beck, "William Faulkner's Style," p. 145 and T. Y. Greet, "The Theme and Structure of Faulkner's *The Hamlet*," p. 340. See also Harry M. Campbell and Ruel E. Foster, *William Faulkner: A Critical Appraisal* (Norman: University of Oklahoma Press, 1951), pp. 97–8. For a recent Derridean reading, see John T. Matthews, *The Play of Faulkner's Language* (Ithaca and London: Cornell University Press, 1982), pp. 202–6.

33. See Frederick L. Gwynn and Joseph Blotner, eds., *Faulkner in the University: Class Conferences at the University of Virginia, 1957–1958* (Charlottesville: University Press of Virginia, 1959), p. 15.

34. See my article, "The Novel as Poem: The Place of Faulkner's *Absalom, Absalom!* in the History of Reading," *Amerikastudien/American Studies*, 31 (1986), 127–40.

Select bibliography

Adams, Richard P. "The Apprenticeship of William Faulkner." *Tulane Studies in English*, 12 (1962), 113–56.

Aiken, Conrad. *Collected Poems*. 2nd edn., New York: Oxford University Press, 1970.

Alexandre, Arsène, M. H. Spielmann, H. C. Bunner, and A. Jaccaci. *The Modern Poster*. New York: C. Scribner's Sons, 1895.

Anderson, Sherwood. *The Modern Writer*. San Francisco: The Lantern Press, 1925; rpr. Darby, Pa: The Arden Library, 1979.

Arnold, Edwin T. "Freedom and Stasis in Faulkner's *Mosquitoes*." *Mississippi Quarterly*, 28 (1975), 281–97.

Atkins, Elizabeth. *Edna St. Vincent Millay and Her Times*. New York: Russell and Russell, 1964.

Baldanza, Frank. "Faulkner and Stein: A Study in Stylistic Intransigence." *Georgia Review*, 13 (1959), 274–86.

Bauer, Roger *et al*., eds. *Fin de Siècle: Zur Literatur und Kunst der Jahrhundertwende*. Frankfurt am Main.: Klostermann, 1977.

Bischoff, Volker. *Amerikanische Lyrik zwischen 1912 und 1922. Untersuchungen zur Theorie, Praxis und Wirkungsgeschichte der 'New Poetry.'* Heidelberg: Carl Winter, 1983.

Bleikasten, André. *The Most Splendid Failure: Faulkner's "The Sound and the Fury."* Bloomington: Indiana University Press, 1976.

"Pan et Pierrot, ou les premiers masques de Faulkner." *Revue de Littérature Comparée*, 53 (1979), 299–310.

Blotner, Joseph. *Faulkner: A Biography*. 2 vols., London: Chatto and Windus, 1974.

Faulkner: A Biography. 1 vol., New York: Random House, 1984.

William Faulkner's Library – A Catalogue. Charlottesville: University Press of Virginia, 1964.

Bowen, Frances J. "The New Orleans *Double Dealer*, 1921–1926." *Louisiana Historical Quarterly*, 39 (1965), 443–56.

Braithwaite, William Stanley, ed. *Anthology of Magazine Verse for 1921 and Yearbook of American Poetry*. New York: Schulte Publishing Co. etc., 1919–22.

Brodsky, Louis Daniel. "Additional Manuscripts of Faulkner's 'A Dead Dancer.'" *Studies in Bibliography*, 34 (1981), 267–70.

Brodsky, Louis Daniel and Robert W. Hamblin. *Faulkner: A Comprehensive Guide to the Brodsky Collection*. Jackson: University Press of Mississippi, 1983.

Brooks, Cleanth. *William Faulkner: The Yoknapatawpha Country*. New Haven and London: Yale University Press, 1963.

William Faulkner: Toward Yoknapatawpha and Beyond. New Haven and London: Yale University Press, 1978.

Bross, Addison C. "*Soldiers' Pay* and the Art of Aubrey Beardsley." *American Quarterly*, 19 (1967), 6–23.

Bruccoli, Matthew J. and Jackson R. Bryer, eds., *F. Scott Fitzgerald in His Own Time: A Miscellany*. Kingsport, Ohio: Kent State University Press, 1971.

Buttel, Robert. *Wallace Stevens: The Making of "Harmonium."* Princeton: Princeton University Press, 1967.

Butterworth, Keen. "A Census of Manuscripts and Typescripts of William Faulkner's Poetry." *Mississippi Quarterly*, 26 (1973), 333–60.

Cabell, James Branch. *The Works of James Branch Cabell*. New York: Robert McBride Co., 1927–30.

Campbell, C. Lawton. "Aubrey Beardsley: An Appreciation." *The Nassau Literary Magazine*, 72 (1916), 63.

Campbell, Harry M. and Foster, Ruel E. *William Faulkner: A Critical Appraisal*. Norman: University of Oklahoma Press, 1951.

Clark, Robert Judson, ed. *The Arts and Crafts Movement in America: 1876–1916*. Princeton: Princeton University Press, 1972.

Cowley, Malcolm. *Exile's Return: A Literary Odyssey of the 1920s*. New York: A. Knopf, 1956.

Craig, Edward Gordon. *On the Art of the Theatre*. London: Heinemann, 1911.

Crane, Joan St C. and Freudenberg, Anne E. H., comps. *Man Collecting: Manuscripts and Printed Works of William Faulkner in the University of Virginia Library*. Charlottesville: University Press of Virginia, 1975.

Eldridge, Paul. "The Carnival. A Divine Comedy in One Act." *The Double Dealer*, 5 (January 1923), 4–21.

Eliot, T. S. *The Complete Poems and Plays of T. S. Eliot*. London: Faber and Faber, 1969.

Ellmann, Richard, ed. *The Artist as Critic: Critical Writings of Oscar Wilde*. London: W. H. Allen, 1970.

Fletcher, John Gould. *Life is My Song: The Autobiography of John Gould Fletcher*. New York and Toronto: Farrar and Rinehart, 1937.

"Miss Lowell's Discovery: Polyphonic Prose." *Poetry* (April 15, 1915), pp. 32–6.

Franklin, Phyllis. "The Influence of Joseph Hergesheimer upon *Mosquitoes*." *Mississippi Quarterly*, 22 (1969), 207–13.

Fredeman, William E. *Pre-Raphaelitism: A Bibliocritical Study*. Cambridge, Mass.: Harvard University Press, 1965.

Fröhlich, Petra. *Das nicht-kommerzielle amerikanische Drama*. Rheinfelden: Schäuble, 1974.

Füger, Wilhelm. *Das englische Prosagedicht*. Heidelberg: Carl Winter, 1973.

Gautier, Théophile. *Emaux et camées*. Ed. Claudine Gothot-Mersch. Paris: Gallimard, 1981.

Gresset, Michel. "Faulkner's 'The Hill.'" *Southern Literary Journal*, 6 (1977), 3–18.

Gresset, Michel, and Patrick Samway, S. J., eds. *Faulkner and Idealism: Perspectives from Paris*. Jackson: University Press of Mississippi, 1983.

Gwynn, Frederick L. and Joseph Blotner, eds. *Faulkner in the University: Class Conference at the University of Virginia, 1957–1958*. Charlottesville: University Press of Virginia, 1959.

Hamblin, Robert W. and Louis Daniel Brodsky, "Faulkner's 'L'Après-midi d'un Faune': The Evolution of a Poem." *Studies in Bibliography*, 33 (1980), 254–63.

Hamblin, Robert W. and Louis Daniel Brodsky, comps. *Selections from the William Faulkner Collection of Louis Daniel Brodsky: A Descriptive Catalogue*. Charlottesville: University Press of Virginia, 1979.

Harrington, Evans and Ann J. Abadie, eds. *Faulkner, Modernism, and Film: Faulkner and Yoknapatawpha, 1978*. Jackson: University Press of Mississippi, 1979.

Hoffman, Frederick J. and Olga W. Vickery, eds. *William Faulkner: Three Decades of Criticism*. East Lansing: Michigan State University Press, 1960.

Hofstätter, Hans H. *Geschichte der europäischen Jugendstilmalerei: Ein Entwurf.* Cologne: DuMont, 1963.

Hönnighausen, Lothar. "Faulkner's Poetry." *The Yearbook of Research in English and American Literature,* 2 (1984), 355–69.

"The Novel as Poem: The Place of Faulkner's *Absalom, Absalom!* in the History of Reading," *Amerikastudien/American Studies,* 31 (1986), 127–40.

Präraphaeliten und Fin de Siècle. Munich: Wilhelm Fink, 1971.

Housman, Laurence and Granville-Barker, Harley. *Prunella or Love in a Dutch Garden* (Boston: Little, Brown and Co., 1919), pp. 72, 76.

Inge, M. Thomas. "Faulkner Reads the Funny Papers." In Fowler and Abadie, eds. *Faulkner and Humour: Faulkner and Yoknapatawpha.* Jackson: University Press of Mississippi, 1986, 153–90.

Kapr, Albert. *Schriftkunst: Geschichte, Anatomie und Schönheit der lateinischen Buchstaben.* Dresden: Verlag der Kunst, 1971.

Kenner, Hugh. *A Homemade World: The American Modernist Writers.* New York: William Morrow, 1975.

Kermode, Frank. *Romantic Image.* London: Routledge and Kegan Paul, 1957.

Kibler, James E., Jr. "William Faulkner and Provincetown Drama, 1920–22." *Mississippi Quarterly,* 22 (1969), 226–36.

Kirstein, Lincoln. "The Eyes of Ez." *The New York Review of Books,* 28, No. 7, 30 April, 1981, pp. 3, 6.

Koch, Robert. "Artistic Books, Periodicals, and Posters of the Gay Nineties." *The Art Quarterly,* 25 (1962), 370–83.

Korenman, Joan S. "Faulkner's Grecian Urn." *Southern Literary Journal,* 7 (1974), 3–23.

Kozelka, Paul, ed. *Fifteen American One-Act Plays.* New York: Washington Square Press, 1961.

Kreiswirth, Martin. "Faulkner as Translator: His Versions of Verlaine." *Mississippi Quarterly,* 30 (1977), 429–32.

"Faulkner's *Marble Faun*: Dependence and Independence." *English Studies in Canada,* 6, No. 3 (1980), 333–44.

William Faulkner: The Making of a Novelist. Athens: University of Georgia Press, 1983.

Lind, Ilse Dusoir. "The Effect of Painting on Faulkner's Poetic Form." In Harrington and Abadie, eds., see above.

"Faulkner's Uses of Poetic Drama." In Harrington and Abadie, eds., see above.

Lowell, Amy. *The Complete Poetical Works of Amy Lowell.* Boston: Houghton Mifflin, 1955.

McHaney, Thomas L. "Brooks on Faulkner: The End of the Long View." *Review,* 1 (1979), 29–45.

"The Elmer Papers: Faulkner's Comic Portraits of the Artist." *Mississippi Quarterly,* 26 (1973), 281–311.

"Literary Modernism: The South Goes Modern and Keeps on Going." In Philip Castille and William Osborne, eds. *Southern Literature in Transition: Heritage and Promise.* Memphis: Memphis State University Press, 1983, pp. 43–53.

"The Modernism of *Soldiers' Pay.*" *William Faulkner: Materials, Studies, Criticism,* 3 (1980), 16–30.

William Faulkner: A Reference Guide. Boston: G. K. Hall, 1976.

Matthews, John T. *The Play of Faulkner's Language.* Ithaca and London: Cornell University Press, 1982.

Meriwether, James B. "William Faulkner." In Jackson R. Bryer, ed. *Sixteen Modern American Authors: a Survey of Research and Criticism.* Durham: Duke University Press, 1973, 223–75.

The Literary Career of William Faulkner: A Bibliographical Study. Authorized reissue, Columbia: University of South Carolina Press, 1971.

Meriwether, James B., ed. "Faulkner's Introduction for *The Sound and the Fury*." *Southern Review*, 8 (1972), 705–10.

Meriwether, Rebecca. "The Copyright of Faulkner's First Book." *Mississippi Quarterly*, 36 (1983), 263–87.

Millgate, Michael. *The Achievement of William Faulkner*. London: Constable, 1966; Lincoln: University of Nebraska Press, 1978.

Minter, David. *William Faulkner: His Life and Work*. Baltimore and London: Johns Hopkins University Press, 1980.

Moore, George. *Confessions of a Young Man*. Ed. Susan Dick. Montreal and London: McGill-Queen's University Press, 1972.

Morris, William. "The Lesser Arts." *The Centenary Edition William Morris*, ed. G. D. H. Cole. London: Nonesuch Press, 1948, and New York: Random House, 1948, 494–516.

Morrison, Gail Moore. "Time, Tide and Twilight: *Mayday* and Faulkner's Quest Toward *The Sound and the Fury*." *Mississippi Quarterly*, 31 (1978), 337–52.

Onoe, Masaji. "Some T. S. Eliot Echoes in Faulkner." In *Faulkner Studies in Japan*, comps. Kenzaburo Ohashi and Kiyoyuki Ono, ed. Thomas L. McHaney. Athens: University of Georgia Press, 1985, 49–51.

Peper, Jürgen. *Bewußtseinslagen des Erzählens und erzählte Wirklichkeiten*. Leiden: E. J. Brill, 1966.

Petersen, Carl. *Each in Its Ordered Place: A Faulkner Collector's Notebook*. Ann Arbor: Ardis, 1975.

Pitavy, François L. "Faulkner Poète." *Etudes Anglaises*, 29 (1976), 456–67.

Polk, Noel. "William Faulkner's 'Hong Li' on Royal Street." *The Library Chronicle of the University of Texas at Austin*, 13 (1980), 27–30.

Pound, Ezra. *Selected Poems*. Ed. T. S. Eliot. London: Faber and Faber, 1928.

Praz, Mario. *The Romantic Agony*. Trans. Angus Davidson, 2nd edn, London, New York, and Toronto: Oxford University Press, 1951.

Pruvot, Monique. "Le Sacre de la vache." *Delta*, 3 (1976), 105–23.

Richardson, H. Edward. *William Faulkner: The Journey to Self-Discovery*. Columbia: University of Missouri Press, 1969.

Rose, Barbara. *American Art Since 1900*. 2nd edn, New York and Washington: Praeger, 1975.

Samway, Patrick, SJ "Faulkner's Poetic Vision." In Doreen Fowler and Ann J. Abadie, eds. *Faulkner and the Southern Renaissance*. Jackson: University of Mississippi Press, 1982, pp. 204–44.

Sanders, Barry, ed. *The Craftsman*. Salt Lake City: Peregrine Smith, 1978.

Schauer, Georg K., ed. *Internationale Buchkunst im 19. und 20. Jahrhundert*. Ravensburg: Otto Maier, 1969.

Schmutzler, Robert. *Art Nouveau – Jugendstil*. Stuttgart: Hatje, 1977.

Seling, Helmut, ed. *Jugendstil: Der Weg ins 20. Jahrhundert*. Munich: Keysersche Verlagsbuchhandlung, 1979.

Sensibar, Judith L. *The Origins of Faulkner's Art*. Austin: University of Texas Press, 1984.

Skei, Hans H. *William Faulkner: The Short Story Career. An Outline of Faulkner's Short Story Writing from 1919 to 1962*. Oslo, Bergen, and Tromsø: Universitetsforlaget, 1982.

Spears, Monroe. K. *Dionysus and the City: Modernism in Twentieth Century Poetry*. New York: Oxford University Press, 1970.

Sponsel, Jean Louis. *Das moderne Plakat*. Dresden: G. Kühtmann, 1897.

Stein, Roger B. *John Ruskin and Aesthetic Thought in America: 1840–1900*. Cambridge, Mass.: Harvard University Press, 1967.

Storey, Robert F. *Pierrot: A Critical History of a Mask*. Princeton: Princeton University Press, 1978.

Swinburne, Algernon Charles. *Poems and Ballads*. 1st edn, London: John Camden Hotten, Piccadilly, 1866.

Symons, Arthur. *The Symbolist Movement in Literature*. London: Constable, 1899.

Triggs, Oscar Lovell. *Chapters in the History of the Arts and Crafts Movement*. Chicago, 1902; rpr. New York: Ayer, 1973.

Verlaine, Paul. *Oeuvres poétiques*. Ed. Jacques Robichez. Paris: Garnier, 1974.

Vickery, Olga W. *The Novels of William Faulkner*. Revised edn, Baton Rouge: Louisiana State University Press, 1964.

Warren, Robert Penn, ed. *Faulkner: A Collection of Critical Essays*. Englewood Cliffs: Prentice Hall, 1966.

Watson, James G. "Faulkner in Fiction on Fiction." *Southern Quarterly*, 20 (1981), 46–62.

Wilde, Meta Carpenter and Orin Borsten, *A Loving Gentleman: The Love Story of William Faulkner and Meta Carpenter*. New York: Simon and Schuster, 1976.

Wilde, Oscar. *Complete Works of Oscar Wilde*. London and Glasgow: Collins, 1966.

Wittenberg, Judith B. *Faulkner: The Transfiguration of Biography*. Lincoln: University of Nebraska Press, 1979.

Wolfe, George H., ed. *Faulkner: Fifty Years After the Marble Faun*. University: University of Alabama Press, 1976.

Wong, Roberta. "Will Bradley and the Poster." *The Metropolitan Museum of Art Bulletin*, 30 (1972), 294–9.

Yonce, Margaret. "'Shot Down Last Spring.' The Wounded Aviators of Faulkner's Wasteland." *Mississippi Quarterly*, 31 (1978), 359–68.

"*Soldiers' Pay*: A Critical Study of William Faulkner's First Novel." Unpublished Ph.D. thesis, University of South Carolina, 1971.

Zink, Karl E. "Flux and the Frozen Moment: The Imagery of Stasis in Faulkner's Prose." *PMLA*, 71 (1956), 285–301.

Index

Italicised numbers refer to illustrations

Weber, Max, 60–2; *Chinese Restaurant*, 60, *61*
Wellers, Winifred, 195; "Women and Orchards," 83
Wheelock, John Hall, 83
Whistler, James Abbott McNeill, 9
Wilde, Oscar, xiii, 2, 4, 9–13, 16, 20, 24, 34–5, 44, 118, 120, 122–3, 125–7, 135, 141–3, 145–8, 150–1, 153, 157–61, 164–5, 169, 172, 178–80, 182, 186–7, 196, 199; "Ave Maria Gratia Plena," 179; "The Critic as Artist," 13; "The Decay of Lying," 120, 148, 158; "The Disciple," 200; "The Doer of Good," 172; *A House of Pomegranates*, 34; *An Ideal Husband*, 199; *The Importance of Being Ernest*, 158; "The New Helen", 146; *The Picture of Dorian Gray*, 201; *Rosa Mystica*, 179; *Salome*, 10–12, 44, 118, 122–3, 125–7, 141–2, 145–8, 150, 153, 158–61, 163–4, 176, 178, 186,

198; "San Miniato," 179; *Wind Flowers*, 196
Williams, William Carlos, 130, 176, 188; "Classic Scene," 176; "Portrait of a Lady," 130
Wilson, Edmund, 1, 187, 190
Woolf, Virginia, 169
Wright, Frank Lloyd, 24–5
Wylie, Elinor, 12–13, 83, 191; "Jewelled Bindings," 12–13

Yale Literary Magazine, 10
Yale Record, 10
Yale Review, 83
Yeats, William Butler, 10, 94, 117, 120–3, 143, 146, 151, 175, 198; "Certain Noble Plays of Japan," 198; *The Shadowy Waters*, 123
The Yellow Book, 9, 118, 185, 187, 198
Young, Stark, 124